Parents in Charge

Setting Healthy, Loving Boundaries for You and Your Child

Dana Chidekel, Ph.D.

Simon & Schuster
New York London Toronto Sydney Singapore

SIMON & SCHUSTER
Rockefeller Center
1230 Avenue of the Americas
New York, NY 10020

SIMON & SCHUSTER and colophon are registered trademarks
of Simon & Schuster, Inc.

For information regarding special discounts for bulk purchases,
please contact Simon & Schuster Special Sales at 1-800-456-6798
or business@simonandschuster.com

Designed by Deirdre C. Amthor
Manufactured in the United States of America

10 9 8 7 6 5 4 3 2 1

Library of Congress Cataloging-in-Publication Data
Chidekel, Dana.
    Parents in charge : setting healthy, loving boundaries for you and your child / Dana Chidekel.
    p. cm.
    Includes bibliographical references and index.
    1. Parenting.   2. Child rearing.   3. Parent and child. I. Title.
HQ755.8 .C448   2002
649'.1—dc21   2001049637
ISBN 0-7432-0202-3

For my husband and my children

Acknowledgments

I wish to acknowledge my extended family for their love and for the support they have offered me. I also wish to acknowledge my many friends and colleagues, too numerous to mention individually, who served as professional resources and who cheered me on. You know who you are. Thank you all.

I offer particular thanks to Bill Persky for many years of love, help, and encouragement. I thank him for maintaining faith in what I could accomplish and who I could become. And thanks to Joanna Patton Persky for all the support she doesn't have to give, but does anyway.

I wish to acknowledge the Sages for—what else?—their wisdom and experience, and their love for me. And I thank everyone at LMP/NYC for their generous efforts on my behalf. A particular thanks to Leann Revson for her creative assistance, to Joe LaRosa for his artistic eye, and to Geraldine Laybowine for coming up with a great title.

Sydny Miner, my editor, has accompanied me through the process of writing this book, trusting me to do my part, and being thorough, good-humored, and respectful in the process of doing hers. I thank her for teaching me what I did not know about writing a book, and for sharing my enthusiasm for the subject matter. Suzanne Gluck, my agent, created opportunities for these ideas to move beyond my computer and into the larger world. I thank her for taking me on. Adriana Trigiani made the introductions that made these relationships possible. I am grateful to her for her generosity, and I am inspired by her accomplishments.

I wish to express my profound gratitude to my mentor, Dr. Lorraine

Gorlick, who encouraged me to begin writing this book, and who supported me throughout the process. I have had the extraordinary good fortune to be taught by Dr. Gorlick for many years. I thank her for her faith in me, her wisdom, her resilience, her humor, her courage, her style, and her grace.

Lastly, how can I express the depth of my love for and appreciation of Dr. Adam Chidekel? He is a supportive, loving husband to me and an inspiring partner in parenting. I'd have to go as deep to express my gratitude to our children for being the individuals who they are, and for giving us the incredible opportunity to love and guide them.

Contents

Preface

Is your toddler making important decisions in your house? Have you ever found yourself in an extended negotiation with your five-year-old? Do you ever wonder at the difference between how well you minded your parents when you were small and how poorly your children seem to listen to you? Is your four-year-old still wearing diapers? Do you shudder to think of taking your three-year-old out to a restaurant to eat?

Parents who consult with me regularly report that they feel their children are running the household. Many report that their children are strong-willed and impossible to control. Never have there been more books advising parents about discipline and child rearing, and never, it seems, have there been so many children who are so ill-mannered and poorly behaved. Many parents feel helpless and don't know what to do. It seems that we need a new way to think about parenting, a new approach. We need this not only to get through each day more smoothly with our children, but also to guide our children today in ways that prepare them to live as adults in the larger world.

This book is predicated on the assumption that early experiences with parents and caregivers are pivotal in shaping the mental and emotional development of children. How parents behave with their children and their understanding of their children's developmental needs have enormous impact on how children come to understand themselves and how they see themselves in relationship to the world. Parents contribute to the contents of children's minds by giving them information directly. More important, parents' interactions with children define the parameters and range of children's minds and feelings, the freedom with which they may use the tools they have been given, the breadth of the lives that they will allow themselves to live, and the ways they will meet all future demands for coping and learning.

This book offers useful tips for dealing with common, short-term child rearing challenges. It also considers the long-term implications of parental actions. If we can be attuned to our children, educated about the depth and breadth of their needs, and aware of how our actions may affect them, then we can make choices that allow them the greatest opportunities to live fulfilling lives. We can raise a society of fine young children who grow into fine adults. As we take better care of our children, so they will grow to become good caretakers of themselves, of each other, and of society as a whole.

I am a clinician in private practice. I am also a citizen of the world. In order to illustrate the ideas I am discussing in this book most clearly, I have used anecdotes. Aspects of these stories are drawn from my clinical practice. No story represents one specific person or encounter, but rather, they have all been constructed to represent common problems for which parents of young children often seek assistance. Some anecdotes are simply my observations of people in the hardware store, on the playground, in the schoolyard, or at the market. Whatever the sources, all names have been changed and other significant, identifying features have been altered to protect the privacy of those involved.

In this book, I am writing about all children—not just girls and not just boys. This undertaking has put me directly in touch with the fact that our language lacks a gender-neutral pronoun. I might have used all "he" or all "she" throughout the book, but that hardly seems fair or accurate. I could have covered all bases at all times, using "s(he)" and "his/her" and "him/her," but I always find this to be distracting when I am reading, so I don't want to subject you to the same. In the absence of being able to figure out a better way, I have elected to make all gender-neutral pronouns in the odd-numbered chapters feminine, and all gender-neutral pronouns in the even-numbered chapters masculine. If you can think of a better way I might go about dealing with the same problem in future books, I would welcome your suggestions.

Parents in
Charge

Chapter 1

Becoming a Parent

When do you become a parent? When you are pregnant? When your child is born? When you sign the adoption papers? We may become parents in the eyes of the law when an actual child for whom we are responsible comes into our lives, but the process of becoming the parent to that child begins long before our child arrives. Becoming a parent is not so much an event that occurs in a particular moment as it is a process that occurs over a lifetime. In fact, the process of becoming a parent begins in our infancy, when we ourselves are parented.

Parenting is a relationship. You cannot parent without a child. Without at least one child and one adult, it is safe to say that there is no parenting going on. In order to parent, you need not be the actual parent to a child. You might be an uncle who cares for a nephew, or a grandmother who cares for a grandchild. Parenting is defined by the existence of a relationship between you and a child, and a level of caretaking and guidance that is a feature of the relationship. Both parent and child participate in and contribute to the experience. And both parent and child are individuals with specific qualities that color and affect the relationship.

There are a number of factors that have influenced you in the course of your life and which have led you to become the parent you are. They make you a different father or mother to your child than your next-door neighbor would be. They influence the way you think and feel about your children and the way you behave with them. They are what contribute to making you, you.

Your child's relationship with you, her parent, during her first years will be the most important and decisive influence upon her throughout the entire course of her life. That's what happened to you too. You were a child. You were parented. Just as your parents had a lasting impact on who you are and how you view life, as a parent you will have that same lasting impact on your child. But why are parents so influential? That has a lot to do with how babies and children learn.

How Babies and Young Children Learn

You, an adult, have a sense of self. You have a sense of who you are, what you believe, and how you fit into the world around you. From this perspective, you can go into any situation and think about how what you are being exposed to does or doesn't fit with you. You can agree or disagree; your reference point is yourself. "Yes," you can say, "I think this is important." Or, "No, I don't agree." Your sense of self is something you have acquired over the course of your life; it is not something you were born with. The older you get and the more you come to know yourself, the more refined your knowledge of yourself becomes and the more discriminating you can be in terms of what you choose to take in from the environment and what you choose to reject.

Babies and very young children do not have a sense of self. They do not have a solidly established "I" on which to base decisions about what to take in from the world and what to reject. In the absence of being able to be discriminating about what will influence them, babies and young children take in everything from those who are closest to them and they store what they take in. Babies and young children could be described as exceptionally sensitive tape recorders with the "record" function constantly in operation and the recording apparatus oriented directly toward those who are most significant in their lives. That means you.

As described by Dr. Lorraine Gorlick, a psychoanalytic psychotherapist in practice in Los Angeles, these "tape recorders" are more like high-tech surveillance equipment. She states, "Unlike tape recorders, which only pick up sounds, babies and young children record you with all their senses: Their eyes record. Their ears record. Their skin records. Their mouths and noses record. But it doesn't stop there. These sensitive tape

18

recorders also record your moods, your feelings, your memories, your hopes, your disappointments, and your wishes. You may have no idea how much of your personality, how much of your feeling, and how much of your life experience your child absorbs. And this will go on without anyone being aware that it is happening or the depth of it. Your babies and young children are picking up on cues you don't even know you are giving, and they are storing this information for future use before they have any capacity to think about or understand it. And it will be used!"

Not only do babies and young children make tapes of you, but they "play back" these tapes as well. Sometimes this is obvious. You may have heard your tone of voice or something you frequently say come out of your child's mouth. You may have seen a look or expression cross your child's face that seems to have been lifted directly from your spouse. You might be tempted to think your young child is imitating you in such circumstances. Not always, and virtually never with a very young child. A person who is imitating another has to see herself as separate from the other, doing something herself that the other distinct person has done. Babies and young children do not have enough of a sense of self—enough of an "I" distinct from a "you"—to carry out such a sophisticated process. Babies and young children don't imitate you so much as they actually *become* you in those moments. They act without any objectivity or self-awareness.

Developing an "I" is a complicated developmental process that occurs over the years of childhood and beyond. There is no "I" at the beginning of life, but you'll see glimmerings of an "I" along the way as your child grows. Your child's sense and awareness of "I" will ebb and flow. You'll swear your toddler has an "I" during the terrible twos. All that self-assertion must mean there's a solid "I" there, right? But then, in the moments between her expressions of grandiosity and bravado, your toddler's sense of self-determination disappears and there may not seem to be any "I" there at all. Your child will go back and forth in her sense of herself as an "I" throughout childhood. Developing a sense of "I" is an incremental process. But one thing remains constant: the "I" your child develops will always contain and reflect vestiges of you, although at certain points in your child's development this will be more apparent than at others.

The idea that we incorporate aspects of our parents in our earliest years without objectivity and without a sense of separateness from them can help explain why what influences us in these first years of life influences us so deeply and lastingly. Adults have an extraordinarily strong penchant to repeat experiences from childhood. Parents who are able to nurture their children most easily often report having had with their own parents relationships that they describe in positive terms. On the other side of the coin, we are all familiar with stories of child abusers having been abused as children and stories of domestic violence victims having come from homes in which there was violence between their parents. When we repeat history, the tapes are playing. And when the tapes are playing, we can't see our way clear to another story until we learn to edit those tapes.

Unlike images and sounds recorded on audiotape and videotape that degrade over time, the memories laid down in early infancy and childhood last. Do you know of families—maybe even your own—where members repeat a particular behavior generation after generation? How many times have you heard yourself say the very thing to your child that was said to you as a child and which you swore you never would say? "Oh my gosh!" we may say. "I sound just like my mother!"

The level at which things get communicated between parents and children and how these things get passed down through generations may seem even spooky at times. An incident from my practice illustrates this phenomenon in a graphic and startling way.

*Seaniah Flynn** came to therapy at the age of nineteen. There had been an ugly divorce between her parents when she was six years old, and her father had raised her as if there had never been a mother, removing all keepsakes and mementos from the household. During the course of therapy, Seaniah set about finding and establishing contact with her mother. One day she came into the office looking ashen. She brought a letter—the first communication she had received from her mother in thirteen years. I asked what her mother had written to her that had moved her so profoundly. Seaniah said it wasn't so much what she had written. It was* how *she had written. To clarify, she pulled out the letter from*

*All names in the text have been changed.

her mother and held it up next to a page that she herself had penned. Her mother's handwriting was almost indistinguishable from her own.

My Parents, Myself

Our parents impart values and beliefs to us directly through what they tell us and through the rules they set. More significant, they influence us by the way they feel and behave toward us and toward others. Young children are adoring, thirsty sponges with no objectivity. They soak up everything parents do, say, and even feel. Your children are sponges who are soaking you up, as you were a sponge who soaked up your parents. As such, your experience with your own parents when you were a child sets the stage for what you will feel about and how you will do many things in your life, including parenting.

The quality of care and nurture that different parents provide and the feelings that different parents have while engaged in caring for their children vary tremendously. Some people look eagerly to examples set by their mothers and fathers to inform their parenting. Others look to examples set by their own parents to tell them what *not* to do. Whatever your memories of those times, they cannot help but have an influence on how you function as a parent to your own children. This applies whether you are happily referencing those early times or actively seeking to disidentify yourself and your parenting style from what was practiced on you. Some people speak about raising children as an opportunity to get back in touch with their own childhoods and childlike feelings. This, indeed, is what happens. Like it or not, invited or not.

Every interaction between you and your baby activates a network of nerve cells in her brain. These networks are her brain's record of these interactions; they can be thought of as one of the earliest forms of memory. They are formed long before your baby develops language or even a sense of herself as separate from the rest of the world. The networks not only record experiences but ultimately become well-worn paths that quietly but pervasively, influence how she interprets events in her world and how she will react to them. Your parents' interactions with you influenced

21

the development of your brain in this way too. If you had an unhappy childhood, don't despair. A well-worn path is not the only way through the woods, but it's the path you'll tend to travel unless you work to clear a new trail.

How much interest did your parents have in you? How much time did they spend with you? How much were they able to consider your needs? How did they consider their own needs? How much authority did they maintain? What were their responses to your transgressions? What basic beliefs did they operate from? How much say did they allow you in decision making? How and how often did they punish you? How much frustration could they put up with, and how could you tell when the limit had been reached? Why did they have you? What were their stated values, and did they behave accordingly? What did you like about them? What drove you crazy? What did they like about you? What drove them crazy?

The answers to these questions and others like them are the emotional legacy you are likely to pass on to your children unless you choose to do otherwise and are willing to do the hard work that making such changes requires. If there is a family history of cancer, you take preventative measures to protect your children. If there is a family history of musical talent, you are sensitized to look for the signs of this in successive generations. In both cases, while there is no guarantee that history will repeat itself in the present, you are open to a greater probability that it will. Similarly, you need to be familiar with your emotional legacy to prepare your children to take advantage of what is good from the past, and to inoculate them against what could be harmful.

The relationships we have with our parents start to influence our relationships with our children before they are born. We have fantasies about who a child will be, who we want a child to be, and how it will feel to be a parent to her. These fantasies are informed by our early experiences, our wishes, our fears, and our needs.

Carina Clay had a contentious relationship with her mother, who saw her as too needy and demanding. Now, one month away from delivering her first child, Mrs. Clay is dismayed to discover she has gained eighty pounds. "The baby makes me so hungry all the time. Maybe she'll be one of those kids who never stop eating. I had a friend whose nipples bled for six months when she was nursing her son. Maybe I'll have to give her bottles. How early can you start them on cereal?" I point out to Mrs. Clay that she seems to be very concerned about the intensity of her baby's needs. Her description of her yet-to-be-born daughter sounds like the way she says her mother describes her—needy, demanding, overwhelming her resources. In Mrs. Clay's mind, she has become her mother, the baby has become her, and the stage is being set for an unhappy repetition of the past.

While having bad experiences with your parents in the past doesn't guarantee that you and your child will have bad experiences together in the present, chances are if your family history is fraught with conflict and misunderstanding, you may be more prone to expect problems, deficiencies, and conflicts between yourself and your children and more prone to interpret what happens between you and your children accordingly.

Consulting about four-year-old Brandon, Mr. Fujimori says, "Last night I asked him what he did at preschool. He said, 'I don't know.' I kept asking, and he kept avoiding my question, defying me. He should be punished for being disrespectful." Mrs. Fujimori said, "I thought he looked confused. I asked him who he sat next to at lunch and what he built with blocks. He told me." I suggest that Mrs. Fujimori's approach is indicated for a child of Brandon's age, whose limited capacity for abstract thought would make it hard for him to respond to more open-ended questions. Mr. Fujimori doesn't buy this: "My son showed me disrespect, and he answered my wife to push my face in it." I ask about each parent's history. Mrs. Fujimori describes a happy childhood in a loving family. Mr. Fujimori's father was a hot-tempered military sergeant who was feared by all his children for his ready criticism and harsh discipline.

Mr. Fujimori's father seems to have expected defiance in his children, and his interpretation of his son's behaviors in childhood was colored by this expectation. History is set to repeat itself in this family. Without some assistance, Mr. Fujimori is likely to keep looking on Brandon through the eyes his father used when looking at him. Mr. Fujimori would certainly not identify a negative relationship with Brandon as a goal. Rather, absent any other models, he is not likely to see alternatives. If you grew up in a family that spoke French, you think in French. Mr. Fujimori grew up in a family that spoke and thought in the language of "conflict." He needs help in recognizing this and learning another way, if it is to be otherwise in his family of today.

Just as you can't learn another language in an instant, so too the process of learning a different way of seeing yourself and others is a gradual one. While it seems like a logical enough proposition to change a perspective that does not work, there is an enormous amount of sometimes disturbing emotion that goes along with making real changes. If you had hardships in childhood, chances are you survived your experience by convincing yourself that things were not so bad after all—by trying to forget your troubling memories, by minimizing the importance of what occurred, or by closing the door on that part of your life and deciding simply to move forward. Real, healing change requires that you remember the things that you may have worked so hard to forget. If you have closed the door on a part of your life that was difficult, healing what was hurt requires you to open that door, go back in the room, and revisit all over again the feelings that you have distanced yourself from. This is easier said than done. But you must do this if you are to offer your child anything better, because offering your child a better experience will necessarily put a spotlight on what you didn't have. You need to be prepared to face this issue and to face the feelings that arise in you.

Mrs. Green's mentally ill mother was hospitalized during long stretches of Mrs. Green's childhood. When she was home, Mrs. Green remembers her as an eerie stranger who shut herself in her room. Her father was not much more available, overwhelmed with providing for three children and coping with his wife's illness. Now Mrs. Green is in therapy, determined to make a nicer life for her son. She says, "I'll be sitting with Darnell in the rocker, singing him a song or reading him a story, holding him close, and it will be such a good feeling, and then the thought will come: 'This is what I missed out on.' And I'll get overwhelmed. I feel how trusting my son is, see how much he needs me. And I'll

24

think back to when I was small and think, 'I needed this too. How did I survive?'"

Mrs. Green's story is a dramatic one; it is not so difficult to imagine how a mentally ill parent would fail to provide important nurture and security for a child. But the story from childhood needn't always be so dramatic to have an impact. A parent who spends long hours at a job, who is preoccupied with his or her own needs for whatever reason, who is uncomfortable with closeness and who pushes you away too much or too soon—all of these more ordinary circumstances can leave you with a sense of loss that, over the years, you are likely to try to turn away from. What Mrs. Green is doing takes courage. To be able to provide maternal love and nurture for her son, she has opened herself to seeing what she needed and to grieving for the closeness with her own mother that she did not have. This is painful but necessary. Were she unwilling to open herself to these feelings, she would have to keep her son and his needs at arm's length too.

Anything from the past that remains unresolved for you is likely to impair your ability to see clearly in the present.

The Sibini family thinks baby Maria, twelve months old, cries too much. When Maria begins to fuss mildly in the session, Mrs. Sibini reacts by bombarding her with toys, wiggling her, singing her songs. The magnitude of Mrs. Sibini's response given Maria's minimal fussing is remarkable, and it is not surprising that under the impact of these frenetic ministrations, Maria's cries escalate. In the interview, I learn that Mrs. Sibini's mother died when she was a young child. Mrs. Sibini states that this is a nonissue for her, as she was too young to remember her mom. But over time, as Mrs. Sibini is encouraged to speak about her mother in our meetings, she is able to get in touch with her grief. She also is helped to recognize that her excessive ministrations to her daughter reflect her fear of her own sadness. As Mrs. Sibini is able to explore what the loss of her mother meant to her, her ability to tolerate her daughter's distress increases. Over a period of several months, she becomes more comfortable with Maria's tears, and strangely, Maria's distress appears to be diminishing.

Mrs. Sibini is so threatened by sadness that when there is any indication of distress in her daughter, she overreacts. This interferes with her ability to see what her daughter really needs and, ironically, creates very real distress and agitation where only minor signs of it existed before.

Along with providing maternal and paternal comfort, parents are also responsible for disciplining children. How your parents disciplined you is likely to have an enormous influence on how you function as a parent. People who were harshly disciplined usually grow into parents who either (1) believe in or are prone to deliver harsh discipline themselves, or (2) swear that what was done to them will not get passed on to their own children. But it is not uncommon for parents who dedicate themselves not to repeat mistakes of the past to find themselves driven, in moments of stress, to act in exactly those ways in which they promised themselves they would not.

Isabelle Linden's mother had a temper, and Ms. Linden swore she would never lose her temper with her own children. She comes to our session in tears. She says, "The other day the washing machine broke and the repairman showed up late. Jeremiah's cutting his molars now, and he's crying a lot. So the repairman is there, I'm now running late to an appointment, Jeremiah is whining, and I just blew up at him. I screamed at him to stop. I felt like throwing him against the wall. And for what? The poor kid is uncomfortable. Well, I'm yelling at him, and this is making him cry harder, which is making me angrier. Finally, I just walked away from him, and then I ended up in tears. I'm afraid I'm turning into my mother. I promised I wouldn't act this way, and I hate myself for it. I feel like a monster, and I can't help myself."

You may swear you will never scream at your children the way your father screamed at you. If you should find yourself raising your voice and you have not allowed for this possibility, the problem is compounded. You are likely to be angry at your child for her misbehavior, but you may also be ashamed of yourself for failing to remain in control. A state of shame is not such a nice place to visit, and no one wants to live there. To get rid of this feeling, you may blame your child for acting in a way that did not permit you to behave in the manner you promised you would. If, on the other hand, you allow for the possibility that despite your best intentions to remain calm at all times, you may find yourself in a situation where you cannot do this, you are more likely not to see yourself as a failure. You can forgive yourself, understand that you are human, understand that humans make mistakes, and realize that one instance of yelling is not likely to damage your child forever. You are more likely to forgive—yourself and your child—and move on.

It is certainly right not to want to inflict bad things that were done to you in the past upon your children in the present. But it is important to keep in mind as well that there is a strong pull from the past—even a horrible past—to repeat itself. Even the most well-intentioned parents may find themselves doing things or wanting to do things that they swore they never would. Being aware of this tendency does not give you license to surrender to your impulses. Rather, it can alert you to be on the lookout for feelings and impulses that you may have assured yourself would never arise. Being prepared puts you in the best position to control yourself and to practice damage control when you fail to behave as you promised you would.

Where You Fit in Your Family of Origin

Your family of origin is the family in which you grew up. Your gender and the order in which you were born into your family of origin can influence the way you feel about and react to your children in your family of today. It is not uncommon for you to perceive the members of the family you have created in the present from the perspective of the experience you had in the family that created you. Though we may appear to be adults on the outside, sometimes we will respond to things that happen to us more as the children we were than as the grown-ups we have become.

Jana Goodwin was the fourth of five children. Her husband, Steve, was the first of four. When their son, John, was two and Jana became pregnant again, Steve withdrew. In therapy, Mr. Goodwin admitted he was worried it would be hard for John to share his mom and dad with a newborn. As we spoke about Mr. Goodwin's history, it became apparent that the pregnancy was

27

arousing memories of his younger brother's arrival. "After my mother went to the hospital, nothing was ever the same. It was like I lost her." Mrs. Goodwin, born into a larger family, had never had the experience of being an only child. As Mr. Goodwin explored the feelings from his past, he was able to see himself as an adult welcoming a baby into his family as opposed to seeing himself as a child at the precipice of a substantial loss. He saw his withdrawal as his effort to distance himself from his wife in antic-ipation of her distancing herself from him, as his mother had dis-tanced herself from him in the past. Mr. and Mrs. Goodwin were able to work together on these issues, and the friction between them diminished.

If you were an only child or a firstborn child in your original family, you may experience the arrival of a baby in the family you create not only as a joyous and much-anticipated event, but also as the arrival of a com-petitor for your spouse's affections, which were previously available entirely to you. The adult in you may want the baby. The child in you may see the baby as an intruder. If you have more than one child, you may find yourself identifying more with the child who has the same place in the birth order that you did in your family of origin—taking her side more often, trying to cut her more slack where you can.

You may also be influenced in how you act toward and feel about your children by their gender. This goes beyond cultural stereotypes of who boys and girls are and how they act. Your response to your child's gender can be specifically influenced by how your parents and other family mem-bers related to you on the basis of your having been a boy or a girl.

Marci Collins, four months pregnant, has felt a lack of excite-ment since getting the news that she is carrying a girl. Ms. Collins describes a happy childhood as the youngest in a family of five girls. Asked how her parents felt about having so many girls, Ms. Collins says that upon telling her family of the baby's sex, her father responded in a joking way, "It figures." Ms. Collins was a tomboy in her youth. Now she says, "It's funny. They used to call me the boy my father always wanted." I suggest that in failing to be excited about her pregnancy, perhaps Ms. Collins is picking up on memories of feelings from within her family. This doesn't negate her parents' love for her, but it does add a dimension of understanding about them and how she grew up. Over the course of several months of treatment as we talk about this, Ms. Collins is able to become more excited about her pregnancy.

There are no hard-and-fast rules with respect to how your birth order, your gender, and the gender of your siblings will affect your feelings about your children or your approach to parenting them. The idea of your position in your family of origin is raised here so you can be aware of it and consider how it may influence you.

Your Temperament

Temperament has to do with your characteristic disposition. It has to do with how you are poised to think, behave, and react. Temperament is there from birth (if not before!). Your temperament is not the same as your personality. Your personality includes your temperament, but your personality has also been shaped by experiences you have had over the course of your life.

Some people are more patient than others. They are more comfortable allowing things to unfold and don't become frustrated or agitated easily. They are not undone when things don't go according to plan. Others are more quick-tempered, more easily frustrated, more oriented to product than process. People have different paces at which they proceed through life. Some talk, walk, and think fast. Others are more methodical. People differ with respect to the intensity with which they approach other people and situations. Some people have more presence; you know the instant they have entered a room. Others are adept at blending in and can enter a situation without disturbing it. Some people are more verbal in their expression of feelings. Others are more inclined to express themselves through physical means. Some people are more bold. Others are more timid. Some people seem to have been born with an eye toward making connections with others. Other people are less socially inclined and are content with just a few close relationships. These represent a small sampling of the dimensions of temperament in which people differ. There are many others.

Much parenting literature has focused on the degree to which children are biologically predisposed to have different temperaments from the beginning of life. As familiar as that concept may be to us, it may be easy to forget that our own behavior is influenced by our temperaments, including our interactions with our children. Being aware of your temperament can alert you to which aspects of parenting are liable to be easier for you and which are likely to be more difficult. If you are parenting as part of a couple, understanding your temperament and that of your partner can allow you to work together to parent your children in a manner that takes advantage of what is best in both of you.

Selma Hasek is a nervous woman who tends to imagine the worst-case scenario in every situation. Her husband, Abdul, is a good deal calmer. The Haseks have a boy, Muhammed, aged two. Over the course of his young life, Muhammed has developed a number of ear infections accompanied by high fever. Mrs. Hasek can care for her son in these circumstances, but she continually has to fight the impulse to panic. Muhammed's illnesses don't feel as threatening to Abdul as they do to his wife. The Haseks know that when Muhammed gets sick, Mrs. Hasek is at her best if her husband can be around, either to care for their boy or at least to provide her with support.

It is important to bear in mind that your temperament is not an excuse for behaving inappropriately with your children. If you have a child with a short temper, you will want to help her learn skills to contain herself so that she can get along more easily in life. Similarly, if you are a parent with a short temper, you need to work to find ways to contain yourself in order to protect your children.

Barry and Jeanine Baron prove that opposites attract. Barry is quick and impatient. A successful attorney, he does not suffer fools gladly and he has little tolerance for mistakes. Jeanine is more easygoing—water to her husband's fire. The couple have two children. Alexandra, eight, is the apple of her father's eye. She's capable and catches on quickly. Nicholas, four, moves at a slower pace, but eventually gets the job done. Now in prekindergarten, Nicholas has little interest in reading. Mr. Baron, concerned that other kids will surpass him, buys flash cards to drill him on a nightly basis. Nicholas may be placid, but he is not passive. The more his father pushes at him, the more he digs in his heels and refuses to use the cards. Mr. Baron is beyond exasperated. Recently, he threw the cards at his son when he refused to respond to them. Mrs. Baron, also not passive, made an appointment for herself and her husband to come to therapy after she witnessed this interaction. In the first session, Mr. Baron is defensive: "So my fuse is short? I've been that way forever."

Being aware of his hot temper does not give Mr. Baron license to express it unfettered. Rather than see this longstanding aspect of his temperament as a license to continue losing his temper with his son, Mr. Baron needs to use this self-awareness to help him steer clear of interactions with his son that are likely to lead him to fly off the handle.

Perhaps this is the place to make a brief mention of the issue of power. What does power have to do with parenting? Everything. Parenthood brings with it a surge of power for which many parents are unprepared. It can be heady and overwhelming, and it can take you by surprise. As a parent, you decide everything for your child—when, how, what, and if she eats; when and where she sleeps; what she wears; with whom she can interact; when, where, and with what she plays; when and with what she will be punished; when and whether she sees a doctor and what you will allow that doctor to do.

Abuses of parental power are rampant. As I write this, there is a story in the news of two teenaged boys who were kept chained in their parents' house in the California desert throughout their lives. These parents didn't consider themselves abusive; they thought they were fulfilling God's will.

The intense power that goes along with parenting and the potential for its going awry is the reason for the elaborate system of checks and balances that we have in place in our society. Doctors, therapists, and others in the helping professions are mandated reporters of child abuse and neglect and are required to report even a reasonable suspicion of such abuses of power. Despite all these safeguards, abuse of parental power goes on all the time. While it is beyond the scope of this book to consider this issue in depth, I mention it here so you can begin to consider the fact that it exists, and to set you thinking about how to use your power over your children wisely, carefully, and responsibly.

Unconventional Paths to Parenthood

The drive to have children and create a family is a powerful one. Increasingly, people who want to be parents find themselves having to overcome physical and emotional obstacles and having to meet challenges they had no way to anticipate when they embarked upon the journey toward parenthood.

A generation ago, parents of young children tended to be married, heterosexual couples in their twenties who had conceived the old-fashioned way or who had gone through a relatively uncomplicated process of adoption. Infertility was not nearly the pervasive problem it is today. Gay couples parenting children were rare at best, and certainly were not in the news. Single parenthood was pretty much never a circumstance a parent entered into by choice and was seen as shameful, unless the parent involved was widowed or divorced. The idea of a woman bearing children into her forties was considered bizarre. Neither in vitro fertilization, surrogacy, nor egg donation were options available for couples who were having difficulty conceiving or carrying a baby to term.

Now, more than one in ten couples is likely to encounter difficulty conceiving. In the course of attempting to become pregnant by unconventional means, many hopeful couples may end up spending extraordinary amounts of money, subjecting themselves to painful and intrusive medical procedures, and enduring a roller coaster of emotional ups and downs on a repetitive cycle of hope and disappointment. The road to adoption—once a relatively straightforward and uncomplicated one—has become increasingly complex, frustrating, and expensive. Older, gay, and single parents may not only have to negotiate issues related to the conception of their children, but are also trailblazing a new sociocultural landscape and have to contend with new social and emotional pressures after the baby has arrived. Recent developments in medicine have also created a subculture of parents of babies who were born very premature and who have survived, with or without significant disabilities.

You may have arrived at the state of parenthood having traversed a variety of experiences and having come up against a variety of obstacles that were all but unknown when you were a child. What you have gone through to become a parent may have an impact on much of your life, and it may affect your parenting style and your feelings about your child or children as well.

> *Eloise Kanter, aged forty-two, endured ten years of infertility treatments and had three miscarriages before giving birth to Zachary—a healthy seven-pound boy born three days shy of his due date. Ms. Kanter consults me when Zachary is six months old, worried that he is not progressing normally in his development. The pediatrician has assured her that his inability to sit upright for more than a minute is not a cause for concern. I examine him and find him to be normal. As I am attempting to reassure Ms. Kanter, Zachary raises a rattle in his mouth and she dives to intercept. A struggle ensues. She emerges with the rattle, which she holds up sheepishly as her son begins to scream. "I know you'll probably think I'm crazy," she says over his crying, "but I can't help but think that he'll bite the end off and choke on it."*

As parents, we have a biological and emotional drive to protect our children. But we also have the awareness that we need to allow children to have certain experiences as a part of living. As in so many aspects of life, we have to strike some sort of balance. Parents who have experienced difficulty in becoming parents may have a tendency to tip this balance toward overprotection when their child finally arrives. Certainly, this is what happened to Ms. Kanter.

When have you ever cared so deeply for something so utterly helpless and dependent upon you? It has been said that parenthood is impossible because in becoming a parent you make the agreement to allow your heart to go walking around outside your body. All parents need to come to terms with this new experience of vulnerability, even if nothing ever happens to threaten their child's life and even if the path to parenthood is smooth. Sometimes, however, that feeling of vulnerability is reinforced by the occurrence of a real crisis.

> *Helga Logan's fourth child, Louise, is a robust two-year-old. But every step Louise takes toward independence makes Mrs. Logan's heart skip a beat. "I had no idea having a girl would be like this," she says tearfully. "I walk around with a feeling of dread, always worried something terrible will happen to her. I wasn't like this with the boys." As I inquire about the history, Mrs. Logan describes Louise's birth—labor and delivery brought on six months into the pregnancy after Mrs. Logan was in a car accident. Louise spent the first month and a half of her life in the neonatal intensive care unit. I suggest that this difficult beginning has very likely had a significant and lasting influence on Mrs. Logan, and I suspect her fear for Louise's survival has much more to do with this experience than it does with Louise's gender.*

It is not uncommon for parents to experience intensely disturbing and uninvited thoughts about a myriad of terrible things that can befall their offspring. The act of becoming a parent transforms your home into a place full of new paraphernalia and the sounds of a baby's coos and cries. But the act of becoming a parent also transforms your home and the larger world into a place full of new and horrible dangers. You cannot watch the nightly news after having a child in the same way you did before you were a parent. Parenthood removes some type of invisible protective covering from every inch of your skin and makes it impossible not to perceive the same environment that, before, had seemed innocuous enough, as a place full of threat.

> *In a support group for new parents, a father described standing at his living room window with his infant son, watching a tree-trimming company across the street use a ferocious mechanical chipper. He says, "I couldn't resist the impulse to take the baby upstairs to get him further away from the machine, even though I*

was perfectly aware that the chipper was forty feet away, that Jack and I were behind closed doors, and that Jack, at three months, couldn't go outside, much less get anywhere near the thing on his own."

If you are adopting a child, the relative ease or difficulty of the adoption may affect your parenting. Where adoption used to be a much more straightforward matter, now many adoptive families have nightmarish and heartrending stories to tell.

Because of a serious illness, Mrs. Sloan underwent a complete hysterectomy in her late teens. The Sloans knew they would not be able to have a biological child of their own, and they planned to adopt. It took them only three months to adopt newborn baby Veronica. But six months later, Veronica's mother changed her mind and took her back. The Sloans were devastated. Eventually, they regrouped and after a little more than a year, they adopted baby Anya. But Anya is fussy and difficult, and after several months, they find they are not bonding. I ask the Sloans if they think the previous adoption experience may be having an impact. "Not at all," says Mrs. Sloan. "Our attorney drafted a stringent agreement so when—I mean if—her mother wants her back, she won't be able to take her." I draw Mrs. Sloan's attention to the fact that she has made a slip—saying "when" instead of "if"— which suggests that she may indeed be anticipating trouble.

When we say something we don't intend to say, our error can give us a glimpse of what may be a truer feeling or thought than what we have convinced ourselves is so. While the Sloans wanted to believe that their family was secure, over several sessions they were able to get in touch with very real fears to the contrary. In spite of the fact that the adoption was in perfect legal order and there was no chance they would lose another baby as they had lost Veronica, they were still anxious. Mrs. Sloan even admitted to a fantasy that Anya's birth mother would come and kidnap the baby. Even though their fears were groundless, the Sloans' feelings were real and needed to be respected and explored. As the Sloans

35

were able to talk about their feelings, they realized that Anya's fussiness was not interfering with their bonding with her; they were keeping their distance from her to protect themselves from another heartbreak. Unconsciously, they reasoned that if they didn't love Anya, then when she was taken from them, the loss wouldn't hurt so much. As they got more in touch with these feelings, Anya's "temperament" changed. Rather than fussing and crying all the time, she quieted and took an active interest in her environment and the people in it. On those occasions when she did cry, she was readily comforted by her parents.

You need not endure a tragedy as an adoptive parent to have your parenting influenced by having taken this route to parenthood. Adoptive parents often know very little, if anything, about the genetic history of the child they are adopting. The same can be said for parents who use sperm or egg donors to conceive a child. In the absence of information or in the presence of just a bit of it, there is room for much speculation and fantasy.

The Sheffields adopted Shawn when he was several days old. When Shawn was three, they came to consult me. The Sheffields know Shawn's birth father had several children out of wedlock and he made a scene at the hospital when Shawn was born. They had seen a television program about attention deficit hyperactivity disorder (ADHD), and they wondered if the father might have had it. Now, based on their son's behavior, they are wondering if he has it too. Shawn runs around the house whinnying, pretending to be a horse. Sometimes he will start to do an activity, like coloring, then abandon it five minutes later in favor of something else. He finds it hard to stay seated at the dinner table for much time beyond when he finishes eating. His parents don't want to put him on medication, but they fear they have little choice.

It has been said the when you have a hammer, everything looks like a nail. The Sheffields are viewing all of Shawn's behaviors through the lens of ADHD and it is no surprise that this perspective is making him look as if he has a serious problem. It is true that three-year-olds with ADHD may run around the house whinnying, have a tendency to shift between activities, and have a hard time staying seated at the table for prolonged periods of time. But three-year-olds *without* this disorder do these things too. The difficulty for the Sheffields seems to arise because in the absence of factual information about Shawn's genetic history, there is ample room for them to imagine all sorts of scenarios and there is no reference point against which they can check the truth of their fantasies. Left unexamined, such fantasies are likely to have a significant influence on how the Sheffields view and relate to their son.

If you have conceived a child through a sperm or an egg donation, you may have been told something about the person who made the donation. The presence of concrete information about your child's biological relatives may also be influential.

> *After years of undergoing different infertility treatments, Mrs. Lawton eventually succeeded in becoming pregnant with a donated egg, and she gave birth, nine months later, to a healthy baby boy. The Lawtons knew their egg donor was a celebrated classical musician. Assuming the gift must be in his genetic heritage, they are pushing Jeffrey, now seven, into a musical life despite the fact that there are no indications that Jeffrey wants to go there. On the contrary, having had piano lessons since the age of two, Jeffrey is developing an aversion to the type of disciplined study that is required of him. He wants to play sports, but his parents are concerned that he may squander a gift.*

Adoptive parents and parents who use sperm or egg donors to conceive a child do not corner the market on fantasizing about their children, but the absence of information or the very small amount of information available to these parents leaves that much more room for invention and interpretation.

If you are parenting as a part of a gay couple, you have to make a number of decisions unique to your situation from the beginning. If you are part of a male couple, you face the question of adoption versus impregnating a surrogate—either someone you know or someone you contract with to assist you. If you are a part of a female couple, you have to decide whether to adopt or whether to carry a child. If you decided on a pregnancy, there is the decision about which of you will do the childbearing and whether you will go to a sperm bank or ask a man you know to donate. Irrespective of whether you are a male or female couple, once your baby arrives, there are decisions to be made about whether a parent or an important figure of the opposite sex will be part of your child's life. Meanwhile, you are likely to contend with pressures from society, which may have a variety of reactions to your new family.

> *Jurgen Stahl and Ryan Nelson adopted baby Nina from China. Mr. Nelson is more outgoing, but Mr. Stahl is more reserved and does not like to attract attention. The problem is that their little family of three is attracting a lot of attention. Mr. Stahl says, "In our community, we are not so unique, but outside of our community, people stare at us. We went to Disneyland together last week, and I felt like a circus animal. People on line were making comments that were insensitive at best. It makes me very protective over Nina. I find myself defensive on her part, fighting back. But I doubt myself. I know how I react will have an impact on my daughter. I think, 'Is this my issue? Or hers? Do I do her a disservice if I try to prepare her for this? Will it be a self-fulfilling prophesy? Would she be better served if we just ignored what people said?'"*

Unfortunately, prejudice has not been conquered. You may think you are inured to its effects, but it can get under your skin. Gay couples who are parenting may face this type of prejudice. Older and single parents may face it too.

> *A forty-six-year-old woman who had recently become a mother spoke of her experience in the hospital: "I find myself so sensitive about my age. Just hours after the baby was born, the nurse comes in, looks at my chart, and says, 'Just in under the wire, eh?' I thought, 'I won't tolerate this.' I told her that I thought her comment was inappropriate and she had no business making value judgments about parents who decided to bear children later in life. She said, 'Oh, no. Sorry. It says in your chart that you were about five minutes away from a C-section when you pushed the baby out. I'm sorry if you misunderstood.' Well, needless to say, I felt like an idiot. Throughout the pregnancy there have been so*

many remarks and looks from people. Even my own mother asked if I was sure I wanted to go through with this! I think I'm just primed to feel criticized."

Like snowflakes, no two parents are alike. Many things have contributed to making you the person and the parent you are. Parenthood may illuminate aspects of yourself that, prior to having children, you were not able to see and can provide an opportunity for you to change things about yourself that you might realize are not productive for you. Then again, parenthood may illuminate positive aspects of yourself that, prior to parenthood, you could not appreciate fully and can provide an opportunity to reconcile negative past experiences that have had lasting effects which may not serve you well.

There is no mandate in parenting to follow in your parents' footsteps, as there is no mandate to take a completely different path. These decisions are up to you. To be the best parent you can be, however, you must develop your awareness of yourself. The better you know yourself and the more awareness you have of what has influenced you, the better able you are to see yourself and your children with the greatest clarity and to make the best choices for you and your family.

Chapter 2

The Toughest Job You'll Ever Love

Before you became a parent, you probably wouldn't have thought twice about the Peace Corps's claim that a job in the Peace Corps is the toughest job you'll ever love. Not having served in the Peace Corps, I would still assert with confidence that it is the job of parenting that deserves this distinction. I don't mean to minimize or disparage the very important work being done by Peace Corps volunteers. I mean to highlight the intensity of the demands and the intensity of the joys to which parenting will expose you. Also, while you can leave the Peace Corps, your tour of duty as a parent, while its requirements may change, is never over.

There are hundreds of books on the shelves in the parenting section with thousands of ideas, techniques, testimonials, suggestions, and explanations to guide parents. Often these volumes suggest that you can simply read the book and get all the information you need, and that, really, this parenting business is not all that complicated. So why don't we all feel more competent? Why so many books on the topic and more being published every year? For that matter, why this one? Because parenting is not simple. We can no more read a parenting book full of good ideas and become perfect parents than we can read a diet book, follow the instructions, and never gain weight again. If things were as simple as they appear on the outside, no one would stay stuck in an unhappy relationship. Smokers would just quit.

We have idealized views of who we will or should be as parents. We have fantasies about the children we will be parenting. Rarely do these notions bear relation to reality—at least not every moment of every day. It is important to recognize some of our views as idealized and to carve a bit of space within them for things to be otherwise when the actual baby arrives. We parents are imperfect and irrational at times. We do our best. There will be joys and delightful surprises along the way in parenting, and there will be challenges the likes of which we could never have imagined. As children can stir in us the most profound feelings of love and joy, so too can they stimulate in us the most profound rage and sadness. It is best to be prepared for this ahead of time, so the difficult times are not compounded by the burden of shame. It's one thing to have tough times with your children. Those times will be immeasurably tougher for all concerned if they are compounded by your conviction that having tough times means that *you* are doing something wrong.

Parenting is a job, but it is a unique one. Doctors, nurses, firefighters, teachers, and others who take responsibility for others' lives and futures complete rigorous, standardized educational programs and must be licensed before they can work within their professions. By contrast, you don't have to take a single course or prove your fitness for duty prior to joining the ranks of parents. And as long as your behavior remains within the law, how you parent will remain your business. This gives you a lot of latitude. As wonderful as freedom is, however, the absence of structure can be a bit daunting. It's nice to know that you can proceed according to your own best judgment, but what if you don't know what your own best judgment is? It's easy enough to land the job of parent. But what, exactly, are you supposed to do once you have it?

Parenting: A Job Description

Parenting in essence involves figuring out what your child needs and providing it for him. It involves responding to his immediate needs, but more important, it involves taking the long view of his life. During his extended stay in your care, your child will be in the process of developing into a person who is responsible for directing himself and participating independently in society. Parenting involves keeping an eye on that independent future and teaching your child the skills and imparting to him the values he will need to make the best possible adjustment to the wide world beyond the walls of your home. Broadly speaking, as a parent you are responsible for guiding your child out of harm's way and into the areas in which he is most likely to prosper physically, emotionally, socially, and intellectually.

Your Child's Physical Needs

As a parent, you are responsible for your child's basic survival. Your child requires food, water, shelter, and regular medical care. He requires a certain amount of rest and sleep. He requires protection from physical dangers. As your child's parent, you need to be educated about child development so you can anticipate the types of dangers he is most likely to get into as he evolves through different developmental stages.

The safety needs of your nine-month-old are different from the safety needs of your five-year-old. With your infant, you make sure he's not left within rolling distance from a fall. Even if he hasn't yet rolled over, you have to allow for the possibility that he will take his maiden voyage on the one occasion you leave him unattended on the changing table for just a second to go grab the phone. With a new crawler and a toddler whose hands reliably will find his mouth, you need to be alert to his propensity to gum everything in his reach and you need to remain aware that his new capacities for locomotion extend the parameters of that reach. You need to make extra sure that you don't drop one of the pills out of your prescription bottle on the floor, and you have to stay vigilant for choking hazards he could come across in his travels. You need to keep the Poison Control hotline number within view of the phone, and you need to keep a bottle of syrup of ipecac around in case your child is accidentally poisoned and Poison Control directs you to induce vomiting. (Actually, you should keep ipecac around until your child is eight or nine, and you need to replace it every year or two before it expires.) In recognition of the fascination he will have for little holes into which his little fingers or other pointed objects might fit, you need to make sure the electrical outlets are capped.

With an older child, the dangers change. Older children move in a larger world. Your baby can't walk himself into the street, but your three-year-old can. A level of vigilance when you are near traffic is required of you when your child reaches this age. Babies can't climb to get into the medicine cabinet, but toddlers and preschoolers can, and they will. You need to work harder to keep medicines out of reach of an older child whose ability to climb may outpace his judgment about guzzling the cherry cough syrup. When the pharmacy asks if you want childproof caps, the answer is yes. When you wonder, "What harm can it do to leave the Liquid-Plumr in an unlocked cabinet under the sink?" the answer is "More harm than you even want to imagine. Don't risk it."

Part of attending to your child's physical needs also involves being sensitive to what he is capable of doing on his own and letting go of him appropriately. Your eighteen-month-old has unreliable balance and a lack of awareness of the danger of being up high, so you're probably going to want to climb up the ladder behind him as he negotiates the slide. Your five-year-old needs more freedom on the playground. Staying too close will interfere with his ability to negotiate the challenge of the playground equipment, and it is this success that ultimately will allow him to keep himself safe. He needs your watchful eye, but he also needs your confidence that he can handle the slide on his own.

There will be times when you can have a fair amount of control over your child's environment, and there will be times when you cannot. Many children spend part of their day with a babysitter or at a day care facility, where you have less control than you have in your own home. You need to investigate any individual who will be caring for your child and any environment in which he will be spending part of his day. Don't hire a babysitter who can't give you references. Make sure to check the references the sitter gives you. Talk to other parents who use your day care. Make sure the accreditation is current. Ask about staff turnover.

When your child goes to play with other children in their homes, you need to assess those environments too. Your child should not be playing at anyone's house if you haven't been there first. Visiting will give you a sense of the people who live in the house and their standards of cleanliness. You can assess directly whether they have a fence around their pool with a reliable latch or whether they keep a pit bull as a pet. Ask if they keep a gun in the house. If so, ask to see where it is kept and where they keep the ammunition. Ask who will be home while the children are playing. Don't assume the parents will be around. A boy in the Los Angeles area drowned last year while visiting a friend. The boys were in the pool and being supervised by a housekeeper who couldn't swim. Ask whatever questions are necessary for you to feel assured your child will be adequately protected, and bring your intuition into play as well. Some hosts may be offended by your questions. If that's the case, the visit is off. Hosts who cannot understand your concerns about safety are not people who should be entrusted with the care of your child.

As the world gets larger for your child, he needs to be instructed in the skills that he can use to keep himself safe when you are not around. You need to assess the dangerousness of situations, and you need to teach him how to do so without alarming him beyond measure. You need to make sure your child learns how and when to speak with strangers, how to cross a street, and what to do if he gets lost. If you have been living in your community without being much of a part of it, when you become a parent you need to get active. Call your local police department and inquire about registered sex offenders in your area. Join your local neighborhood watch. Pay more attention to what is around you, and teach your child to do so too.

This chapter presents a smattering of good ideas that might serve to get you thinking about these issues, but you should educate yourself further on these matters. There is nothing more important than your child's safety. You should read up on child development and on other child safety matters too. *Protecting the Gift,* an eye-opening book by Gavin de Becker, sheds light on a number of aspects of child safety that you may never have considered. I have recommended this book to parents who have consulted with me as well as to my family and friends. I'm recommending it to you too.

Your Child's Emotional Needs

Your child needs to know you love him. You've heard, and perhaps recited to your spouse, the promise "to love and cherish, in sickness and in health, so long as we both shall live." With your child, this promise must be implicit. He needs to know that you, his parent, cherish him by virtue of his simple existence on the planet. And while you can promise these things to a spouse and renege, the same does not go for your child. He needs to know that your love for him is forever, no matter what, even if you may be displeased with his behavior at times.

As a parent, it is your job to communicate your love to your child in ways he can understand. You can write a love letter to your baby, but in the years before he learns to read, you need to find other ways to convey your adoration. Thankfully, this is not usually difficult. Parents who love their children take an interest in them and enjoy them. This gets communicated in words, and it gets communicated in action. As a parent of a baby or young child, you need to hold him, gaze into his eyes, sing to him, play with him, laugh with him, read to him, handle him tenderly, revel in the softness of his hair, be astonished at the perfection of his nose, celebrate his achievements, suffer with him his frustrations, keep your word to him, minister to his boo-boos, and call him from the office. If you are ordinarily not a demonstrative type of person, parenting is your invitation to loosen up a bit and show affection more directly to your child than you may be accustomed to doing with others. You cannot spoil a child with too much love.

As a parent, it is also your job to help your child understand his emotions. The wider the emotional world available to him, the richer the life he is likely to lead. You may not like some of the feelings he has, but it is your job to help him understand these feelings so he can understand and accept himself. It is also your job to teach the ways in which his emotions can—and cannot—be expressed.

Your Child's Social Needs

The world in which you are raising your child and the one that you are preparing him to join is populated by a lot of other people. But it isn't enough for us to be in a world with others. We also have to know how to contact and interact with them. As a parent, it's your job to help your child learn how to exist in the social world. This means providing him with opportunities to socialize and with some instruction and guidance in how to do so. It means teaching him manners and appropriate rules for interaction.

We do not live in a well-mannered society. Perhaps your community is an exception; for your sake and that of your children, let's hope so. In the main, manners seem to have gotten lost. Beyond the relative absence of "please," "thank you," and "excuse me," we are likely to come up against much more blatant evidence of graceless living. People talk on cell phones in movie theaters. Telephone customer service representatives seem as likely to disconnect you after you have been holding for twenty minutes as to help you. Television talk shows allow adults to erupt in physical violence. And the local news is at the ready with stories of road rage—a critical breakdown in manners with lethal results.

What does this have to do with being a parent? Not only are you an individual with responsibility for your own behavior, but as a parent, you are raising an individual, or maybe you are raising more than one. You need to bring manners into the equation and to recognize their importance. I have yet to meet a child who was born polite. Good manners are a product of socialization. Parents civilize children. Or they don't. In either case, as children form part of the community at large, we all live with the consequences.

Good manners go beyond saying "please," "thank you," and "excuse me." Your child needs to be taught which fork to use, not to interrupt others who are speaking when he has something to say, and to allow someone else to proceed before he charges through the door. He needs to be taught how to greet someone to whom he has been introduced ("How do you do?" or "It's nice to meet you") and how to depart from a situation ("It was nice to see you" or "Thank you for having me"). Having good manners means meeting a person's eyes when you are speaking to him and using a nice tone of voice with enough volume to be understood. Having good manners means you don't flee from the table the moment after you cram the last bite of dinner into your mouth.

What does it take to rear a child who says "please" and "thank you" to others? What does it take to rear a child who chews with his mouth closed, who does not interrupt conversations, who allows others to go through a door before pushing ahead, who takes turns in games, who asks for permission to be excused from the table? I'll give you a hint: The words "patience" and "seemingly endless repetition" should go somewhere in your answer. Before you can remind children to mind their manners though, you have to teach them manners to begin with. Children need to be taught *explicitly* what is expected of them. This does not mean criticizing them when they are rude. This means telling them in advance what to do, what to say, and how you expect them to behave. It is only after what is expected of them has been made clear that the reminding and repetition part of the enterprise begins.

Your child will need an extraordinary amount of reminding about manners; you need to be prepared for this and be prepared to be consistent. Often I meet with parents who, after making a good start with all the best intentions in this direction, slack off. They start by reminding their child to "say please," but they get tired of repeating this, so they do so inconsistently. What message does this send? It says manners are not all that important. It says they are optional. A child who is only required to use good manners when a parent is in the mood to remind him learns that manners are only for when you feel like using them. He learns manners are not something to which he needs to make a commitment.

But it is not only endless reminders that create mannerly children. Your child learns first and foremost by what he sees you do. I have yet to see a polite child spawned by a rude mother and father. Parents who do not show each other consideration or who do not interact appropriately in the larger world spawn offspring who treat others much the same way.

Anna Graham was not enjoying the Mommy and Me group she recently joined at a local church with her three-year-old son, Jesse. Some of the mothers were cliquish and exclusive. Other mothers were downright mean. One of them failed to intervene when her son repeatedly pushed Jesse out of the way to get to a toy. When Anna stopped the boy, the mother angrily approached her, telling her to mind her own business and not to discipline her son. Several years later, I met with administrators at the church nursery school to discuss providing a series of talks for parents. Asked what topics would be of interest, the administrators immediately identified the children's cliquish behaviors and bullying as significant issues.

Is this surprising? It's an elegant, if unfortunate, example of the degree to which children are bound to manifest behaviors according to their parents' example.

Socializing children properly creates an opportunity for you to brush up on your own skills. A mother in my office, actively engaged in fostering manners in her three-year-old, described an interaction with her husband: "We were in the kitchen in the morning. I was pouring a cup of coffee, and my husband said, 'Can I have a cup?' Before I even realized it, I found myself responding, 'Please?' Thank goodness we both could laugh about it."

It is important to recognize that when you are directing your child to be more mannerly, you need to be mindful about setting a good example for him in the process. Whispering a reminder into a child's ear at a social event is much better manners on your part than is screaming "Did you say thank-you, Sadie?!" across the room.

In addition to being instructed in good manners, your child's social needs include his need to be taught how to negotiate his emotions in a public situation. You need to teach him the way to be gracious if he has lost in a contest or, for that matter, if he has won. You need to teach him how to manage his jealousy in a situation where someone else gets something that he wanted, and how to limit his triumph if he gets something that another person covets. And you need to teach him to control and to channel his expression of anger in situations that frustrate him.

In the long and short term, having good social skills will open opportunities for participation for your child that would not be open to him otherwise. We enjoy socializing with those who are gracious. We tend to avoid boors. In the long term, an individual who knows how to transact interpersonal business gracefully is likely to proceed in the world with self-confidence and is likely to have a lot more friends.

Your Child's Intellectual Needs

Part of your job as a parent involves providing your child with the opportunities to develop his intellectual abilities. Intellectual abilities do not only involve the amount of information your child has amassed. They have to do with his attitudes toward learning and his relationship with his own curiosity. It is not your job to make sure that your child has encyclopedic knowledge of any subject. Rather, he needs you to support him in developing his capacity for thinking and reasoning, so when he comes across a problem or question for which he does not have the answer, he will have the resources to think it through. It is your job to understand something about how his intellectual life develops so you can provide the materials necessary to support him. You will find a more complete discussion about how to do this in Chapter 4.

Defining a Parental Role

Your parental role is the foundation from which you minister to and provide for your child. It guides you in your decision making along the way. It is a mission statement of sorts—a system of beliefs about what being a parent means to you and an understanding of your position in relation to your child. Defining your role as a parent is your job, not your child's. You need to have a coherent perspective about who you are in relation to your child, and you need to be fairly consistent in your approach. You can play certain aspects of parenting by ear, but your understanding of your role cannot be up for grabs.

Does defining a parental role mean you are going to be rigid? No. It means you can be flexible within boundaries that you define. It's all well and good to be sensitive to a child's temperament and personality, but who you are and your beliefs about the main tasks of parenting need to remain consistent. An English teacher, by analogy, may accommodate a visually impaired student by getting books on tape, but if a student does mathematics in her class during reading time, she doesn't allow it. She understands that her job is to teach her students English.

In defining your role as a parent, keep in mind the degree to which your children will learn from you by mimicking your behavior. It's all fine and good to preach exercise, broccoli, and healthy living, but if you are eating potato chips and smoking cigarettes, and the most exercise you've gotten in the last week is from shaking your martini, you're going to get into trouble if you want your child to do otherwise.

In the not-so-distant past, defining a parental role was not much of an issue. Before the 1960s and 1970s, parents were parents, kids were kids, and everyone seemed to know how to proceed and what to do because there were fewer socially acceptable choices. We no longer have a culturally defined and generally agreed upon "right way" to act as parents; we define for ourselves what this role means to us and how we will behave within it.

A generation ago, parents clearly saw themselves as superiors to their children; it is presently in vogue to view everyone more as equals. To the degree to which both parents and children are human beings deserving of basic respect and courtesy, this holds true. Beyond this, however, parents and children are *not* on equal ground, and it does everyone a tremendous disservice to proceed as if it were otherwise. You need to have a belief about who children are in relation to their parents, and that belief should include that the balance of power is unequal and you're the one with more of it. An appropriate parental role has authority at its core.

What Is Authority and Do You Have It?

Contrary to what your three-year-old may tell you, no one in a family is at his best when the children are in charge. This statement could be extended to include the notion that no one in a family does his best when young children have an undue amount of influence in decision making. And no one does his best when the rules for decision making are not clear and consistent. Inconsistently enforced rules are no rules at all. If you are inconsistent, or if you say one thing and do another, your household will be in chaos. Perhaps it already is. Perhaps that is why you picked up this book. If that is the case, then welcome. You are in the right place.

As a parent, it is not your job to win any popularity contests with your child; please don't think you are doing him a favor by trying to become his best friend. Your child will have classrooms and schoolyards full of friends. By contrast, the number of parents available to him is limited.

As a parent, you need to take authority. Taking authority is not the same thing as being authoritarian. Authoritarian approaches to parenting (which I do not recommend) are covered in the next section of this chapter.

Authority in parenting has everything to do with leadership. This means that *you* are in charge. *You* determine the course of action. *You* are steering the ship. What *you* say goes. You may elect to open certain topics for negotiation, but it is *you* who are in charge of determining which topics are open, and *you* who are in charge of determining how far the limits of the negotiation will extend. Authoritative parents do not spend time convincing their children to go along with their ideas.

You cannot "try" to be authoritative. This is akin to "trying" to quit smoking. When you try, there is a weak link in the chain, a place where resolve and commitment are not strong. If parents are trying to take authority, the presumption exists that authority is not within their domain, and children know this. A parent who is trying to take authority is a parent who does not have it. Such a parent's efforts to be authoritative will buckle under pressure. When a parent's authority buckles, the household comes crashing down.

Taking authority with children means you make the rules; you determine the consequences; you carry out the discipline. You are in control. Your position as the leader is as negotiable as the law of gravity, meaning not negotiable at all. You are not apologetic to your children for taking this role, and you are not ambivalent about it.

Does being an authority mean you're a meanie? Absolutely not. Actually, the more authority you allow yourself, the nicer you become. When you have the courage of your convictions, your directives become factual and objective. The nagging, negotiating, wheedling, and second-guessing that can take up so much space in your relationship with your child are gone. You need not speak in a cajoling, angry, or injured manner. Your children suffer less because they can trust your words. You suffer less because you also trust your words.

A mother was observed with her five-year-old son outside a rest room in a busy mall. The mother had an armful of packages. Two younger girls were fidgeting in a double stroller. The boy held his crotch, presumably to staunch the imminent flow. The mother was pleading: "Just go in, Max. It doesn't smell so bad." "It does," he said, "I want a different bathroom." "Come on," she said. "You could hold your nose." "No way! I gotta go, Mom!" At this moment, one of the girls wriggled free of her seat belt. While refastening it, the mother changed her approach. Instead of pleading, she became matter of fact. "Max," she said, "this is the only bathroom around. You have to use it." Max registered this new interaction, his facial expression changed to one of resignation, and he took a step toward the door. Unfortunately, Mother, still occupied with his sister, did not see this. She added, "Please." And everything changed.

51

Max stopped his progress toward the door, his face screwed up in consternation, and his objections and the struggle with mother started anew.

This scenario is an eloquent example of authority gained, and then lost in an instant. Politeness certainly has a place in interactions between parents and children, but this "please" was not polite. This "please" left room for negotiation. This "please" said "No authority here."

Authoritative parents do not engage in a lot of negotiating. Authoritative parents do not waffle. Does this mean that being authoritative means being rigid? No. Once you have established your authority, you can provide some leeway because you do this in the context of your position. What does this mean? For example, say you have told your five-year-old that it is bedtime. He asks for five more minutes so he can finish playing his computer game. You can allow it or not, as long as it is you who are making the decision and as long as you are not capitulating to whining. Authoritative parents do not make decisions based upon wanting to avoid unpleasantries with their children. Authoritative parents do not make decisions because their children have worn them down. They make decisions based upon their beliefs about everyone's best interests. They consider the long- and the short-term consequences of their decisions.

In order to ensure that the parameters remain clear with their children, authoritative parents are not likely to allow for the extra five minutes before bed on a frequent basis. Authoritative parents, however, may decide to institute a five-minute warning before bedtime on a regular basis. This doesn't compromise their authority. In fact, most children are much better able to accommodate changes if they are given some warning and have some time to prepare. Good parents understand their children's needs. They understand that different children have different temperaments and may need different parenting styles. They do what they can to accommodate these differing needs. But they do not accommodate by compromising authority.

How do you become an authoritative parent? You assume the role. Does this mean you will not make mistakes? No. Does this mean that after making one decision you will never reconsider? I certainly hope not. As part of being a parent who takes appropriate authority, you are going to find there are times you will want to change your mind:

The Franklins set a seven-thirty bedtime for their six-year-old daughter, Serena, at the beginning of the school year. She objected strenuously. They stood fast. But Serena remained awake in her room, staring at the ceiling for an hour every night and she still awoke refreshed in the morning, so they extended the bedtime to eight-thirty. This worked fine until Serena got involved in after-school activities. Then she was more tired and started having trouble getting up in the morning. The Franklins changed the bedtime to eight o'clock, discussing their reasons with her, and sticking fast despite her protests. The protests did not last long, and the eight o'clock bedtime worked well for the rest of the year.

Parents who take an authoritative parenting role define the boundaries of children's lives. Within the structure and consistency of these boundaries, children can experience freedom. Authoritative parents and their children understand that to step outside these boundaries is a transgression. Misbehavior occurs. How could it not? We are talking, after all, about children. We are not talking about robots. But authoritative parents deal with misbehavior in a predictable way that makes some sense.

This raises an important point. Your children experience many feelings, both positive and negative, from very early in life. They need to find a way to express these feelings. You need to help your children to channel the expression of these feelings appropriately. Your child will get angry. You need to direct your child to give that anger expression in words or by other nondestructive means while clearly forbidding kicking, biting, and other such behaviors. These restrictions are ultimately comforting to your child; they allow him to understand that despite the intensity with which he may feel something, his real destructive power is limited.

Authoritative Versus Authoritarian Parenting

A number of parents who balk at the idea of being more authoritative with children confuse the concepts of authority and authoritarianism. Loath to embody the latter, they abdicate the role of setting firm limits on children's choices. There is an enormous difference between being an authoritative parent and being an authoritarian parent; however much good authoritative parenting can do, authoritarian parenting can do just as much damage.

Authoritarian parenting is defined by its goal of absolute, unquestioning obedience. Authoritarian parents are rigid. They inspire fear. They don't admit uncertainty to children, and they are also unlikely to admit it to themselves. Authoritarian parents believe they are always right, and they tend to believe that there is only one way to do things: their way. In some households this provides the environment in which power struggles thrive.

> *The Mellons complain that three-year-old Natasha is willful. "A week ago I serve her milk in a blue cup," says Mrs. Mellon. "She says she wants a pink one. Dinner is on the table, and I refuse to change it. She begs, cries, and screams, and eventually we send her to her room with no dinner. Since then, she's asking us for a pink cup every night." I ask if they are complying. Mrs. Mellon says, "Whatever cup I grab from the cabinet is the one she gets." I ask why they are proceeding this way. Mr. Mellon says, "It's a ridiculous thing that she's fixated on. Natasha has to learn she cannot control us."*

The Mellons see Natasha struggling with them, but it is they who are struggling with her, and they are struggling over something trivial. Selecting a pink cup from the cupboard would not inconvenience Mrs. Mellon. There is no indication that Natasha is trying to control anything more than a small element of her world. The cup is a nonissue that has only become an issue because the Mellons are making it into one. In parenting, there are enough issues that can erupt between parents and children. Parents need to be selective and pick their battles. The Mellons are not selective. They are ready to take up arms on every minor point.

Authoritarian parents like the Mellons place a high value on control and tend to see interactions with their children in this context. They see themselves as the arbiters of what is important. Never mind that anyone with experience of preschoolers will tell you that seemingly trivial things like the color of a cup that gets used at dinner or the shapes into which the halves of a sandwich are cut are enormously—and maddeningly—important to kids of this age. If it is not important to authoritarian parents, there will be no accommodations made. By contrast, authoritative parents choose to focus on things that are more significant. Authoritarian parents tend to go to battle on anything that whispers of an encroachment on their control.

Discussions between authoritarian parents and children about things that have been forbidden do not occur, because what's the point? At best, children learn nothing is going to change. At worst, children know that parents will misconstrue their attempts to start discussions as their being obstinate and difficult. Children who have parents who take appropriate authority have the opportunity to question and learn about thinking things through; children who are parented in an authoritarian manner don't have such opportunities. It is not difficult to see how this type of approach limits learning.

> *Jordie Gleason's preschool teacher observed him picking at the skin behind his ears. A visit to the pediatrician ruled out a medical condition, and Mr. Gleason laid down the law: No more picking. But Jordie won't stop. The pediatrician suggests psychological consultation. In the first session, asked why he thinks his son is engaging in this behavior, Mr. Gleason says he doesn't know and doesn't care. He wants to know what type of punishment will be the most effective to stop it. When I suggest we try to understand what is driving the behavior, he scoffs, "Everyone wants to try to figure everything out these days. My dad would have given me a swift kick in the rear, and that would be that."*

Mr. Gleason did not return after this first appointment. He had come to my office to learn punishment strategies that would provide a quick fix to his son's problem. When it became apparent to him that this was not in the cards, he was not interested. In this situation, I could no more assert a point of view that differed from his than his son could. Rather than being willing to see his son's behavior as an attempt to communicate something, Mr. Gleason simply sees it as defiance of his rules. He cannot understand the behavior, and therefore, from his point of view, there must be nothing to understand. When children are parented this way, communication between them and their parents is limited because parents insist communication be transacted on their terms or not at all. However, children often do not have the language or impulse control that would allow them to comply.

As a parent, you are the world to your young child. The way that you are is the way of the world. You are modeling, teaching by example, whether you intend to or not. Because authoritarian parents discourage questioning, their children may make a "tape" of this approach. Some may respond by not questioning much of anything over the course of their lives. They may believe that curiosity is wrong. Because there is no model for working out problems or misunderstandings in the parent-child relationship, when difficulties arise in future relationships, people parented in this manner may be passive and silently resentful. If all questions have been met with "Because I said so," then this is what the person parented in this way will come to expect in every interaction. It is not difficult to see how such a person would stop trying to understand others' meanings and motives, and how poor his relationships could be as a consequence.

In 1967, before there were more regulations governing the treatment of people and animals in psychological experiments, Dr. Martin Seligman conducted an experiment in which a group of dogs were placed on a metal grid through which they received mild electric shocks. Initially, the dogs tried to get away, but barriers were in place preventing escape. When they found they could not leave the situation, the dogs stopped trying to do so and passively accepted their fate. When barriers preventing their escape were removed, the dogs remained on the grid. Dr. Seligman named this phenomenon "learned helplessness." Children who are parented in an authoritarian manner are prone to develop "learned helplessness" so far as their interpersonal relationships are concerned.

Not all children parented in an authoritarian manner become passive; they may become bullies. An authoritarian parent is something of a bully. Those children who may be more temperamentally prone to express their feelings actively rather than to internalize them may identify themselves with this aspect of the authoritarian parenting experience.

Misty Morello, seven years old, is referred for mandatory counseling by the school after bloodying another girl's nose.

Misty is one tough cookie, and all the kids in school are afraid of her. Mrs. Morello brings her to the appointment one-half hour early, and she knocks loudly and insistently on the door to my inner office, despite a sign in the waiting room that says "Please have a seat. Dr. Chidekel will be with you at the appointed time." When I open the door and point out to Mrs. Morello that she is early, she complains about having to wait and threatens to leave. She is clearly unhappy. When I come to the waiting room at the appointed hour, she demands a fee that is half of what I had quoted her over the phone. Her anger at my refusal to accommodate is palpable. As we begin to talk about her daughter's fighting, she tells me with pride, "No one pushes Misty around."

If "eat or be eaten" is the choice, some children would rather be perpetrators than victims. This has been described in psychology literature as "identification with the aggressor." It could be said that Misty Morello has gotten tough by following her mother's lead and identifying herself with her mother. There may be an aspect of self-preservation to this because you would be hard pressed to imagine how a child any less tough than Misty could survive in Mrs. Morello's household.

Children of authoritarian parents may also grow up looking for external rules and structures with which to comply rather than being able to think through things on their own and make independent, well-reasoned decisions. If these children do not develop a pattern of passive acceptance, they may become authoritarian, like their parents. Such children are bullies who demand that others comply with their rules. Other children with authoritarian parents may become actively disobedient, purposefully defying those in charge in order to get the kind of attention that they have learned will not be available to them if they behave more cooperatively. And some children with authoritarian parents may disobey more blindly. Their operative principle: If there's a rule, I break it. In the absence of having a way to work through their complicated feelings, these children may misbehave in a reflexive, knee-jerk way.

Being the Boss Is Not Always Fun

Your doctor knows that in order to be safe against certain terrible diseases, you have to endure the discomfort of being inoculated against them. Doctors don't like inflicting pain, but they give injections anyway because it's their job to keep you healthy. So it is in parenting. You need to take corrective action to prevent problems down the road, even when taking such action is unpleasant.

As a parent, you are the boss, and you will remain the boss until your children are grown and living the independent lives for which you have prepared them. Being the boss, being in charge of children, looks different as children age and progress through different developmental stages. By analogy, in a business, entry-level workers and managers both need supervision, but the quality of supervision is different given the different level of skills that the workers in each category of experience have attained. Your two-year-old needs to be supervised much differently than does your six-year-old, but both still require supervision. Being in charge of both means making decisions according to what you believe is in everyone's best interests, whether your child likes it or not.

Kaeisha Dalama's big present for her fourth birthday is tickets to the Ice Capades, but Kaeisha wakes up the morning of the show with a sore throat, a cough, and a fever of 101.5 degrees. She insists she doesn't feel bad and says she still wants to go. But while she begs, her parents maintain that they cannot let her attend if she is sick, as much for her sake as for the sake of others to whom she might be contagious. The Dalamas feel terrible about the situation, and they tell her as much. They would take her on a different day, but this is the last performance. They offer to make it up to her by taking her to a ballet or concert once she is better, but she is so angry with their decision that she won't talk to them.

The Dalamas are making a decision here for reasons of health and safety. They know that they cannot place others at risk of catching Kaeisha's illness. They also know that as the day goes on, Kaeisha is likely to feel worse and probably wouldn't enjoy the show anyway. Kaeisha doesn't see it that way, nor is she expected to. She is a child. Her inability to take this point of view is exactly why she does not get to make the decision here. The Dalamas' decision, while well reasoned and sound, is not going over well with their daughter. And as the bosses, they have to tolerate this and stand firm. None of us like to see our children upset, but it is sometimes our job to make decisions that make them unhappy.

As a parent, you will make many unpopular decisions for your children that they are not equipped to make on their own. If your child is diabetic or is allergic to a particular food, you are going to have to restrict his diet in a way he will not necessarily like. It doesn't matter how much a child with a peanut allergy wants to eat a peanut butter sandwich that is served at a party. This is not his decision to make. If you are not willing to take charge in this situation and take the heat when the protest occurs, the consequences could be catastrophic.

You may also have to make other decisions for your child that the immaturity of his intellect does not permit him to make. For example, your child can't be on the soccer team and the baseball team if they both practice at the same time. To you, this is logical. You understand that a person cannot be in two places at once. To your child who cannot appreciate this fundamental logic, it may be an outrage. You may have to make the decision about which sport gets sacrificed, and no matter which direction you go, your child may remain unhappy. All you can do is empathize with your child about how hard it is to not be able to do all the things that sound like fun.

Sometimes we will make unpopular decisions for our children that differ dramatically from decisions that other parents make for their children. These are decisions we make on the basis of our values and our beliefs. If you have certain standards for healthful eating, your child may complain that he is the only one at school who doesn't get potato chips and Oreos in his lunch. If you limit television watching in your household, be prepared to hear complaints after your child visits a friend and discovers that in that house, the kids watch as much TV as they want to. Be prepared to contend with the parental version of peer pressure as your children try to argue against a rule with some version of "But *Johnny's* parents say it's okay!"

59

Bobby Baretta, seven years old, is mad. All his friends get to play on a particular baseball team, and his mom and dad have said no to him. Mr. and Mrs. Baretta describe the atmosphere in the particular club as cutthroat, and they believe the coach, who is prone to yell, emphasizes winning at great cost to the kids, many of whom spend entire games on the bench because they are not as large or well-coordinated as their teammates. Bobby is not interested in joining another club with a different coach because his friends are all on this team. The Barettas consult me to determine if they are making the right decision.

In addition to standing firm on a correct decision, the Barettas can use this opportunity to expand Bobbie's ability to think critically and creatively. They might point out that he doesn't like it when they yell at him, and ask him what makes him think he would like yelling any better coming from the coach. They might ask him why he wants to join this team. Is it to sit on the bench with the rest of his small friends? Or does he want to play with them? They might help him think about starting another team with a leader who is more friendly and fair, and asking his friends to join him.

In life, no one is happy all the time, and so it goes with children and parents. Your children will not be happy all the time. Neither will you. This is not a bad thing. Pleasant, smiling times between you and your child cannot be your criterion for success as a parent. To expect happiness and smooth sailing constantly is to take an idealized view of the human condition, which is neither practical nor desirable. Every day can't be a sunny one. Of course, if it never stops raining in the relationship between you and your child, this is an indication that you need to get some help. But the occasional cloudburst is to be expected and not a cause for concern.

The Future Is Now

As a child, John spent a summer at his grandparents' farm. Shortly after he arrived, a big draft horse gave birth to a tiny chestnut filly. John and his grandfather were present at the birth, and his grandfather directed him to rub the foal with a burlap sack while the mama gave her a bath with her big, rough tongue. John named the foal Delilah. Over the course of the summer, John and Delilah could always be seen together when John didn't have chores to do. Within a week, they had developed a game: John would do a special whistle when he came through the pasture gate. Delilah would run up to him, and John would pick up her front legs and place her dainty, little hooves on his shoulders. Soon, Delilah learned to rear up and place her hooves on John's shoulders by herself. And so they played for the rest of the summer until John went back to the city to go to school. He came back to the farm a couple of years later and went straight to the pasture to see Delilah. He did the special whistle. She remembered! She galloped straight toward him, and reared up over him—all twenty-five hundred pounds of her. As he watched her dinner-plate-sized hooves bearing down on his shoulders, John, terrified, flung himself under the fence and narrowly escaped serious injury.

This story is offered to prompt you to think about how you interact with your children, to consider the types of behaviors your children engage in, and to think about what those behaviors might look like down the road. Clearly, some things that look cute coming from a baby or young child do not necessarily look cute coming from an older child or an adult. In fact, some behaviors that seem innocuous enough in babies and small children can be significant problems for that baby and for others later in life if they persist.

- When a baby is first learning to eat solids and covers his face in strained peas, there is hardly a parent who does not run for the camera. We are not running for the camera, however, when this child spoons yogurt into the VCR, or when this adolescent leaves hairballs in the shower and dirty clothes and towels all over the bathroom floor. We are not delighted when we walk or drive through neighborhoods where trash is strewn freely about the street and walls are covered with graffiti.
- When a two-year-old starts to say no and indicates the first hints of temper, the stamping of little feet, the hammering of little fists

against our thighs, and the dramatic flinging of a little self on the ground can seem cute. We are not charmed, however, by an older child's screaming temper tantrum in the toy store. We are not delighted at the behaviors of a school bully.

• When a new runner is told to stop, but instead of halting in his tracks, heads for the farthest reaches of the room as fast as his little legs will carry him while looking over his shoulder with an impish glint in his eye, it is tempting for parents to turn his behavior into a game. It is not a game, however, when a child heads into a busy street and the directive to stop is taken as an invitation to run faster. And who is laughing at the astounding proliferation of police pursuits on television?

A family is, among other things, a group. Parents are the group leaders. Children are group members. This applies to single-parent households with one child as well as big families with two parents and many children. Group behaviors have been studied and written about extensively, and researchers have discovered some basic principles. Among them is this: For a group to be productive and cohesive, group leaders and group members need to maintain awareness of the group's reason for existence and group goals. What does this mean for parents and families? It means that parents who function best in their roles are those who have overarching ideas about those roles, who have an eye toward the future, and who interact with their children accordingly. With this in mind, it is useful to turn your attention, as a parent, to the question of what you foresee for your child in the future.

What does it mean to foresee a future for your child? Contrary to opinions held by some parents, it does not mean starting a two-year-old on the cello to ensure he becomes the next Yo-Yo Ma. Far from being constructive, that type of behavior leads to a host of other problems. Foreseeing a future for your child means recognizing that there will be a future and your child will be part of it. This means taking the long view and preparing children to participate as adults within the community, to make decisions, and ultimately to prepare the next generation that they will create for another future beyond that. We are talking about the continuity of our species and the continuity of a civilized society.

Foreseeing a future for children involves recognizing certain qualities that can be developed in them to allow them their best chance at success in society. Keeping an eye on the future also involves recognizing certain negative qualities in them that will need to be limited. Politeness, attentiveness, respect for others and self, social interest, an ability to tolerate and regulate feelings, curiosity, a willingness to try new things, and personal responsibility are often mentioned as qualities to which parents aspire for their kids. Greed, destructiveness, cruelty, and dishonesty are considered those that will need to be limited.

Young children are malleable. They are learning the shape of the world. While it may be difficult to foster and teach certain behaviors to young children, it is infinitely more difficult to do so when they simultaneously have to unlearn old ways of doing things. With babies, toddlers, and young children, you have as close to a fresh canvas as you are going to get.

> *Ethan Sharpman, sixteen years old, is out of control. He spits on his parents and destroys objects in the house. He was kicked out of school for cursing at the teachers. When his parents attempt to mete out consequences for his bad behavior—grounding him, taking away privileges—he defies them. They say Ethan has been a problem since he was little. They have tried not to come down too hard on him as he always had a negative reaction to any form of discipline. As a toddler, he kicked a hole in the kitchen wall when a toy was taken from him. Recently, they thought giving him a car would increase his independence and make things better. But within two months, he got two moving violations. His license was suspended, but he has been driving anyway. When his parents tell him he cannot, he curses and leaves. They don't feel they can live this way any longer. What should they do?*

The Sharpmans are in big trouble, and the future is not bright. During Ethan's formative years, the Sharpmans failed to go on record by setting and enforcing limits. But the damage goes deeper than this. The Sharpmans have not simply failed to teach Ethan anything about limits. Rather, in failing to set limits and in capitulating to his threats and misbehavior, they have consistently communicated to him that his anger is powerful, that he cannot be contained in any system of rules, and that he is unstoppable. He has obviously taken these messages to heart, as even the court's decree that he is forbidden to drive has failed to make a dent in his behavior. In failing to set and enforce limits for Ethan early on, the Sharpmans created a circumstance in which society will have to set them. Ethan is the type of child who is likely to end up in prison—the ultimate Time Out.

"Any Port in a Storm" Parenting

Maureen Greco is mother to five-year-old Tyler, who recently started bed-wetting and has developed nervous tics. She says she wants to bring him to see me, but since he recently underwent extensive oral surgery, he has developed an intense fear of doctors. I ask the purpose of the dental work. She explains: "When Tyler was little, he would only go to sleep without a fight if I let him have his bottle. The pediatrician told me not to give it to him, but Tyler would scream and cry for hours without it. I figured what was the harm? Any port in a storm, right? So I let him have it. Well, needless to say, the pediatrician was right. Tyler has had four root canals, and now we not only have dental problems, but all these emotional problems on top of it. I wish I'd been stronger."

For most adults today, the demands of life are enormous before parenthood even enters the equation. Children increase the complexity of life immeasurably. With limited time, a job or two to hold down, a spouse to satisfy, bills to pay, a house to clean, meals to cook, and children to rear, we are functioning at or beyond our limits of energy on a daily basis. When minor problems erupt with children—when they are disruptive, when they cry, when they persist in asking for the same thing over and over again despite being told no as many times—we may feel we have no reserves to call upon. We may be inclined to do what seems easiest to smooth the waters and buy some immediate peace. This is "any port in a storm" parenting.

With so many demands being placed on parents and so much stress, many parents stick a finger in the dike when they see a leak, focusing on just getting through one day at a time, crisis by crisis. It's easy to lose sight of the big picture, of a child's future. But it is the child's future—everyone's future really—which is at stake. As illustrated by the story of Tyler Greco, "any port in a storm" parenting may fix a problem in the moment, but it has the potential to lead to much more serious problems down the road.

It is not only incumbent on us to get through each day with our loved ones intact. It is also incumbent on parents to give some thought to the individual who is being developed in the process and consider the implications of their actions. If you take a long view, you can see that the stress of parenting is likely to be less if you can resist the temptation to do what is easiest and act, instead, in your child's long-term best interests. Taking a long view of parenting means looking at things differently.

- Brown tree snakes were brought over to control the population of rodents on a South Pacific island a number of years ago. The reptiles grew so numerous that while they solved the rodent problem, a snake problem arose in its place.
- Kudzu, a vining plant that is indigenous to Asia, was brought to the United States because of its ability to grow rapidly. It was planted in the southeast to address a problem with erosion. Now the erosion problem is fixed, but there is a significant problem with the kudzu, which has choked out most of the native vegetation.

You may not be interested in tree snakes or kudzu, but I hope you are interested in the principles these stories illustrate: What might seem like a good idea today may create unanticipated consequences in the future. Of course your foresight is no guarantee that things will work out as you planned. The less thrown you are when something takes a surprising turn, the more likely you will be able to see a potential opportunity in it and the greater chance you will have to instill this type of resiliency in your children. As a parent, you are best served when you take what action you can to prevent problems in the future, but remain prepared for surprises nonetheless and greet them as gracefully as you can.

"I just want to get through the next fifteen years," said a father of a three-year-old in a parenting group. "Then my son is on his own."

This is an old cliché, but the truth is, once a parent, always a parent. It may be comforting to remind yourself that your children will one day reach the age of majority, but this does not relieve you of the responsibility to do the hard work of parenting for those years when your children are with you. At times, it may seem that there's no energy left to resist a child's will and you can't imagine listening to whining or crying for one more instant. Find the energy. Your young child may have many feelings, but he doesn't have judgment. The whining and crying of today is small potatoes compared with what you may be opening the door to for yourself and your child in the future by capitulating.

Don't Expect a Good Night's Sleep

No one who hasn't had a child knows what to expect as a parent. It doesn't matter how many times you have been told what it's like or how many books you may have read to prepare yourself for the experience. No one's expectations match up with the reality of the child who arrives, and no amount of preparation can really prepare you for what it will feel like to be a parent. So in the absence of really being able to prepare, what can you do? Expect to be surprised. Expect to be caught off guard by how things really feel.

Jenna Wayne, thirteen months, is in constant motion. She needs to be watched like a hawk to be kept out of danger. Jenna's father says it's impossible for him to watch a simple football game because of Jenna's constant activity. Jenna's mother complains that she can't cook a proper dinner because the baby needs to be watched. They're eating take-out more often, and Mrs. Wayne can't get to the gym, so she has yet to shed her pregnancy weight. Weekends, far from being the idyllic family time that both parents always anticipated, are chaotic. The pressure to get Jenna her meals, ensure she gets down for naps, and try to have any fun is overwhelming them all. The household is getting increasingly tense. Last night was the final straw. After whining and crying all day, Jenna was up at two in the morning with a fever. Her parents were up with her for an hour before she was finally able to get to sleep.

Children change your life. They do so in ways you can anticipate and in ways you cannot. One thing, however, is certain: Once your children arrive, you will not be able to do many of the things you did prior to having them, in the same way. Children get sick. They wake up early in the morning and sometimes in the middle of the night. They cry and are not always easily soothed. When they start talking, they repeat the same question over and over again. They whine. They are selfish. They don't like to share. They are not uniformly thrilled at the arrival of a sibling. These are not the reasons people *want* children, but these experiences and others like them are part of the deal, nonetheless. To have a child and to expect things to happen otherwise is to court disaster. It guarantees that a tone of resentment will pervade the household, and it sets the stage for your child to grow up with a negative opinion of himself based upon your attitude toward his very appropriate needs and expectable, ordinary behaviors.

Remember back to a time you were sick. Imagine that when you told someone close to you that you weren't feeling well, he was angry with you and said, "Oh great! Again? So *now* what do you need?" or something similar. Imagine going to a restaurant where the waiter was irritated with you as he wrote down your order. Imagine him setting your plate on the table with an angry flourish. How do you feel? Now realize that as unsettling as these experiences would be, you are an adult who has already formed a sense of self. You don't need to rely on those who treat you poorly. You can call another friend to minister to you when you're ill. You can leave a restaurant. You also have a relatively mature coping system. About the people who treat you poorly, you can think "What jerks!"

Your young children have no alternatives beyond you; they are utterly dependent. If you are angry about having to give a bottle to your baby in the middle of the night, he cannot go elsewhere. He cannot conceptualize an "elsewhere." If he is sick in the middle of the night and your irritation with having been woken by him limits the comfort you are able to give him, he cannot find an alternative.

Children have fundamental, nonnegotiable needs. You do not get to choose whether to meet these needs or not, and you are not within your rights to view your child's expression of these needs as anything personally directed against you. A baby who needs a diaper changed is not being capricious. A toddler who needs a nap is not getting cranky on purpose to ruin your afternoon at the zoo. You are within your rights to get irritated with your spouse for keeping you longer in the hardware store while you want to get to the gym. You are not within your rights to get angry with your four-year-old for interrupting your sleep with a scream of terror after he awakens from a nightmare.

Until the age of nine or ten or so, your child is too young to have a developed sense of himself. Babies and young children don't think "What idiots!" of their parents. Rather, they are egocentric in their thinking and are liable to refer everything that occurs—negative and positive—to themselves. When their needs are greeted with annoyance or irritation, they are liable to develop a feeling that their needs are too great, and that they are inherently rejectable or unworthwhile. Children treated this way are liable to expect to be rejected when they are feeling most vulnerable, and they may seek this kind of relationship when they're adults because it is what is most familiar. We certainly don't wish this for our kids.

A father in therapy complained that his two-month-old baby was awakening every two hours. "Last night I was up with her for three hours. First she wanted to play. Then she starts crying. I couldn't get her to stop. I woke up my wife and practically dropped her in her lap. I said, 'You deal with her!'" I empathize with how difficult it can be to be sleep-deprived and to have to deal with a baby's seemingly irrational needs in the middle of the night. But I also ask the father, "Suppose your daughter is fifteen years old, going through the emotional ups and downs that go along with that age. One day, her boyfriend comes to pick her up. When she sees what he's wearing she insists on changing clothes even though they are already late and she looks great. The boyfriend explodes at her, 'For God's sake, get in the car. Don't be ridiculous. I came all the way over here, and I can't be expected to wait for you while you change your stupid clothes!' What would you do?" "No one's talking that way to my kid," says the father.

Based on their experiences with you, your children are concluding what they have a right to expect. The inner world is shaped in such a way that it recognizes what has become familiar to it during growth.

There is yet to be a parent who reports having been thrilled with being awakened at three in the morning to be vomited on by a two-year-old. We can all agree that being vomited on is disgusting. But for the parent who expects otherwise, it is more than disgusting. It is a betrayal. Conversely, a parent who realizes and accepts that into every parent's life a little vomit must fall may not be pleased with what has occurred, but is not likely to feel so betrayed and angry. This parent is not likely to convey a message to the child that what he has done—and could not have helped doing—is wrong.

In the absence of anger and feelings of betrayal, there is room for compassion. We've all been sick. We all know how unpleasant it is, and we all know the world of difference that a kind word or a soft hand on our brow can make. A parent who is not surprised at a child's illness is more likely to be able to offer a soothing hand, a tender voice. A parent who expects such occurrences as an inevitable part of parenthood is not so likely to be preoccupied with his or her own needs in such a circumstance. A child who is met with compassion can become a compassionate person. He can call up the memory of softness and consideration. He can apply it to himself, soothing himself when he feels needy and vulnerable. And he can offer it to others.

When people talk about learning from experience, this is what they are referring to. You cannot create a kind child by simply explaining kindness to him. You cannot create a kind child simply by sending him to religious school and indoctrinating him in your religion's values and principles. You cannot create a kind child by punishing him when he is unkind. If you want a child who is compassionate, treat him with compassion. If you want a child who is confused and conflicted, explain to him that he should be caring and generous toward others while you make it clear that you resent his needs.

And You Thought All That Was Behind You

Your experience of being a parent cannot help but put a spotlight on your experience as a child being raised by your parents. In the course of parenting your children, memories of and feelings from your childhood will come to you unbidden, whether you welcome them or not. Sometimes they will announce themselves. "Ah, yes," you will say as you bring your child to the dentist for the first time and a memory of your first cleaning and the pack of sugarless gum you were given at the end of it rushes back. Other times, memories will sneak in more surreptitiously, and you won't even be aware that you are under their influence.

Sarika Quetzie wonders what is wrong with her. She dropped Jamal at his first day of kindergarten four hours ago. She sobbed all the way home, and she is now standing in the middle of her kitchen, still sobbing, with no end in sight. Mrs. Quetzie had prepared herself for the first day of kindergarten and the milestone it represented in her son's growth, but she had no idea she would respond so strongly.

Actually, Mrs. Quetzie might find her way to some relief if she were to realize that her crying is not so much about her son's growing independence from her. Rather, Jamal's separation from Mrs. Quetzie has opened a floodgate of feeling left over from a series of separations from her own parents when she was small. Parenting will bring back such memories. You won't always be able to anticipate your reactions, but if you orient yourself to think this way, you may be able to see your way clear when you find yourself in the grip of a powerful feeling that seems way out of proportion to the event which brought it on.

Just as parenting will cast light on memories of your childhood, so you have an opportunity when parenting your children to see and understand aspects of your parents that you could not see before. As a parent raising a child, you revisit the past in your memories, but you do so with a foot in the world of adults. You have an opportunity to gain perspective on things which happened that you could not have before, when you had only a child's point of view from which to look at events. Sometimes this can allow you to be more compassionate or understanding about things that transpired between you and your parents.

A mother of two young girls comes to consult me when she finds herself at her wit's end with their bickering. She says, "I remember my sister and me going at it like this. I remember one

70

Christmas day I made some comment that if my sister was going to mix the waffle batter, then I wasn't going to eat the waffles. My mother screamed, sent me to the neighbor's house, and took away all my Christmas presents. Eventually, she gave them back, but I have always remembered that day. As I think back on it now, I can't say I agree with what she did, but I can certainly understand where she was coming from.

Parenting can also give us a new perspective on family myths. Family myths are old ideas about how things are in our family. A family myth can become like a mantra that is repeated so often, we no longer hear it or process the meaning of the words. "Aunt Jane was such a good cook." "Grandma Betty was such a generous person." "Your mother loved you kids more than anything." Such ideas seem to be immutable truths. Becoming parents to our own children, however, often puts the spotlight on these beliefs and leads us to question them. This is not always an easy process. There is a strong pull to hold on to these ideas and leave them undisturbed because they comprise fundamental aspects of our family identity. They are the foundation stones on which rest much of our family as we have understood it. It can be unsettling to let these ideas go, yet it can be very useful to do so as well.

Stella Arbois is irritated with her six-month-old baby's need for two middle-of-the-night feedings. Not only is she exhausted, but adding to her burden is guilt about her exhaustion and irritation. "My mother had seven of us and never gave a thought to herself. I've always been told I was never grateful enough for what she did for me and my siblings. I didn't realize just how hard it must have been for her until now. I called her this weekend and told her how tired I was. She said, 'Well, now you know what I went through with all of you.'" I reflect that this hardly seems like a response from a mother who is as selfless and generous as Mrs. Arbois's mother has been reputed to be. Mrs. Arbois says she never thought of it this way, but in fact, she is aware that when she got off the phone, she felt more hopeless than she had felt before she placed the call.

Is it not difficult to see the seeds of resentment in Mrs. Arbois's mother's response to her daughter. This interaction prompted Mrs. Arbois to question the idealized image she and the rest of her family members held of her mother—the family myth of her mother's unlimited and ungrudging generosity. As she was able to see her mother in a role that was less idealized, Mrs. Arbois was able to begin to see herself in a different light too. She saw herself not as an ungrateful wretch—an image of herself that had followed her from childhood into her adulthood and was clearly in painful evidence now—but rather, as an all-too-human and tired mother whose feelings of frustration were entirely expectable and acceptable. She saw that they did not invalidate her affection for her baby and her delight in being a mother, but that they existed alongside these feelings. Illuminating the old family myths and taking her mother off her pedestal opened the way for Mrs. Arbois to have a nicer relationship with herself. She could accept her own feelings and needs, and this allowed her to become a good deal more tolerant of her baby's feelings and needs too.

The Toughest Job You'll Ever Love: Why You'll Love It

Your children will surprise you. They will love and cherish you beyond all reason. They will matter to you down to the center of every cell in your body. Your children will be creative in ways you yourself have never imagined. They will attend to the things in the world that you would as easily have stepped on or over, and they will show you the magic that is there. They will make you laugh. And laugh. And laugh. Your children will marvel at simple things you show them. They will make you reach into yourself to find ideas and feelings and answers that you had not known you possessed. They will honor you with an opportunity to be trusted at a level you could not imagine existed prior to having them. Raising them will give you a tangible sense of continuity into the future, and a deep feeling of continuity with the past. Your children will call upon what is best in you, yet sometimes bring out what is worst, and they will forgive you and keep loving you anyway. They will show you what love without conditions really means. They will open new social worlds to you, giving you things in common with other parents and providing opportunities for sharing with them a time in your lives that is unique and extraordinary. Your children will give you the opportunity to learn things you thought you already knew all over again, through their eyes. They will strip you of assumptions that you didn't even know you had made, and they will bring more life into your life in the place of them. Your children will bring forth in you tenderness and vulnerability that you might never have realized you were capable of feeling. At other times they will call upon strength in you that you could not have imagined you possessed.

I recognize that not all parents feel this way about their children. You may be reading this and think that I have described never-never land. Or you may interpret this to mean that this is what is expected of you, and you may think that if you are having a parenting experience which feels otherwise, this means you are doing something wrong. I hope you don't feel this way, as it certainly is not my aim. Rather, I have attempted to describe the best that it can be in parenting—a parenting peak experience, if you will. It's a state of relationship and feeling you may recognize in a moment here or there when you are playing with your children. It may come over you when you look in on them when they are sleeping. Or it may be a feeling you get when your child crosses your mind in the course of your workday. If you have not had this experience, don't close the door on it as a possibility. If you convince yourself this isn't possible—and I promise you that it is—then you won't recognize it when it is happening. But if you believe it is possible and hold out hope and faith in yourself and your children to have this kind of experience, then you will see it when it is there to be seen. And you and your children will be the richer for it.

Chapter 3

How Parents and Children Experience the World:
Sometimes the Twain Shall Meet

If you are preparing to move to a foreign country, chances are you're going to do a little research before you pack your things and sell your house. You might buy some travel guides, go on the Internet, or speak to others who have moved there. You'll do so in recognition of the fact that you'll be entering a different culture. When people from different cultures come together, all are better served if there is an understanding of the ways in which values, language, customs, and perspectives may be similar and how they may differ. This prevents misunderstandings and allows for smoother communication.

As parents, we may not realize that the same appreciation for cultural differences that we readily apply to people from different countries can be put to good use in a household populated by adults and children. If you have young children, you don't have to get out your passport and board a plane for a crosscultural experience. You need not look beyond your front door.

It could be said that young children and adults occupy the same space while inhabiting different worlds. In the eighteenth century, the French philosopher Rousseau said, "Childhood has its own ways of seeing, thinking, and feeling, and nothing is so foolish as to try to substitute ours for theirs." In this chapter we will take a look at "ours" and "theirs." If you are preparing to be a parent, this will help you get a bit of perspective on the way children experience things. If you are already a parent of a young child, this chapter may give you a new understanding of your child's perspective and give you a new understanding of how she thinks and what she feels.

The Culture of Early Childhood
Versus the Culture of Adults

When you go on vacation, how much fun is it to explore the cruise ship or the hotel, set out to discover an unfamiliar city, see new things, eat in new places, look at different scenery? Vacations are restorative—not only in that they represent time away from familiar obligations, but also because they give us a chance to look at the world with new eyes and forget a bit about the pressures of our everyday lives.

Children are on vacation all the time. They have minimal external obligations, and they have a different understanding of, and experience with, time. They don't need to change locations to see the world with new eyes; their eyes *are* new. Every day is a discovery. Most of us adults are jaded, and we fail to see so much of what is in the world around us. Rushing from one place to another to accomplish what we need to do in the course of a day, we are likely to fail to see the places in between. Children, on the other hand, are all about the in-between. Do you doubt this? Try to get a young child through a revolving door for the first time. The concept of "late to where we're going" is not factored in. "Where we're going" is paramount in your mind. "Fun door" is what your child has discovered, and that's where her mind is.

Nothing is self-evident or obvious to children. In the absence of having developed the habits that adults have, children are constantly creative, combining and recombining elements of life in a variety of ways that delight and astonish us old fogies. There is nothing fogyish about kids. Children are not stodgy. They are not old-fashioned. Quite literally, they are new-fashioned—fashioning in the course of their days decisions and objects and ideas that are unlike anything that has come before.

Young children are not limited by the constraints of what appears to us to be common sense or convention because they haven't had a chance to learn them. In the absence of knowing what they are supposed to think or do, children come up with their own ideas. Children don't respond to things according to preconceived notions because young children are relatively new to the world. They don't have much "pre." Without a lot of "pre," children are free to think of the things that they encounter in their own unique ways. They are relentlessly creative. They can't help it.

Where adults (hopefully) have common sense, children have child sense. Applying common sense to child sense when necessary is one of the responsibilities of raising kids. But it is equally important for parents to apply common sense judiciously. Common sense is necessary to get everyone safely through the day, but there's not much fun in it. Child sense, by contrast, is delightful. Being privy to child sense is one of the gifts of raising kids. The opportunity to see things through a child's developing eyes is part of the fun of parenting. It's delicious.

> *A five-year-old boy was returning from a trip to a local ranch with his parents. The trip had been fun and educational. The boy had learned from the rancher about the animal origins of his hamburgers and chicken nuggets. In the car on the way home he looked as though he was turning something over in his mind. Finally, he piped up. "Mom?" he said. "Do the cows know that they're made out of meat?"*

All of us once had child sense. Over time, as we have grown and have had experiences in the world, things that once were new and interesting have stopping capturing our attention. The first time you drove a car, you attended to every detail. You had to think consciously about which was the gas pedal and which was the brake. You had to remind yourself to signal, to look over your shoulder, and to look in the rearview mirror before a lane change. When you become a more experienced driver, you do not need to be so deliberate about the small acts that make up driving. You don't need to remind yourself consciously to look over your shoulder before a lane change, for example. Driving is not an activity unto itself, but rather it has become a means to an end. While you remain vigilant about the activities around you when you are in the driver's seat, the small movements that make up the act of driving have become relatively automatic.

Young children, however, are not on automatic pilot. Like Zen monks, children meet what are to us mundane experiences in daily life as things that are fresh and new. It is we, the adults, who walk to the mailbox to get the mail without considering it a real possibility that rather than walk, we might skip or walk backwards. Just because. It is we, the adults, who sit down to eat dinner without thinking that we might, before digging in, make up a song about our carrots. Childhood is the time for this. Childhood *has* the time for this. Adulthood has less time for this.

It was Saturday. John Steiner, five years old, had been on a walk with his parents, and they had tickets to a puppet show in the afternoon. Mrs. Steiner: "I made hot dogs for lunch. John squirts ketchup on his plate and says, 'Look. It's red like the roses we saw in our neighbor's yard.' I agreed, but I told him to hurry and eat. He takes a bite, but then he's using the hot dog as a brush and painting ketchup all over the plate. Then he's turning the hot dog into an airplane, zooming it over his plate with sound effects. He says, 'Mom do you remember when we went camping and we cooked hot dogs on sticks?' I tell him we're going to miss the puppet show if he doesn't hurry. He takes a bite, but then he's talking about the camping trip—the stream we crossed, the mosquito bites he got, the snake we saw. I don't understand why he can't focus. Do you think he has attention deficit hyperactivity disorder?"

Every child has attention deficit hyperactivity disorder if we measure her according to her ability to sustain attention on what we think is valuable. We are all familiar with the phrase "Stop and smell the roses." This is a directive from adults, for adults. This is not something you need to tell a child. A child not only stops to smell the roses, but she's liable to want to touch them, taste them, water them, and dig around in the dirt they are growing in to see what it feels like and to discover what treasures it might contain.

How Children Experience Time

Time is an abstract concept. You can't hold it in your hand. You can't portray it in a picture. You can't taste it or hear it or smell it. Yet anyone reading this—presuming you are over the age of six or seven—has some understanding of it. How did you come by this? What is your relationship to time? And how was it different for you when you were younger?

We adults rarely occupy the moments in the day through which we live. At any given moment, we are likely to be thinking about what we need to do later, or thinking about something that has happened previously. This way of being in the world has its downside. It leads us to miss things around us. But it is not all bad. It allows us to prepare for the road ahead, to anticipate difficulties in order to avoid them, and to anticipate opportunities in order to take advantage of them.

As adults, our understanding of ourselves in relationship to time lets us use our memory of past experiences to make decisions in the present to meet future goals. For example, if you are presently on the horns of a parenting dilemma, you might recall that in the past you profited from reading a book. You decide to buy this book to help you resolve your problem so it will not follow you into the future. Perhaps you buy this book on tape because you recall that in the past, despite your best intentions, print books that you have bought remained unread because of your hectic schedule. This ability to use the past to make decisions in the present makes you more effective at meeting the demands of your adult life. It also makes the world a less threatening place because it gives you more of a sense of control. You recall a past in which you have acted upon the world, and you, in this way, can gain confidence in your ability to cope in the present and future.

In living a grown-up life, you need to function with an awareness of yourself in relation to time or you are going to get yourself in trouble. Consider the following scenario: You arrive at the airport Christmas Eve, bags in hand, attempting to book tickets to a distant state only to discover that all the seats have been sold out for months. Unable to travel, you return to your home only to discover that your gas has been shut off because you missed the deadline to pay the bill. You are cold, but you are also hungry, so you set out on a shopping trip only to discover that all the markets are closed for the holiday. What do all these things have in common besides being component parts of a miserable Christmas Eve? The failure to plan ahead.

Intuitively, we know we cannot rely upon children to plan ahead. It is our job to make sure there is drinking water in the beach bag and that a jacket gets taken for later in the evening when it gets cold. While you are provisioning the car for the journey (common sense), your child is chasing butterflies in the backyard (child sense). Your mind is on the future. Your child is in the right here, right now.

The ability to think yourself back and cast yourself forward in time not only makes you a more effective planner, but it also gives you your sense of self. You remember who you have been in the past and what you have done. You imagine yourself in the future. You may want to change or improve yourself, but you will still be the same individual with the same history. This goes a long way toward permitting you to tolerate some of the unpleasant things in life. You understand that some things, while not enjoyable, are transient. You may not want to get an injection at the doctor, but you understand that the experience will be short-lived and the sooner you get it over with, the better. Your young child, by contrast, may be terrified of the injection. Without the memory of having lived through things and come out on the other side of them, your child experiences any threat as a dire one. And of course without this sense of herself in time, your child has no ability to recognize that if she hadn't been screaming and hiding under the examination table for the last ten minutes, the shot would already be done and she would be on her way home with a Barbie sticker from the receptionist. You can try to reason with a young child and explain this, but she is not likely to know what you are talking about because she hasn't yet the capacity to understand time.

Once you develop a concept of time, the relationship you have to it will depend upon the life you lead. In most adults' lives, time is a constant companion. In the course of a day, most parents will have to make lunches in the morning, cook breakfast, drive a carpool, run errands, put in a full day at the office, pick up the kids from day care, bring them home, cook dinner, supervise baths, read bedtime stories, make phone calls, and pay bills. As an adult, your daybook, weekly planner, or Palm Pilot becomes an extension of your arm. You have a certain amount to accomplish and a certain amount of time in which to do so. You have a sense of how much time things should take. You need to keep time in mind constantly in order to make sure that you are able to do what you need to do.

A mother of four returned from a two-week vacation and said, "Being away that long was the ultimate in luxury—not the place we stayed. That was pretty standard. But simply in the fact that for the first time in longer than I can remember, I lost track of time. I didn't even have to keep track of what day it was, much less when I needed to drive carpool or keep a doctor's appointment or get the kids to karate or dance class. It's like a constant noise that you're not even aware of until it stops. You don't realize how much the daily grind wears on you until you get away from it."

The ability to see ourselves through time and make future decisions based upon what happened before is clearly within the purview of adults. Why? It's not because young children don't want to think in these ways. It's because their life experience and their brain development do not permit it. As an adult, to understand yourself in relation to time, you needed:

- *To live through multiple experiences in the world.* There is no way you are going to understand time without having had plenty of opportunity to live through some of it. Children have had limited time to have experiences.
- *To be able to find recurring patterns among your experiences so you can reference them effectively.* When you look back in time, you have to have a way to organize your previous experiences. For example, you may be distressed that your spouse is going on a business trip, but you can look to the mental category "Previous Business Trips" and be comforted as you recall how, in the past, your spouse has called you at a certain hour to let you know he or she arrived safely. You can also look to the mental category "Airplane Travel" and recall that a trans-Atlantic trip will involve a change in time zones, which means you and your spouse have to make a plan about when phone calls can be made. The part of your brain that permits memories to be stored and retrieved according to these different categories is not developed in young children. Children have to develop abstract thinking before they can group experiences in such categories.
- *To develop the language to represent your experiences.* Children's capacity for abstract and conceptual thinking progresses throughout the early elementary years along with the language that they need to describe the concepts and ideas they are discovering. Until

they have the words to describe and label what they have experienced, children will be limited in their ability to organize and get access to their memories.

- *To be able to stop yourself from responding to your first impulse in a situation.* When we think of the physical abilities children develop in the first years of their lives, we are most likely to think about the developmental milestones of sitting upright, crawling, walking, jumping, and climbing. Along with these abilities, children are developing physically in another way that is no less meaningful, but which tends to be less celebrated. That is, children progressively develop the ability to sit still. The ability to sit still and inhibit your first impulse to act in a situation is essential if you are to develop an understanding of yourself in relation to time. It permits you to pause in a given situation, reference your previous memories, and imagine the outcomes of different courses of action before you decide how to proceed. The part of a child's brain that permits her to stop herself from responding to her first impulse develops slowly throughout childhood and is not fully mature until adolescence.

Children benefit from their parents' understanding of, and relationship to, time because parents get children to school, to the puppet show, and to the doctor in a reasonably timely fashion. Parents buy children jackets before the weather turns frigid and start the roast cooking in advance of the dinner hour. Adults, however, profit from children's relationship to time in important ways as well. Have you ever had the opportunity to walk through an area where previously you had only traveled by car? Walking, you see the red of the neighbor's geranium against the aqua windowpane, the small purple flower growing at the base of the mailbox, the lizard that peers at you from under the front steps. Where adults speed through, children walk. When we slow our pace to join a child in the present moment, we are enriched by the details around us. While putting the roast in the oven ahead of time ensures that the body will be fed, slowing down and noticing details in the world nurtures the soul.

How Children Think

Mrs. Kivlitz was on the phone with five-year-old Marika. Marika was distracted, and Mrs. Kivlitz found herself having to repeat questions several times. She was growing increasingly frustrated. Finally, she said, "Marika, if you are on the phone with me, you have to listen. When you don't answer me, I don't know if you've heard me, if you still have the phone, or if you've walked away. I don't know what you're doing because I can't see you." There was a pause. Then Marika asked, "Can't you see my ear?"

The world of adults is populated by people who are (for the most part) able to think logically. This developmental achievement is reached in small steps.

When they are born, babies do not differentiate anything from anything. The world is a mass of sensation, and babies do not have awareness of themselves as distinct from it. A baby's sense of herself as distinct from everything that is not herself develops in the first few months of life. As babies begin to get an inkling of themselves as whole entities, they also begin to get a sense of other whole entities. For example, from a breast, an eye, a scent, and a tone of voice gradually develops a stable sense of a mother to whom all these parts belong.

Until your baby is eight to ten months old, things that she cannot actually see do not exist. Your baby cries mightily when in need because in your absence, she cannot be soothed with the memory of your comfort. There is no future and no past because she cannot yet conceive it. If you are not in sight, there is no you anywhere. There is only now with whatever feeling it contains.

When they are between eight and ten months old, babies develop a concept that things that cannot be seen continue to exist. You will recognize this stage when you can no longer remove an object from your baby's grasp and hide it without occasioning a protest. Your baby may cry when you leave now, not because you have ceased to exist, but because she has a concept of you as someone who continues to exist and who can be summoned, even when you are not in view.

When the concept of the permanence of things develops, a baby's thinking is still concrete and dependent on actual physical objects and experiences. She may remember that things that are not in view continue to exist, but she does not have an abstract concept of what those things are. Your twelve-month-old understands "ball" by holding one. But, if you show most twelve-month-olds a picture of a ball, they will see the physical properties of the actual picture—the paper, the frame, the colors and lines on the page—but will not recognize what the picture depicts. The idea that one thing can represent another thing—that there is a concept of "ball" in addition to the actual thing that can be held and thrown—comes along in the second year of life.

Concepts that we adults take for granted have their foundations in the physical experiences babies and young children have in the world. Think of the word "heavy." Could you explain the meaning of this to someone who had never held anything in her hand? Could you explain "warm" to someone who had never had the physical feeling of temperature? Even depth perception is founded on early physical experience. Your baby crawls and reaches for something and has the experience of having to reach farther for the object that is smaller. You don't teach depth perception by explaining to a child that the farther-away object looks smaller, or that the thing that is partly obscured by another thing is farther away. That is something you learned, initially, through the same physical experiences that your child will come to on her own. Dealing concretely and physically with actual objects in space allows children to develop concepts of "behind," "in front of," "farther," and "under." Your child will not learn what "wet" means without having experience with liquid. Your child won't learn "fast" without the experience of movement.

Through actual experiences in the world, the foundation for your child's logical thinking and her understanding of abstract concepts is being laid. This process is as biologically wired into your child's scheme for mental development as sitting, walking, and crawling are wired into her scheme for physical development. You can trust your child to develop in these ways.

A six-year-old was on an airplane with her father. She was drawing a horse race. She drew circles behind the horses' hooves

*to represent the dust they were kicking up. Behind the first horse
she drew two circles, the second horse had three circles, and the
third horse had four. She explained to her father, "Look, he's
going slow because he has two circles, and he has three circles so
he's faster, but he has four circles so he's the fastest." Then she
paused. "Hey," she said, "two circles, three circles, four circles.
That's like numbers!"*

There is no class that your child can take to make logical, conceptual
thinking develop faster. And there's no reason to accelerate the process. In
fact, there are ample reasons *not* to do so.

We live in a time in our culture that values youth, competition, and
speed. Many parents will proudly crow about a child not having crawled
before walking, or having spoken in phrases and sentences before the age
of twelve months. Viewed through the lens of our contemporary cultural
values, such precocity seems enviable. "What a smart child!" we may
think. "How advanced!" But viewed through the developmentalist's lens,
these precocious achievements are not necessarily positive.

We live in a time when to determine a child to be average in any
domain is tantamount to calling her inferior. But average is not bad, particularly when we are talking about child development. Certainly, we
aspire to average fetal development. We consider it average for the baby to
be born somewhere between thirty-eight and forty-two weeks gestation.
Falling outside this window places a child at risk. Does this mean every
baby born at thirty-four weeks is going to have problems? No. There are
babies born at thirty-four weeks who have no problems at all. But when a
baby comes early, we pay more attention because an early birth is an
anomaly that can be associated with later problems.

As there is a wisdom to normal fetal development—each day in utero
has a particular purpose with respect to preparing the child for survival
outside the womb—there is a wisdom underlying the normal course of
development *after* a child is born. A progressive pattern of abilities develops that tends to follow a particular sequence. This sequence reflects the
progressive maturation of connections inside your child's brain. It is really
rather miraculous, and you have a front-row seat from which to watch it
all unfold. Did you know your child will scribble vertically before she is

able to scribble horizontally? Watch, and you will see that when she first draws a circle, she will begin at the bottom and proceed clockwise. It is only later that she will start drawing circles at the top and proceed counterclockwise. Long before your child's language emerges, an entire pattern of communication skills will precede it. Before you celebrate the word "doggy," for example, celebrate the finger that can draw your attention to the family pet by pointing.

Normal development is defined by the sequence of abilities that unfolds in a child, and by age parameters within which most children acquire each new skill. For example, one child walks at nine months and another walks at sixteen months. Neither raises the pediatrician's eyebrows because both are considered normal. Neither early nor late walking within normal parameters is associated with any positive or negative outcome in a child's life. Children who walk early are no smarter than those who walk later. Really.

Of course, there are children who achieve developmental milestones in a sequence that varies from the normal pattern. Just as a premature birth *may* presage later problems for that child, so too a variation of the developmental pattern, including the very late *or* very early achievement of a milestone, may indicate the potential for the development of later problems. As is the case with a premature birth, when there is an anomaly in development, we simply pay a bit more attention as such a child grows to ensure that there is not something amiss that merits clinical attention. For example, we may understand that there is a need to be concerned about a child who is not walking by her second birthday. We may not be so attuned to the need to be concerned about a baby who rolls from front to back at the age of four weeks, but the early achievement of this milestone may signal an unusual quality of muscle tone that may be associated with a disorder. It seems obvious that a child who has no words at the age of two and a half needs to be assessed. When a child speaks fluently and with adult-like intonation at sixteen months, however, this too merits attention. Speaking so early may be an early sign of a particular type of learning disorder, particularly if the child speaks excessively, repeating words with no understanding of their meaning, and produces multiple utterances unrelated to the activities at hand.

I'm not trying to panic you. I simply want you to see normal, average child development as something to celebrate in its own right. It's an invitation not to feel bad if your child is not ahead of the curve or ahead of every other child in the Mommy and Me class, and not to feel triumphant if she is. This is an invitation to take pressure off of you and your child.

Between the ages of two and six, your child has specific, nonlogical qualities to her thinking, that are a part of the normal development of her mental abilities.

- *She will tend to see everything in reference to herself.* It gets dark because she has to go to sleep, the sun moves when she moves, the door is for her to go through, and the rain makes puddles for her to splash in.
- *She will be fooled easily by appearances.* She believes a ball will sink in water because it's big. If you pour water from a short, broad vessel into a tall, narrow one, she has no sense that the amount remains consistent and will tell you the taller vessel, because it seems bigger, has more.
- *She will attribute consciousness to everything around her and see everything as potentially coming to life.* The moon sleeps at night, the sun wakes up, the mountain is following her in the car, and she is writing with a friendly pencil.

You cannot talk a child who is at this "illogical" stage in intellectual development past it any more than you can talk a child into growing taller. Getting taller and thinking more logically are both developmental processes that require the right conditions. To help your child achieve physical stature, you provide good food, ample rest, and access to regular health care. To permit your child to develop intellectually, you need to provide concrete learning materials and hands-on, active learning experiences. Does this mean scheduled classes? No. Your four-year-old child may tell you that the sun moves when she moves. Please don't think that she needs to be disabused of this notion by being enrolled in a peewee astronomy program at your local planetarium, where she will learn the relative positions of the planets in their orbits in space. Your child may learn to parrot what she's taught in such a circumstance and she may impress your friends when they come over for dinner, but this is not true learning.

One day when your child is at a picnic or at the park, she will look up from the blanket where she's been sitting to discover that the sun is in a different place in the sky while she hasn't moved an inch. This is a discovery that will excite her. This is true learning.

What Makes a Child Secure?

Because she is limited in her ability to engage in abstract thinking and because her relationship to time is different from yours, the things that make you feel secure and the things that make your child feel secure are very different. Your young child is likely to be more directly in touch with her basic needs than you are, and she does not have the ability to experience her needs being filled in abstract or indirect ways. For example, you, the adult, understand that working to make money fulfills the need for safety. Working allows you to provide food and shelter. Maybe you have a stock account with a broker, contribute to a 401K plan, or are working on making partner in your firm. These work-related activities provide you a sense of security for the future.

By contrast, your child has no sense of the relationship between work and safety. Safety to your child is your arms around her; you are nearby. If she thinks about your work at all, she most likely sees it as something that takes you away from her. You can explain to your crying five-year-old, who wants to spend the day with you, that you are going to work to make the money that's necessary to send her to school and buy her clothes and toys. This explanation might make you feel better, but it is not going to help her. She is presenting you with a feeling, and you are meeting her expression with logic. To the pain associated with your departure is now added the pain she feels at being fundamentally misunderstood. Does this mean you stay home from work in response to your child's tears? No. But understanding the fundamental difference between the meaning you and your child ascribe to your departure may help you to understand that empathizing with her sadness is likely to provide her with comfort, whereas any sort of logical explanation you provide is likely to increase her distress.

The culture of adulthood values accomplishment, making money, being recognized by others, spending time with friends, having some time to relax, staying organized, meeting obligations in a timely manner, looking attractive, and staying healthy, among some other things. Your children value your presence, time spent with you, time to relax and ponder, and time for exploration. This allows children to discover the world and to discover themselves in relation to it.

The Gift Is the Relationship

We all have the impulse to provide for our children, but there is such a thing as too much stuff. Let's say you are expecting your second child. You anticipate diapering and feeding your infant, and you feel it would be helpful for your four-year-old to have a baby of her own to practice on. What do you do? One mother might go out and buy the most elaborate and realistic looking babydoll on the market, buy a small replica changing table and crib, and purchase a box of real diapers for her child to practice with. A different mother provides a doll. She and her child discover the paper towels in the kitchen can be used as diapers, and they figure out how to fold them. They hunt for something to use as adhesive and find the Scotch tape. The mother helps her child learn to use the dispenser. Mom supervises the cutting of some scrap fabric, and together, they glue the fabric to a shoebox to make a bassinet. The first child has the fancy stuff. The second child has the relationship. Which one would you rather be?

Some years ago, Rene Spitz, a pediatrician, came across vast numbers of babies who had been held in orphanages during World War II. Each of the babies had her own crib. All were fed. But many of the babies died. What were they lacking? Touch. The babies were not held by caregivers. While there are many things in our world that change over time, there are certain basic, underlying things about people that do not. Dr. Spitz's discoveries provide a dramatic and concrete illustration of our fundamental need for others. We are social beings. Wired into us is a need for community, for affiliation, and for relatedness. No matter how fancy the trappings of our external lives—no matter how much stuff we accrue, no matter how high a position we attain in our careers—this need for connection with others remains.

As an adult, you have learned certain rules of interaction that allow you to understand the community and to see yourself as a part of it. Your knowledge of these rules and your ability to apply them can be thought of as your social skills. Over the course of your development, you learned how to join a discussion, to work as a member of a team, not to interrupt others, how to ask for what you need, to let everyone have a turn, not to comment aloud on another's deformity, not to hit others with whom you are angry, not to grab things you want from other people, and not to push ahead in line. You have developed some capacity to deal with your feelings in a private way when you are in a public setting. You didn't study these skills in a book. You developed these skills in the course of living your life and interacting with other people.

Your child is in the process of developing social skills as part of a natural process of her development. She is largely taking her lead from you, mimicking aspects of your interpersonal behavior that are so subtle you may not even be aware of them. She is also learning standards of interaction through the experiences she has in your house, in school, at other children's houses, in day care, and in other places her child life naturally takes her. She is not learning social skills on the Internet. She is not learning social skills on television. She is not learning how to live with and understand others and herself by reading books.

Your child started learning these skills as a baby in interaction with you, her parent. Everything did not need to go smoothly in the dance between you to provide her the opportunity to establish a solid foundation for her social self. In fact, research has shown that in the interactive dance between babies and their caregivers—the cooing back and forth, the vocalizing, the smiling—there are numerous episodes of bad timing and multiple misunderstandings. You and your baby will, at many junctures, fail to appreciate accurately the meaning of each other's emotional displays, and your reactions to each other, in turn, will be off the mark and out of sync. Not only will this occur, but this is a *necessary* part of your baby's social development. Through negotiating these moments of disharmony and then working with you to get back to a more coordinated state, your baby learns something about regulating herself and the relationships in which she interacts. This is the beginning of her ability to do so.

Once your child is past infancy, the ways you, an adult, and your young child are able to establish, develop, and maintain relationships with others remain very different. As an adult, you have an abstract concept of yourself as someone with particular values and interests. You can make friends on the computer with someone you have never seen. But your young child is limited in her ability to engage in abstract thinking, and her relationship to time and her capacity for memory is different from yours. As such, she needs proximity to others to establish a social interaction.

If you understand this fundamental difference between how social experiences function in the lives of children and adults, and how different children's social needs are from those of adults, this can allow you to take a look at some common social conventions of the present day with a fresh perspective. After reading and reflecting, you might find you organize things differently for your children than the prevailing cultural norms would have you do.

The Hazards of Overscheduling

Things have changed quite a bit over the past forty years or so in many ways. The world we live in today is complex. It moves fast and contains opportunities and choices that have not existed before. But there is a cost to progress, and much of the cost is being borne by children. The price we pay for progress, increasingly, is childhood.

Until the late eighteenth century, childhood was not viewed as a separate and unique time of life. Children were seen as small adults who were taken care of until they could be put to work in whatever capacity they could physically tolerate. Child labor was the norm, and it wasn't seen as a violation of anything. In the nineteenth century, the concept of childhood as a unique time of life was developed. Societal reforms began in earnest. Pediatrics was introduced as a separate discipline in medicine. Rather than being seen as adults in miniature, children were increasingly seen as growing people in need of adult care, guidance, and protection. Childhood itself was seen as needing protection. In the early twentieth century, child labor laws were created in the United States in keeping with the idea that the needs of children and childhood were unique.

As recently as thirty or forty years ago, the culture of adults still tended to see children in this light. Read the following description of a classroom, and try to guess what year in school it is describing. Prepare yourself to vote for preschool, prekindergarten, kindergarten, or first grade.

> *In this class, children play alone in small groups, have a mid-morning snack, have periods of quiet work between active work and play periods, and have frequent changes of activity. There is a relaxed schoolroom atmosphere free of pressure to perform where children learn to write their names over the course of the year in large letters, learn the numbers 1 to 10 according to things they can physically hold in their hands and manipulate, select their own activities, choose from abundant housekeeping and transportation toys, have large crayons and brushes available for work at the easel, and have lots of picture books available for looking at.*

What do you think? Preschool? Pre-K? Kindergarten? If you're like most contemporary parents, chances are you voted for one of these. In fact this is a description of first grade in the 1950s. I found this in *Real Facts from Real Schools* by James K. Uphoff, Ed.D. It's an excerpt from a 1954 New York State Education Department publication entitled *The Elementary School Curriculum: An Overview.* The degree to which school has changed over the last fifty years reflects how much our concepts of children and childhood have changed.

In his book *The Hurried Child,* Dr. David Elkind talks about children in the relatively recent past being viewed as growing people in need of adult care and guidance. By contrast, we presently tend to view children as superkids with great powers who are competent to deal with and benefit from anything and everything life has to offer. What happened? Did children fundamentally change between the early 1950s and today? Do brains develop differently or faster than they used to? No. Rather, the culture changed, and our concepts of childhood have changed in response.

The space and time for childhood that were carved out two centuries ago are in the process of being chipped away at as children increasingly come to look like and be seen as little adults. We dress them in more adult clothes. We fill the hours of their days with structured activities in which we expect them to apply themselves and excel. We see the formative years as a time when children can begin to start their participation in activities in order to get a leg up on others for the future.

Mrs. Ramden came to consult about day care placement for two-year-old Gerold. One facility was much more expensive than the others she had investigated, but she figured it was worth it after she heard their curriculum. "The lady on the phone said they were modeled on European educational principles. They have a Spanish immersion program in the morning, and then they switch to French in the afternoons. On Tuesdays they have a Japanese culture day. All day, every day, in the different languages, they teach phonics and numbers. The lady said that nearly all of their kids are reading by the time they're three and that they're way ahead of the other kids by the time they start formal school."

Most contemporary parents, like Mrs. Ramden, respond to this day care description positively. "Ooh! Reading by three!" we are likely to say. Immediately, we assume that a child's reading so far in advance of other children would be something of value. My advice to Mrs. Ramden? Save your money, and save Gerold's childhood while you're at it. Put him in a good, old-fashioned child care situation where he can run and play and get dirty and discover and not "accomplish" a thing.

We presently live in a time when earlier and faster are assumed to be better, and if that isn't enough, the idea of being ahead of others seals the deal. This was not always the case. It's hard to imagine that as recently as a generation ago, parents who pushed children to precocious academic achievement were viewed as bad parents. These days, it seems to be the opposite. As one mother in a preschool parenting group said, "I think my daughter is the only one of all of our kids who doesn't have the phonics game. Am I doing something wrong?" Earlier, faster, and better are cultural values that are so ingrained that we may fail to question if taking action on these bases is the wisest choice. With respect to children, it is not. There is no reason to push children to precocious academic achievement, and in fact, there are many reasons not to do so.

You can hammer phonics into a young child, but why? A child cannot read with comprehension until she has some life experience to reference while she's reading and some memory and capacity for abstract thinking to permit her to be reflective about what she's read. While there are a few children who confound our current understanding of neuroscience and read spontaneously and with comprehension by the age of three, these children are few and far between. In my experience, these are *never* the children who are pushed by parents to read or who are drilled with flashcards or immersed in toddler phonics programs. Rather, these are the kids whose parents say something to this effect: "I thought George had memorized that book, but one day we were driving and he started reading billboards and I realized he was really reading!" The earliest years are not the time to spend in front of flashcards. The time a child would spend being drilled in phonics is the time she could otherwise be spending having hands-on, direct experiences to feed her brain and guide its wiring in the way nature designed.

When we push children to excel beyond peers, or to do things faster than nature intended, we are smothering childhood with the values of adulthood. We are placing too much adult sense where child sense should be, and we are interfering with very important developmental processes. Children are scientists. They can be trusted to be curious about the world they live in. Just as there is a drive to walk, there is an inherent drive to mastery and discovery. A child who is placed in structured classes at a young age may fail to develop her own inquiring mind. Taught how to think by others, she is deprived of the opportunity to discover curiosity and exploration on her own.

Sand, mud, crayons, paper, blocks, pebbles, roly-poly bugs, Tupperware, dolls, paints, grass, flowers, glue, rubber bands, glitter, music, stuffed animals, musical instruments, sticks, leaves, tricycles, bicycles, a variety of textures and flavors in foods: all of these are things from the world of childhood that give children a chance to explore, manipulate, question, recall, and label. To allow your child's mind to unfold and develop, you need to provide access to materials like these and you need to provide time. Plenty of time. Plenty of unstructured time without scheduled activities. Giving your child access to hands-on materials and giving her the time to find her own way of combining and recombining them is essential to permitting her to form her own foundations of logical thinking and her own ability to differentiate belief from reality. Time and hands-on materials provide your child an opportunity to develop emotional resilience and confidence in her ability to solve problems. Unstructured time in the world allows your child to develop a theory of herself and others.

> *At her sixth birthday, Sandra Keller received a child's version of an appointment book. It's likely to be useful for her because Sandra has a full and busy life. She attends kindergarten until two o'clock every afternoon. After school, Mondays she goes first to ballet and then to piano. Tuesday afternoons are computer class. Wednesdays have been playdate days, but she's scheduled to start Kumon math to give her a leg up for first grade. Thursdays she takes an art class. Fridays are karate. Saturdays she plays in a soccer league.*

I have yet to meet parents who say they enrolled their children in classes and activities in the service of limiting their future possibilities. Most parents will say that they place their children in classes to develop skills to place them in their best stead for the future. This is a nice idea, but it is out of sync with biologically, neurologically determined facts of children's intellectual, social, and emotional development. The psychoanalyst and developmentalist Erik Erikson, in *Childhood and Society,* describes early childhood, particularly ages four through eight, as the time when your child's initiative and creativity are naturally coming to fruition. When organized activities are imposed on your child at these ages, she becomes occupied with learning skills instead of having the opportunity to grow in her ability to conceptualize her own projects, discover her own questions, and figure out her own ways of answering them. Far from growing into an adult who has an edge over others, this child is more likely to grow into an adult who is dependent on others for direction. This is not a leader. This is a child who cannot even lead herself.

Parents often place their young children in structured classes because they think this will be fun for kids and that children will be bored if they are not given enough to do. The danger of this point of view is that it becomes a self-fulfilling prophecy. Like wild animals raised in captivity who never develop their inborn potential to hunt for themselves, children who are robbed of the opportunity to come up with their own games and entertain themselves at those times in their lives when these capacities are developing may very well become dependent upon others to determine their good times.

The tendency to be bored absent a structure created by others may very well be a trait passed down through generations. Adults, in general, tend to have a good deal more difficulty simply "being" in the course of a day. Many adults like to have planned activities and want to be entertained. Without considering the developmental differences between themselves and their children, adults may simply assume that their children's requirements and preferences are comparable to their own and act accordingly.

Some parents want to provide classes to ensure that their children develop an appreciation for different things available to them in life.

> *Mrs. Giraud had four-year-old Natalie in ballet classes. The problem was ballet class met at one of the few times during the week when Natalie could have spent time with her very busy executive father. Natalie was resisting ballet, but her mother was insistent. Asked why, Mrs. Giraud said, "I want to make sure she has an appreciation for the arts." I suggested that Natalie was more likely to grow up associating ballet with a lack of understanding in her relationship with her mother and with painful separation from her father. This seemed to be a recipe for a resentment of the arts, not appreciation.*

The most salient thing a child will take away from having something shoved down her throat is a sore throat and a desire to avoid the thing that created the pain.

How do you give your child her best chance for an appreciation of the arts, or anything else for that matter? *You* appreciate it. If you want the best chance of raising a child who enjoys music, then fill your house with music and *you* enjoy it. Things that are part of your life become part of your child's life. There are no guarantees that your children will grow up liking what you expose them to, and they will be within their rights to decide such things. All you can do is create the opportunity, and you do so most effectively by living the thing yourself.

Rethinking the Birthday Party

There is a free monthly magazine for parents in Los Angeles, the last pages of which are dedicated to advertisements by companies who will provide party entertainment for children. Parents can rent moon bouncers, magicians, people dressed in character costumes, puppet shows, petting zoos, reptile handlers, and pony rides. For many parents, the idea of a party without some rented entertainment of this sort is as alien as the idea of a party without cake. Characters or clowns run the entertainment. "Happy Birthday" is sung. Cake is eaten. Visiting children are given a party bag at the door, and they go home. Presents are opened later. Thank-you notes get written—sometimes by parents with or without the child's help. Occasionally, the thank-you notes are the fill-in variety with a preprinted message and a line on which a child—or, more often, her mother or father—fills in the particular gift given.

The child's birthday party of the past bore some resemblance to this contemporary party, but the version of today seems to have had its soul ripped out. We have forgotten what is valuable. Or more accurately, we seem to be confusing what is valuable for adults with what is valuable for children.

What exactly is a child's birthday party? In an increasingly adult-dominated, entertainment-focused world, we seem to see a birthday party as a two-hour vacuum of time that we are obligated to fill with structured activities and constant hoopla. But this is not the main point. The essence of a birthday party is the social event it is for the children who attend. First and foremost, it is a community experience. In creating a party and inviting others, you are creating a small community of several hours' duration. The activities that are provided are meant to be in the service of the experience that the children will have together. A birthday party is one of the many community experiences we provide for children not only to celebrate a happy event, but also in the service of preparing them for life in the larger community of adults.

It seems that over the last generation, a slow leak has sprung in the birthday party and much of its essence has drained out. We provide the appearance of an experience that often may only imitate the real thing. We have all the ingredients, but we have lost the feeling. The success of a birthday party is not to be measured by the entertainment you provide or how good the dip tastes. The success is measured in the contact between participants, the relationships they have with one another, and the social experience overall.

The Party Bag

Have you given out party bags at the end of a party, or has your child come home with one? For many adults, the party bag has become another (expensive) thing to buy as a part of party preparations. Where does it come from? What is its purpose? Are you interested? You need to be. If you are not interested in thinking about such things, you put adult life where child life should be. In the place of meaning, you stick social protocol.

If you came home from childhood birthday parties in your day with a party bag, I'm willing to bet it wasn't something you picked up at the door on the way out. The contemporary party bag is, in many cases, an insipid stand-in for what used to be a collection of goodies that were collected during the interactive activities of the party itself—as prizes from games and contests, as things given out to children during the course of the puppet show, as windfall from the piñata that everyone rallied round and collectively tried to break open. As such, rather than a bunch of stuff in a bag for a child at the door—a token parting gift—that bunch of stuff was associated with the community experience a child had at the party in the course of amassing it.

An article that appeared in the *Los Angeles Times* on October 22, 2000, noted one mother spent close to seven hundred dollars on party bags for her four-year-old's birthday party, and the article cited other parents bemoaning this fact because they felt the pressure to keep up. The article said that young partygoers are disappointed if there are no bags, or if the bags aren't interesting, and cited a six-year-old's party in which one of the main activities involved making elaborate art boxes, at the end of which the partygoers were dismayed to discover that these boxes were their parting gifts. Thank goodness this article inspired a great deal of negative response. Clearly, something has gone seriously awry.

Experiments in social science have demonstrated that if you take an experience that is inherently pleasurable to a person—something she does on her own just for fun—and you start paying her to do it, when you remove the payment she will no longer pursue the activity independently. The payment apparently alters the experience and diverts the person's attention away from the inherent enjoyment of participation. This has applications to the party bags in the child's birthday party of today. Increasingly, as children expect to be "compensated" for participation, the inherent pleasure and meaning of the party may be obscured, and the fun of the celebration may be lost.

The Presents

Mrs. Garrett talks of preparations she is making for her daughter's upcoming seventh birthday "I told all the mothers, 'Please, no more Barbies.' At this point we could add or take away ten Barbies from the Barbie box, and I can't honestly say that Junie would even notice. In fact, there's nothing Junie needs at all. The whole present thing is a little overwhelming. The last thing we need in the house is any more stuff."

The "stuff" one child gives to another is not the point of the present. Perhaps you've noticed that while your child may get a momentary thrill from a new thing, this often is not lasting, and even the most anticipated and cherished toy soon ends up among others jumbled in the toy closet. The real gift is not the toy. The real gift is the connection between one person and another that occurs in the process of giving and receiving. Who needs another bottle of bubbles? But if that bottle of bubbles is opened and played with among the children at the party, it is no longer a bottle of bubbles. It becomes an experience shared by children—a communal event.

If you are playing tennis and you are served a ball, you don't wait until the other player has left the court to return it. By analogy, there is tremendous satisfaction for children in giving and in seeing their gift received. There is a relationship between the giver and the receiver. The real gift is the experience; the object itself is merely a thing that provides the chance for a relationship to occur.

A generation ago, it was unheard of to leave presents unopened until after party goers went home. Opening gifts was as much a part of the party as was eating the cake. While this tradition is maintained in some communities, there are some parties at which not only are gifts not opened communally, but even to consider doing so is thought to be the height of bad taste.

Gift opening after the fact is another concept that has clearly been applied to the world of children from the world of adults. You, an adult, can open a gift from a friend, sustain the thought of that person, and feel the relationship to her symbolically, through the gift. Children do not think symbolically when they are young. A pile of presents opened after the fact is just so much more stuff in a child's life. It loses its connection to the giver, and it loses a good deal of its meaning in the process.

Gifts opened publicly can be played with communally, and this extends everyone's fun. At a recent party, a six-year-old boy received an elaborate nylon tunnel habitat that was opened and fanned out over much of the backyard. All the children at the party instantly started crawling through it. Giggles and squeals of delight abounded. Imagine if this boy had opened this gift once everyone had gone home.

Mrs. Martin wants to spare her son Marlon the jealous feelings she imagines will arise if he has to watch a birthday boy open so many gifts.

When we immunize children against diseases, we expose a child to a small amount of something toxic in order to allow her to build antibodies against it. Antibodies prepare a child's body to minimize the harm should she encounter the toxin at a later date. Without a bit of exposure, a child who later meets the bacterium is going to be vulnerable to its effects. The principle underlying immunization has social applications as well.

Mrs. Martin fails to see the opportunity the party provides for helping Marlon with his socialization over the long term. Marlon might very well feel jealous when gifts are opened, but rather than being protected from this feeling, he is much better served by having an opportunity to experience it and be guided through it by his parents.

One day I was at a birthday party for a five-year-old that was held at one of those places set up for children with large slides, netted climbing apparatuses, huge containers of plastic balls for rolling around in, and the like. After an hour of play, the children retired to a private party room. There was pizza, singing, and cake. Presents that had been displayed in the room were bagged, unopened, and transported to the car. The kids went back to the play area, and shortly thereafter, everyone went home. The manager at the facility stated they do thirty or forty parties each weekend. I asked at what proportion of these parties the gifts were opened as part of the party itself. "Oh, hardly any," said the manager. "In fact, we discourage it. The kids only have the party rooms for an hour, and besides, you know how kids are. You don't really know how they are going to respond. I mean, they might open something and say, 'Oh, I already have one of these,' or something like that. There's always a danger that they'll say the wrong thing."

Well, of course they will say the wrong thing. Children should be coached ahead of time about the manners to use in such a circumstance, but we should not be surprised when they forget and make mistakes. The question is, when did this become something to hide and avoid at such great cost? In the course of living through childhood, we can expect children to feel jealous, to act without grace, to fail to use manners. Childhood is the time to help children through such experiences to prepare them for life ahead. If we can see the birthday party as one of the small communities we create for children to give them an opportunity to become more socialized, then we need not feel we need to protect them from acting in these ways. We can see the opportunity that such venues present instead. We do children no favors in shielding them from feelings that arise in the context of interpersonal experiences. We do them favors when we accompany them through experiences and give them tools they will need to cope in the future. The birthday party is a venue in which children can prepare for a lifetime of graceful giving.

> *"I'm afraid that Sayeed wouldn't take well to having the other children play with all his things. I don't think he would want to share them."*

Your child may have a special toy. The things she opens as a part of a community at her party do not fall into this category. Parents who anticipate sharing difficulties are frequently surprised that their children are not as covetous of the new things they receive as parents had anticipated. Things opened communally tend to retain their communal feeling, and children do not seem to have the tendency to see them as exclusively their property. Occasionally, a child receives something that is uniquely special, or that she has been anticipating, and that she doesn't want to share. This can be respected, and the thing can be put away until later for independent play. Most children will accept this and, in the heat of the gleeful moment, will fall into the community of party goers and the fun of playing with the collection of other new treasures.

There are children who are exceptions to this rule. They understand the concept of "mine" and are quick to apply it to everything within their view. With a younger child—aged two or three—this is often a quickly passing storm. A Time Out for regrouping can often do a world of good (see Chapter 7 for a discussion of Time Out). Also, such children can often be distracted or their attention redirected in a manner that extinguishes the tears or tantrum. But what if you have an older child with a pervasive sharing problem? What should you do? Should you open presents later to spare her—and yourself—the difficulty of coping with this experience? No. The community experience of a party and the opportunity for learning it presents is for all children, the birthday child no less than for the other party goers. A child who hoards and cannot share is a child who will miss out on a lot over the course of life. If your child has this difficulty, it will be helpful to talk with her about it and prepare her for what will happen at the party so she is not taken by surprise; but don't expect her to be able to accommodate seamlessly, and be prepared to cope if she has a negative response. A few spilled tears at a birthday party are a small price to pay in the grand scheme of things. Ultimately, if the problem is a pervasive one, if may be worth seeking a professional consultation.

If you already include gift opening in your parties, you have seen how excited children get at seeing their gifts received and you have seen the energy in the interaction between the giver and the birthday child. If you don't include gift opening as a part of your parties, start now.

Thank-You Notes

There is nothing that more dramatically illustrates what has become soulless and automatic in interpersonal relationships than the modern invention of the fill-in-the-blank thank-you note. Perhaps you've seen this thing. It has a preprinted "heartfelt" message—something like "Dear———, Thank you so much for the———. I *really really* like it, and I'm *so* glad you gave it to me. Love, ———"

A thank-you note, in theory, is an expression of gratitude. It represents the time someone has spent being thoughtful about what someone has done for her. It is a small gift in return. It is good manners. At best, the fill-in-the-blank thank-you note does none of these things. At worst, the fill-in-the-blank thank-you note is an insult to relatedness. It is an ill-mannered version of good manners; it recognizes that there is an obligation, and fulfills that obligation in the most graceless way. If you want to raise children with some style and grace, you have to act with some style and grace and encourage them in these directions. This means you have to write your thank-you note messages from scratch.

Writing thank-you notes is a chance for you to go on record about good manners and proper behavior. Even for young children, aged three, four, five, and even six, whose abstract thinking and memory are relatively limited, taking part in writing thank-you notes is important. A child may not be able to evoke the memory of the individual who gave her something, but participating in the act of writing notes is important in that it lays the foundation for a future of good manners.

It's never too soon to involve children in the writing of thank-you notes. Mrs. Cleng, the mother of newborn Claudia, was overwhelmed with the task of writing notes to thank those who had sent her baby gifts. Claudia clamored for her attention in every waking moment and could not stand to be put down. When Claudia slept, Mrs. Cleng was too exhausted to summon the energy for writing. What was Mrs. Cleng to do? Put Claudia in her Snugli baby carrier and write the notes together. Did this contribute to the development of Claudia's good manners? It's hard to say. At worst, it provided Claudia and her mom a new kind of shared experience, and it satisfied Claudia's need for Mom as well as Mom's need to get her notes written.

When your child is two or three years old, she can participate in much the same way. You sit her on your lap and model how it's done. "Let's see, Aunt Ethel gave you the paintbox. Remember, you made the beautiful painting that's on the refrigerator? Let's write, 'Dear Aunt Ethel, Thank you for the paintbox. I made a painting, and mommy put it on the refrigerator.' How's that? Should we say anything more?" Be open to your child's input. Incorporate it. It will also be useful to keep in mind that at these ages, your child may be limited with respect to how long she can remain seated. You might want to plan to write only two or three notes at a sitting.

As your child is five, six, and seven, she can take a more active role in thank-you notes. She can draw pictures for the gift giver. When she has learned to write her name, she can sign notes. She can be active in writing the text if you take her dictation. You can remind her of what someone gave her, and ask her what she would want to tell that person or ask her what she thinks of the gift. Take down what she says verbatim. When she has learned to write a few words on her own, let her do it.

If you aim to raise children who live lives of depth and meaning, then you need to allow things to be meaningful. Thank-you notes present another opportunity to do so.

Chapter 4

Communicating with Children:
A How-to Guide from Birth and Beyond

Imagine you are in an alien culture where people do not speak. Suddenly, one of your hosts taps his toe on the ground and looks at you. He does it again, then a third time, each time more emphatically. You are bewildered. If he keeps doing this, chances are you'll begin to ignore him. If your host does other strange things like this, you are liable to conclude that in this culture, all gestures are meaningless.

Now imagine this same host taps his toe on the ground and then places you in a chair. He does this several times. It will not be long before you apprehend the meaning of this gesture. "Aha!" you will say, "Toe tapping means 'sit down'!" Beyond understanding this gesture, you are liable to conclude that in this culture, all gestures have meaning and chances are, you will be interested in understanding them.

How Children Learn the Meaning of Language

When we talk about taking appropriate authority with children, we include the need for children to comply with our directives. But before children can comply with what is expected of them, they need to understand what these expectations are. It is important for us to define our terms before we hold children accountable for them.

The Truman family is working on getting control over sixteen-month-old Carter's behavior. When they enter the office, Carter's mother tells him to sit in her lap. He sits in a small chair instead. She speaks more sharply, but he ignores her. Carter picks up a Kleenex box. His mother tells him to put it down. He does not. Father raises his voice, but Carter keeps plucking tissues. At this point, the Trumans ask what they should do. I suggest they remove the box from him and place it on the table while telling him, "Put the box down." When mother tells Carter to come sit in her lap and he does not come, I suggest that rather than say it louder, she pick him up and place him there. I propose that rather than being obstinate, Carter is confused and needs to have the meaning of these directives illustrated for him. Gradually, the family comes to realize that instead of yelling, they get more satisfaction if they define their words by action. I suggest that this is the way that Carter will learn not only the meaning of their words, but also that his parents mean business when they speak to him. They try this approach at home for a couple of weeks and report success.

It is useful to think about your child developing language much as you might think of a foreigner learning to speak. Children are not born understanding the meaning of words. You will need to illustrate the meaning of words by examples and with actions if you want your child to come to understand them. How do you teach a baby what "no" means? This is not best accomplished by yelling "no" loudly when he is doing something you want him to stop. You may startle him and this may distract him from his activity, but he is not liable to understand your meaning. You teach no by saying the word "no" while you remove the forbidden object or while you remove the baby from the forbidden situation. When a toddler climbs a chair, you teach the meaning of "get down" by saying this while you remove him from the chair. Saying "get down" to a new climber without reinforcing your words by removing him is fruitless. Does repeating "get down" in a sterner voice get your point across any more effectively? Not any more than someone's yelling at you in Portuguese would help you understand the meaning of what he was saying (presuming, of course, that you do not speak Portuguese). Not any more than a puppy will sit if you yell "Sit!" at him repeatedly while failing to push down on his back end.

Of course, yelling in such circumstances creates additional problems

beyond a lack of understanding. It's liable to create a distressing environment in which your child will be distracted from what you are attempting
to teach. It also introduces an unpleasant element into your relationship.
Would you look forward to your interactions with a foreigner who was
regularly getting angry with you for not understanding his language?
Probably not. Over time, it's likely you would feel frustrated or angry. You
would probably prefer to avoid him.

Increasing the volume and intensity of your commands is not the same
thing as being firm with children. Being firm with children presupposes
being fair. Yelling words your children have not completely understood
and calling their lack of response anything other than confusion is not fair.
It leads to unnecessary misunderstandings.

> *Mr. Kelly reports that his twenty-month-old son, Alexander, is
> being contrary. One day, Alexander was playing with the VCR,
> and Mr. Kelly told him to stop while removing him from the
> machine. Later, Alexander again played with the machine, and
> this time Mr. Kelly needed only to say, "Get away from the VCR"
> for Alexander to move on. A few days later, however, when the
> same thing happened again and Mr. Kelly told him to stop,
> Alexander kept on playing. Mr. Kelly believes this was intentional
> misbehavior. I suggest that while Alexander has complied once,
> he has not, in fact, mastered the meaning of these words. Mr. Kelly
> is counseled to continue to illustrate his words with action.*

As bright as our children may appear to be, it often takes a while for
them to master and understand different things that they are being taught.
You may have the world's most precocious two-year-old, but that doesn't
mean that he will understand what you intend when you tell him to clean
up his room. And then, even if you explain the meaning to him detail by
detail—pick up the socks, put them in the hamper, put the books on the
shelf—this doesn't mean he will remember to do these actions the next
time. It's entirely human to require a process for instruction, to require
repetitions of a lesson, to forget something after we think we have grasped
it. Recently, an adult patient spoke with me about going to the hardware
store, where she was shown how to rewire a lamp, only to get home and

find that she could not remember how to do it. Keeping these very human proclivities and limitations in mind allows us to be more forgiving of kids. Damage can be done if we are quick to ascribe negative motives to a child whose only "crime" is a lack of understanding or memory. So illustrate your meanings to children, and then illustrate them again. Expect things to be forgotten, and you will not feel betrayed or let down when this occurs.

What About Your Tone?

Meaning what we say also involves using a tone of voice that matches the content of what we are saying. A mismatch between what is being said and the tone in which it is being said is a common source of misunderstanding between parents and children. Consider the following:

> *Mrs. Greenberg calls to make an appointment. She explains to me that her two-year-old daughter, Jenna, is "out of control." I ask in what way. "Just a sec," she says to me. Then she covers the phone. I hear her say, in a singsongy voice, "Jenna? You need to get off the table, honey. We don't go on tables. It's dangerous." A listener who had not heard this mother's words, only her tone, would have thought she was calling "Yoo-hoo! Anyone home?" Apparently, Mrs. Greenberg is not successful, because she tries again, still singsongy: "Jenna, honey, Mommy is going to be angry. You have to get down from there." A pause. "Right now, honey. Right this instant or Mommy is going to be angry and you'll get no dessert and no videos and you'll have to go to your room right now." I hear Jenna giggle and Mrs. Greenberg sigh. She comes back to her conversation with me. "You see?" she says, "This is a perfect example. This is why I need your help."*

What is remarkable in this interchange is not only the number of threats that are not being delivered upon, but the singsongy tone in which the whole interchange takes place. Tone is a critical aspect of communication for adults and for children. With a young child, using a tone that reinforces your message is even more important than it is with an adult. At the age of two, Jenna has a limited vocabulary, and because of this, she is likely to rely even more heavily on her mother's tone to understand what is really expected of her. Further difficulties arise in a circumstance like this when parents, unaware of the mismatch between the tone and content of their speech, become frustrated and angry with their children for failing to obey.

There are many circumstances that will arise in which Mrs. Greenberg's soft, nonauthoritative tone of voice will not allow her to get her meaning across to her daughter. Other parents, different from Mrs. Greenberg, may go to the opposite extreme. They may tend to speak to their children with a harsh, demanding tone. But these parents may not get their meaning across any better than parents who err on the side of speaking too softly.

The White family comes for consultation because of behavior problems with their four-year-old son, James. No sooner does Mr. White start to talk about the difficulties at home, than James gets down from his chair and starts walking toward some toys in the room. "Get over here!" says Mr. White in a voice as sharp as a slap. James barely acknowledges his father. "Stop that! Get over here!" he yells again. James keeps wandering. Mrs. White pipes up, "James! James! You get over here and listen to your father!" James continues walking toward the toys. Mr. White explains that this is the problem. His boy does not listen, and instead he does as he pleases. How, they wonder, can he ignore them when clearly they talk to him in a way that suggests they mean business?

Before a child will comply with a directive, you have to make sure you have got his attention. A harsh or loud tone gets a child's attention not by its sheer volume, but by the degree to which it differs from what has come before. It cannot work if there is never anything softer. Like an airport ground-crew worker who eventually stops hearing the deafening whine of the jet engines, James has acclimated himself to a certain level of noise within his family. At first glance, the Whites' style of communication might not sound like a monotone, but it is. It is simply a monotone that is taking place at a high pitch. The first intervention for Mr. and Mrs.

White involved helping them get James's attention. And it was deceptively simple:

>   *After James had made his way to the toys, he began playing with them. His father yelled "James!" with no response. I suggested to Mr. White that rather than speak so harshly to his son, he speak in a barely audible whisper. He balked, then tried it. The effect was startling. Where what had been conveyed in a roar had produced no effect on James's behavior, his father's whisper stopped James in his tracks. I encouraged Mr. White to whisper again. James turned around with a quizzical expression. His father whispered once more, and now James got up and came toward him, asking "What?" I encouraged Mr. White to speak even more quietly. Now James grinned, moved closer, and asked again what his father was saying. A game evolved. Not only was compliance eventually achieved, but there was a nice interchange between father and son.*

When children are spoken to in a tone that is consistently harsh, not only are they likely to tune out, but they are likely to feel—and rightly so—that there is nothing to lose. James was going to be spoken to in this manner irrespective of what he did or didn't do. So he did what he liked and suffered no greater consequence than he would have by being compliant. Parents who speak to children in this way don't leave themselves much room to move. There's not much room to get any louder, should a point need to be emphasized.

You may have to use a sharp tone now and again to get your child's attention, but once you have it, you don't have to shriek at him to get your point across. Rather, once you've got a child's attention, you need to make good use of it. You need to mean what you say.

Mean What You Say

A mother, father, and six- or seven-year-old boy were observed in a mall next to a small choo-choo train ride. Father took his son to the gate. "One ride, Justin," he said, "and then we're going to eat dinner." Father joined mother at the table and both tiredly waved as Justin happily rode around the track for the designated period. When the train whistle sounded and the train came to a stop, Father beckoned Justin to come over. "One more time?" Justin asked. "No," said his father. "Dinner is getting cold." "Please, Dad, just one more?" "Justin," said his mother, "Daddy told you one ride, and you had it. Get off the train." "Just one more ride. Please, please, please!" "Oh, for crying out loud, Justin," said Mom, looking utterly depleted. "One more ride. But this is it. You understand? I don't want to hear about it again." Father wearily got up and paid the operator and Justin rode again. Many unattached observers had the sense that this was the second of many rides.

Have you ever played a slot machine? First you fed it one coin, then another. At some point, there was a payoff—maybe just a few nickels, but a payoff nonetheless. That's the way slot machines are. You know that if you feed them enough, eventually they will deliver. The amount of your reward is never certain, but the fact that there will be a reward, eventually, is guaranteed. And you will be tempted to feed coins until it happens.

The same principle that holds true for the slots—keep at it and eventually it will give you what you want—is the basis on which a number of children interact with their parents. If your child knows one of your decisions can be reversed with sufficient whining and pleading, you are going to have whining and pleading until there's a payoff. And as with the slots, he may not know how long it will take or just what the payoff will be, but he knows he will gain something.

Your children do not come into the word rational and reasonable. They do not come into the world intuitively understanding what limits are and what words mean. They learn the meaning of limits and words based upon your portrayal of them—what you say and how you follow up. They do not inherently know that the word "no" has finality. You illustrate no by saying it and by maintaining its integrity. A child who wants more dessert and who is told no is not a child who should receive another cookie before bed. The child who is told no and whines and pleads until parents acquiesce is a child who is learning that the meaning of "no" is, in fact, "keep asking."

In our culture today, people's words tend to be a good deal less meaningful than they used to be. Have you been kept on hold for forty minutes while a computerized voice repeats, "Your call is very important to us"? Have you bought the new and improved version of anything lately and been hard pressed to discern a difference from the older version? How can we buck such trends in society? If you want a society in which people's words are trustworthy, raise children who uphold this value to populate that society. How do you raise children who are good for their word? Be good for yours. This means you have to deliver on what you say.

Meaning what you say to children is not only a way to increase their compliance with your demands. It also has everything to do with personal responsibility. You demonstrate personal responsibility when you deliver a promised punishment or a promised reward. You demonstrate it when you make good on your word. A child who is told the truth—for after all, this is what it means to mean what you say—is more likely to grow up speaking the truth. The child for whom you follow through on promised consequences today is the child of tomorrow who keeps his word to others.

When you are reliable, your children can feel safe. As much as a toddler may scream against your prohibitions and butt up against your rules, he is comforted by the consistent presence of those rules and prohibitions. How safe would we feel in a society in which courts arbitrarily enforced the law? Not safe at all. We are contained and are able to function most effectively in a society in which laws exist, in which they are clear to all, and in which they are reliably upheld by those who are charged with this responsibility. This is a society we can understand. So too is your child best able to get on with the all-important business of growth and development in a household in which you, his parents, remain reliably more authoritative than he is.

Against certain unyielding standards, children can try out a variety of positions and strategies. The standards give children a chance to come to know themselves better. They will be comforted to know that no matter how far afield they stray, they can find you in much the same position in which they left you when they embarked upon their wild ride. The parents who maintain consistency in their position when they enforce sensible rules that may frustrate children are the parents who remain firm in their position on the most important elements in children's lives. These are parents who will not be swayed in their love for their children, in their dedication to their well-being, and in their responsibilities as caregivers.

This may sound very logical and sensible, but putting it into practice in real life is a different ballgame. We are human. We get tired. You are not a failure as a parent if you fail to stick by everything you say. But if you continually capitulate to whining, you have become a slot-machine parent. Your children will learn "no" means "yes, if you keep at it long enough," and they will dedicate seemingly inexhaustible energy to playing you into the ground once they learn there's a possibility for a payoff. Capitulate to whining and you set the stage for negotiation on every unpopular point you make in the future. This is likely to be at best irritating and at worst infuriating and potentially destructive to the relationship between you and your kids.

How Do Children Think?
Some Concrete Facts About Abstract Thought

Samantha Dole, four years old, has just finished most of her peanut butter and jelly sandwich and potato chips for lunch. She tells her mother that a monster ate her chips. "Samantha," says her mother in a gentle, teasing voice, "you're full of baloney!" "I am not full of baloney," says Samantha. "You are," says her mother. "I am not," insists Samantha with a bit of an edge in her voice. "You are, you silly goose," says her mother, a bit bewildered and trying to lighten something that has become inextricably charged with seriousness. At this point, Samantha bursts into tears. "I am not full of baloney!" she cries. "I'm full of peanut butter and jelly!"

When we talk about being clear with children, it is important to understand, from a developmental point of view, what is required to accomplish this goal. We have already discussed the idea that babies come to understand words according to the actions that accompany those words. If you do not provide these actions to make your meaning clear, babies will not understand you.

How does their relationship to language change as children get older? At two, three, and four years old, children have developed some words and their vocabularies increase. Some children develop language very well and seem to be very sophisticated. Others develop it more slowly. Irrespective of how sophisticated their words may seem, all children's thinking at these ages is "concrete thinking."

What is concrete thinking? Well, if you asked this question of a concrete thinker, he might tell you that concrete thinking means thinking about cement. When people think concretely, they cannot recognize that words may have any meaning beyond their literal meanings. While this makes for a very limited and dull adult, concrete thinking is a normal phase in the development of young children. Because toddlers think concretely, they do not understand puns. They cannot interpret proverbs. Ask a young child what "Don't judge a book by its cover" means, and you will get a response along the lines of "If you have a book, it has a cover and you can't judge it." Concrete thinking means not being able to generalize beyond an immediate situation. For a concrete thinker, baloney is baloney.

As young children's brains develop, concrete thinking begins to be replaced by abstract and conceptual thought. Children come to understand that things in the world have common features by which they can be grouped. Conceptual thinking gets increasingly sophisticated as children have more experience in the world. You may be able to get your just-turned-three-year-old to look at a bucket of assorted blocks, plastic utensils, and large beads and pick out all the red ones. Tell this same child, however, "Pick out all the things we eat with" or "Pick out all the things you can stack," and the conceptual operation will most likely be too demanding. He is not liable to be up to the more complex conceptual task until another year or two has passed and his understanding of concepts has become more sophisticated.

Abstract thinking allows people to understand that things are not what they appear to be. Abstract thinking allows people to understand that things that are presented can be seen in more than one way. Where the two- or three-year-old child comes to understand that things belong in categories, the four- and five- and six-year-olds come to understand that there may be more than one category to which things can belong simultaneously. As abstract and conceptual thought develop in children of these ages, they begin to enjoy jokes. They take particular delight in puns beginning around the age of six or seven. This is the age of "knock-knock" jokes. The delight young children take in puns seems to be a delight in their discovery that something has two meanings simultaneously.

Abstract thinking allows people to generalize beyond an immediate situation and make inferences beyond what is presented to them directly. It is essential to bear in mind that children cannot make inferences until they have developed the foundation for abstract thought. Inference requires a person to hear or see one thing, and to understand it to mean something else.

A toddler's inability to think abstractly and make inferences is *extremely* important to keep in mind when you speak to your young children. If you are aware of these developmentally based limitations, you will be in a position to impart lessons to children in a way that renders them most likely to be understood.

> *Mrs. Reiss wanted to improve her relationship with her three-year-old daughter, Laura, but things were not going well. One weekend she thought it would be fun for them to work in the garden. There were a number of spent blossoms on her perennials, and Mrs. Reiss figured it would be fun for them to pluck them off together. Laura had a grand time plucking dead blooms off the stems. But she also had fun plucking off the buds and vibrant blossoms. Mrs. Reiss became frustrated trying to teach her the difference between what should and should not be plucked, and finally gave up the whole enterprise and brought her inside. The next day, however, Laura went outside and started plucking on her own. She had made it through a stand of dahlias before Mrs. Reiss saw what was going on, screamed at her, brought her inside, and gave her a Time Out. Now what?*

Mrs. Reiss felt justified in her anger at Laura, but it is not her little girl who has made the error. Rather, Mrs. Reiss is the one who has made the mistake. Making subtle distinctions between valid and spent flowers demands a level of categorical thinking that three-year-olds do not possess. Mrs. Reiss's first mistake was in expecting this level of discrimination from a child of three. Her second mistake was in assuming that Laura was behaving badly and punishing her for what seems, fundamentally, to have grown from a lack of understanding. Laura wasn't being bad. Chances are she even thought she was being helpful.

These types of mistakes will happen. We do not always make accurate judgments about what our children can comprehend. When we recognize we have asked our children to understand something that is developmentally beyond them at the moment, we may be inclined to try to reteach the lesson, figuring that with enough repetition, eventually it will sink in. But this approach sets a child up for more failure, and it sets up a parent for more anger. Actually, a better strategy is to take a step back. Mrs. Reiss needed to make new rules for Laura. "No touching the flowers" would be a good place to start. Such an intervention is likely to do as much for their relationship as it is for the garden.

When they are young, rather than making fine discriminations, children tend to learn broad rules. When socializing a puppy to be a family pet, it's not a good idea to give the puppy old shoes to chew, because the puppy will not make the distinction between these shoes and the pristine Italian loafers in the closet. Mrs. Reiss taught Laura to pick flowers from the garden even though it was not the lesson she had meant to impart. Keeping in mind inherent limitations in toddlers' abstract thinking limits the potential for such misunderstandings.

What's Not Okay About "Okay?"

It's sundown at the park, and the voice of one mother is heard across the sand: "Karen, we're going now, okay?" Karen, three and a half, continues to play. Her mother says, with slightly more urgency, "Do you need my help putting on your shoes? Karen, honey? We need to go!" No response. "Come on, Karen, okay? Daddy's going to be mad if we're late." Karen plays on.

Do you recognize yourself in some version of this picture? If not, you are the rare contemporary parent.

What's going wrong here between Karen and her mother? Well, the answer to the question would depend on whom you ask. Karen would be likely to tell you that nothing is wrong except that her mother is getting annoyed with her for reasons she cannot comprehend. Ask Karen's mother what's wrong, and she will tell you that her child doesn't listen to her.

While Karen's mother believes Karen is being uncooperative, she does not appear to realize that she has not told Karen to do anything. Rather, Karen's mother has posed questions to her daughter, asked favors of her, and given her a series of choices. Karen may well be listening to her mother, and given these circumstances, she is entirely within her rights to keep playing. She's not being defiant. She's just being concrete. Karen has probably not understood the subtext of what her mother is saying. She hears questions as questions. She does not translate, "Do you need my help putting on your shoes?" to mean "Sit down and put your shoes on." She's more liable to think, "Why would I need help putting on my shoes? I'm playing in the sand."

As adults, we have accomplished the ability to engage in abstract thought. We understand a phrase like, "Honey, we need to go now, okay?" as a directive that indicates that we need to get moving. If you understand that toddlers are concrete thinkers, you will understand that a toddler at the park will hear "Honey, we need to go now, okay?" as a legitimate question as a favor being asked of him. He will perceive that his opinion on the matter is being sought, and that he has just been given a choice. He will see himself as entirely within his rights to continue to play in such a circumstance. And he *will* be within his rights to do so. This is important to understand because if you phrase something to a toddler in this way and he doesn't jump to his feet, then you will understand that his failure to do so is not a consequence of his willfully ignoring you. Rather, it is a consequence of his developmentally based inability to infer meaning from what you have said beyond what you have directly presented to him. If you understand this, then you will not get angry with him in this circumstance. You will recognize the need to rephrase your directive.

Giving children clear directives is an essential component to their optimal development. If we present our children with choices that are not choices and are continually frustrated with their responses in these circumstances, what template are we creating for them in future relationships? We are sowing the seeds for them to feel perpetually misunderstood and unjustly accused. You are not within your rights to perceive a child as not listening to you if he does not get up at "We need to go now, okay?" You are, however, within your rights to perceive a child as not listening to you if he keeps on digging in the sand after you say "Samson, we're going now. Pick up your shovel and bring it to me."

There are parents who balk at being so direct with children. They see this type of communication as harsh and mean. One young father in a parenting group where this idea was brought up responded, "So you're just supposed to order them around? That seems so cruel."

It is not cruel to tell a child what to do. On the contrary, it is likely to be much crueller to be unclear when we tell children what we want of them. When we do not give a child complete information and instead rely upon him to infer the meaning of our words and act accordingly, that child will not necessarily reach the conclusions and make the decisions we would wish and *we* will not necessarily be able to keep from taking this somewhat personally. We may attribute a child's failure to infer our meanings as a lack of cooperation. Conflict, frustration, and power struggles thrive in such soil.

> *Walker Trill and his parents were in the living room, and Walker got up on the coffee table and started to do a dance. Mr. Trill tells the story: "I said, 'Careful, Walker, you're going to fall.' He kept dancing. I must have told him five times that he was going to fall. Sure enough. He fell and he knocked over a vase of flowers. He was crying hysterically, but I was so angry. I said, 'For God's sake, Walker, why don't you listen?'" It was pointed out to Mr. Trill that Walker, just turned three, is by virtue of his age, a concrete thinker. While an adult might have understood "You're going to fall" as an adequate warning that meant, "Stop dancing on the table," Walker was not yet able to make this inferential leap. The next time such a situation arose, the Trills were counseled to be much more direct. Mr. Trill said, "Now I get it. Next time I should say something like, 'Walker, get down. Come dance in the playroom instead.'"*

Saying we need to be direct with children is not the same as saying we should become a society of dictatorial parents. There are circumstances in which children have choices, and there is as much of a need to be clear in our language at such times as there is a need to be clear when we are presenting a directive. What is essential is for us to recognize when a choice is really a choice, versus when there is no choice though our soft language is conveying otherwise.

"Okay," you say, "but my problem is not with a three-year-old child. My problem is with my seven-year-old. How do I get him to listen to me?" The answer here is pretty much the same as for younger children, though for some different reasons. Your second grader can make some inferences. This, however, is not an invitation for you to be indirect, since your second grader may infer a different meaning from the one you intended.

When you are indirect, not only may your child fail to understand exactly what it is you expect, but he also may not understand exactly how serious you are. Maybe *you* don't know how serious you are. Being direct forces you to focus your thoughts and clarify your intention.

> *The Kerrys need to leave the house at eight-thirty to get seven-year-old Jerome to school. At ten minutes after eight Mrs. Kerry comes through the living room. "You need do your teeth and hair," she says. Five minutes later, Jerome has not moved. "You're going to be late for school if you don't turn off the TV," she says. After another five minutes, Jerome is still engrossed, and now Mrs. Kerry is angry. "Dammit, Jerome, didn't I tell you to turn that thing off?!" she yells. After she recounts the story in our session, I point out to Mrs. Kerry that the answer to her question is no. She did not tell her son to do anything, much less provide a time frame in which he should do it.*

"Turn the TV off now" is the type of statement that is more likely to get action because it leaves no room for interpretation. "Turn the TV off now" is a clear command.

Giving Clear Commands

Giving clear commands to children lets them know that you mean business. Give an indirect command and you have no leg to stand on if your child does not comply. Be clear in your meaning and his compliance or noncompliance comes into sharper focus. This provides a reference point for various consequences, both negative and positive.

What is a clear command? A clear command is a simple imperative sentence. It is not a favor you are asking. It is not an invitation. It is not a question. It is not a threat.

A clear command is not unduly long. If you want your seven-year-old to put on his shoes, take out the trash, put a new bag in the trash can, turn off the TV, get his books, and start his homework, you would be best off breaking these up into two or three commands to be given separately.

A clear command is simple: "Take out the trash" is an example. Its meaning is clear. "Please take out the trash" is another clear command. Being polite does not undermine the seriousness of your intention. It allows you to model the good manners you wish to instill in your children, while still allowing you to make your purpose known. But "please" belongs in a command only the first time around. If you have to repeat a command a second time, drop the "please."

"Will you please take out the trash?" is not a command at all. It is a question. It is not too difficult to imagine a child saying "No." It is also not difficult to see how quickly this could degenerate into a child's being called sassy or smart-mouthed and the start of a conflict that is entirely avoidable.

Say "Take out the trash, okay?" and you are asking for a favor. Parents who are anxious about appearing mean or heavy-handed often phrase things in this way. If children don't agree to the favor, parents are irritated. After all, they've been such nice guys in how they've asked, right? Wrong. It is not nice to speak indirectly to your children and then to hold them accountable for not doing what you expected.

"Take out the trash or you get no TV" is a threat. Make a statement like this and your child is within his rights to choose one or the other. Chances are this was not the outcome you were hoping for. You want the trash taken out, yes? Is it of consequence to you whether your son watches TV that evening? Probably not. A threat in this instance is not being used appropriately. This is not to say that threats cannot be made to children, but a threat is not a command and shouldn't be confused with one.

Giving clear commands is an essential component to gaining your children's compliance. But what happens if you've given the command, and it was a good one, and it doesn't work? Read on.

1-2-3: The Pause Between Direction and Action

You are living in a household with a toddler. You must establish a rule of governance that lies somewhere between a dictatorship (where you, not your toddler, rules) and a democracy. A toddler's main aim in his emotional life is to develop a sense of autonomy. Parents certainly don't want to step on their toddler's toes during this developmental stage, but nonetheless, rules still apply and parents must find a way to maintain proper order. How do you appropriately limit your toddler's sense of grandiosity and omnipotence, without squashing his thrill at independent action? Providing an opportunity for your toddler to make limited choices is one strategy. This means giving your toddler the opportunity to feel he has some say in the way his life is going. Does this mean you open the refrigerator for your two-year-old and ask "What do you want?" Absolutely not, and anyone who has done so with a two-year-old almost certainly has not done this again for at least another year or two. The entire refrigerator and its contents is too big a world for such a small person. Modest choices—"Do you want pizza or a hot dog?"—are indicated for your toddler. Within these confines, your toddler can feel powerful and can perceive himself as a director of his own destiny. And you, his parent, can have your sanity and authority preserved.

Toddlerhood is also the domain of no. Just as your three-year-old wants to feel powerful by selecting his lunch, so he feels powerful by asserting no when told to take off his shoes in preparation for the bath. So the bath is running, dinner is cooking in the oven, and what does the self-respecting parent do with the unwilling bather? Does he pick up the gauntlet and engage in a power struggle? No-yes-no-yes-no . . . and so on? Perhaps, but then no one is happy. A better strategy is, for lack of a better name, "1-2-3." That is, you tell your child that you will count to three, and by three the thing needs to be done, or you will ensure it is done. You will impose your will.

By giving a child the opportunity to make good on the directive by the count of three, you accomplish many positive things. 1-2-3 allows your child an opportunity to determine when he is going to choose to put himself into action, within a reasonable limit. 1-2-3 is good not only for toddlers; it works for older children as well. 1-2-3 allows you to turn the encounter into something of a shared game.

> *Mrs. Zacharias had terrible problems gaining compliance from five-year-old Kaela, and whining and irritation were the norm in the house. After a month or so of implementing 1-2-3, Mrs. Zacharias reported, "Not only is Kaela listening, but she's started to race to see if she can do what I've told her to do before I even start counting. Where there used to be whining, now there's giggling. I tell her, 'You're so fast, Kaela! How did you do that so fast?' and she eats it up! We're having so much more fun now."*

Certainly, 1-2-3 does allow for more fun and it allows your child a bit of space in which to make a shift, mentally and physically, from one activity to another.

The ability to transition quickly from one activity to another is something we may take for granted as adults. It is not, however, an ability with which babies are born. It has a technical name: "set-shifting," which refers to the ability to shift from one mental set to another. Like reaching, grasping, walking, and jumping, set-shifting is a developmental achievement that depends on brain maturation. You may be familiar with the idea that your child's nervous system develops from the center outward. What does this mean? It means your baby grasps before he can stand because his hands are closer to his brain than his feet are. The nerves that go to his feet are longer, and they take more time to "come on line." The same developmental processes that are occurring to link up the nerves in your child's arms and legs are also occurring within your child's brain. That is, the central, deeper parts of his brain are linking up and developing connections before the parts farther from the center and closer to the surface come on board. What does this have to do with set-shifting? The part of the brain that lets your child engage in set-shifting is far from the center toward the front of your child's head. It's an area that won't mature until your child is nine or ten years old.

What does this mean for your child's behavior? It means that if you expect your two-year-old to stop what he's doing and change activities immediately after you issue a directive, you are going to be disappointed. Your two-year-old can no more accomplish this than he can accomplish threading a needle or jumping rope. 1-2-3 respects a young child's neurological limitations; it allows your child's brain the time to make the shift, and it allows him the time to put his body into action. 1-2-3 also makes clear the intention that your directive is to be carried out.

Bear in mind that you are liable to be tested on this matter, and it is critical that you make good on your promise, or this strategy will be useless for you. So what will this test look like? It looks like you, at bathtime, telling your mostly unclothed son that he needs to remove his shoes, and it looks like your son, with a glint in his eye, not making a move in that direction. It looks like you counting "1-2-3," and the only thing that has changed is that the glint in his eye has grown sharper. A loudspeaker might as well go off in the room, announcing "Testing! Testing!"

All right. So this is a test. Let's call this one pass-fail. How do you pass? You perform some variation of picking him up and taking his shoes off for him, despite his kicking and screaming in revolt. You plunk him in the bath, and before you know it, the storm has passed and he's happily sudsing his hair. The more cheerful and equitable you remain, the quicker you are going to get to happy sudsing. This seems simple enough, yes? So how do you fail? Let's say you've counted to three with no compliance. You get into trouble if you tell him again. You get into trouble if you count again for him. You get into trouble if you start yelling or making threats. The point is this: Your child has to know that you mean business or 1-2-3 becomes an empty threat. Empty threats are almost useless as tools to get the behaviors you want from your child in the short term. In the long run, they have grave and far-reaching implications. Empty threats can foster in your child a sense that you are not trustworthy.

Empty Threats

Emma, three, has apparently confused her macaroni and cheese with Play-Doh, and she is up to her wrists in it, squishing and squashing and watching it emerge from the spaces between her fingers. Her father tells her to take her hands out of her food and use her fork. Emma does not comply. "Emma," says her father, "take your fingers out of your food or I'm taking away your bowl." Emma doesn't move. "Emma," says Father, "I'm serious." No response. "Emma!" yells Father, "Emma Jean! What did I tell you? Take your fingers out this instant, or I will take that bowl away and you will have no more dinner!" Emma makes no indication she has heard. "Don't test me, young lady!" yells Father. "Don't test me or you are going to go to bed hungry."

Emma's father makes multiple promises to take away Emma's dinner. Notice that he does not follow through. Notice that the threat does not work to change Emma's behavior. Emma keeps playing with her food, and why shouldn't she? Chances are this is not the first time such threats have been made to her, and she has learned that the promised consequences will not come to pass. If, on the other hand, this is the first time these threats have been made to Emma, then she is on her way to discovering the hollowness of her parent's words. Empty threats not only do not work to control a child's behavior, but they have a more far-reaching consequence of teaching a child that words have no meaning and that parents cannot be trusted to tell the truth.

As a parent, you must deliver on any threat you make. This seems easy enough; however, there are a number of considerations you need to keep in mind. You need to know when to use threats and the kinds of threats to make. You also need to be prepared for the sacrifices you will need to make in the course of demonstrating to your children that your words mean business. And you need to be prepared for some of the immediate consequences you may have to live with when you live by your word.

When parents are not secure in their authority, they tend to overrely on threats, using them too often and too quickly.

When five-year-old Kenton comes in with his parents, he has difficulty remaining in his seat, as directed, during the interview. His parents tell him once, then twice, to sit down. When he is up out of his chair a third time, his father asks, "Do you want to play

Nintendo tonight or not?" Kenton sits, but only for a minute. The
threat is repeated multiple times over the course of the hour. No
one is happy.

Kenton's parents have abdicated their authority. Kenton sitting down should not be open for negotiation, which is exactly what happens when the Nintendo enters the discussion. Kenton should not be listening to his father in order to earn a privilege. He should be listening, he should be sitting, because his father has told him to do so. When Kenton's father introduces the Nintendo, he provides an alternative. Now Kenton may either comply or not comply, if he's willing to pay the price. The threat is a meaningless one evidenced by the fact that it gets repeated so many times.

What is a parent in such a situation to do? Make good on the threat by taking Nintendo away after Kenton pops up for a fourth time? And then what? By the end of an hour, such an approach could end up denuding a child of every toy and game in his closet. And *still* the parents wouldn't be getting the behaviors they want.

While Kenton's dad may indeed keep Kenton from playing his Nintendo game once the family gets home, this consequence will take place at a great distance from the infraction. While this is not exactly an empty threat, it might as well be for all the power it has to change Kenton's behavior. The example provides a good illustration of the importance of making a consequence not only something that will be carried out, but something that can be carried out immediately.

Jennifer Griffin, five years old, won't stop bothering her
three-year-old sister, Amanda. She has a plastic horse that she
adores, and she continues to tickle Amanda's cheek with its mane
and tail. Amanda is crying and pushing her away. Mrs. Griffin
tells Jennifer to stop repeatedly, but she shows no signs of listen-
ing. Finally, Mrs. Griffin tells Jennifer that if she does not stop,
she will not be able to attend a friend's birthday party the follow-
ing weekend. Jennifer continues to harass Amanda.

Mrs. Griffin thinks she has pulled out the big guns here, but the consequence that Mrs. Griffin has threatened is too distant and clearly has no impact on her daughter. A more immediate consequence with more relevance to the situation was suggested.

Mrs. Griffin was counseled to warn Jennifer that if she touched her sister with the horse again, the horse would be taken away from her and kept away until the following day. Jennifer made another move, the horse was removed from her, and a significant temper tantrum ensued. Mrs. Griffin was counseled to hold firm, which she did. Over the course of several months' consultation during which she practiced such techniques, Mrs. Griffin reported that Jennifer's misbehavior decreased markedly. Once Mrs. Griffin was able to make the consequences immediate and instill confidence that they would be carried out, Jennifer became a good listener.

Immediate consequences you can impose on your child will always be more effective than those that take place at some future date. For one thing, it's usually easier to make immediate consequences relevant to the situation at hand. Jennifer, for example, was misbehaving with the horse, and so she lost the privilege of having it. Immediate consequences have the additional benefit of helping parents accomplish short-term goals. In this case, for example, taking away the horse removed the instrument of torture directly.

Have you, as a parent, ever found yourself in a situation where your child was misbehaving and you threatened to take him home if he didn't stop? And if so, did you make good on your threat when he didn't stop what he was doing? Most parents do not. There will be times when following through on a threatened consequence will involve considerable sacrifice for you as a parent.

John, five, is at a baseball game with his family, but he is having a terrible day. He wants peanuts. He wants popcorn. He wants an ice cream. He wants everything he sees, and he seems to be getting most of it after he whines and cries enough. People seated near the family breathe a sigh of relief when father delivers the ultimatum: Any more tears and they are leaving. But then John wants a hot dog. He cries and whines. Dad stays firm, repeating his threat to leave. And repeating it. And repeating it. The sighs of relief from those seated near them turn to sighs of exasperation as everyone recognizes there will be no reprieve.

The scenario cited above, and a multitude of variations upon it, are all too common. Parents have a variety of explanations for why they don't follow through on a threat to leave once they have made it: They are afraid of hurting a host's feelings. They feel that leaving a social gathering would constitute bad manners. They were having a good time at an event, and they didn't want to go. Their other child is behaving well and having a good time, and they don't want that child penalized for the misbehaving child's actions. All of these defenses are deadly. If you threaten to remove your child from a situation and you don't get compliance following this threat, you must act on it. This means you will miss out on some things yourself. You may miss the end of some movies if your child acts up in the theater. You may miss the cake if your child acts up at a birthday party. You may go home early from the beach. Once you tell your child that this is the consequence at hand, you must follow through.

So should you ever make such a threat? If you don't want to leave a place, maybe you think it's a good idea never to threaten your child with such a dire consequence. This is a fine idea, to a point. By all means, find alternative consequences if you can. However, there will be times when it is appropriate to remove a child from a setting, and this means removing yourself too.

When is it right to leave a situation? One does not allow a child to ruin someone else's experience. If a child is being obnoxious at the movies and disrupting others and he persists in doing so, this is not a time to start taking away the candy and popcorn. If a child is so completely exhausted that he cannot stop a tantrum at a party, you pick him up and get in the car. You do this not only to model personal responsibility, but you do it to protect your child from the consequences that ensue from being aggressive or destructive toward another. You prevent your child from acting in these ways to protect the children around him, and you do so to ensure he is not burdened later with concern over what he has done.

The Montague family was going to a child's birthday party. Their five-year-old daughter, Melissa, had been irritable all day and had already had one tantrum in the car. Her mom and dad were excited about the party because they rarely had a chance to see the birthday girl's parents. When they arrived, arts and crafts were being done at a corner table. Melissa approached a girl using a bright pink marker. She tried to grab it, and when the girl wouldn't give it up, Melissa hit her on the head, raising a welt, and started pulling her hair. Her parents rushed to intervene. Melissa was in a full-fledged temper tantrum, kicking her feet and flailing her hands. The Montagues told her if she didn't calm down and apologize, they would leave. She continued to kick and scream, and they picked her up and headed for the door.

Are our children happy to be removed in such a circumstance? Do they express gratitude to us for saving them from themselves? Less often than we might wish. The fact of the matter is, when we craft appropriate consequences and follow through on our warnings, children do not greet these events with pleasure. We need to recognize that when we take such a position with our children, they are liable to be angry and express all manner of unpleasant emotions. We need to be prepared, in such an instance, to ride out the storm.

Communicating effectively with children boils down to saying what you mean and meaning what you say. Knowing how children are capable of understanding language and understanding how they are able to think about what is said to them at different stages in their development puts you in the best stead for effective communication with your children. This creates the potential for fewer misunderstandings and more harmonious interactions all around.

Chapter 5

The Many Faces of No

Imagine you have just moved to a town where there are no laws governing driving. People drive wherever they want—on roads, on sidewalks, across people's front yards. There are no speed limits. There are no traffic lights or stop signs at intersections. Want to make a U-turn? Go right ahead, anywhere you like. Signal if you feel like it. Now imagine you have to get yourself across town this morning. How free do you feel to travel on the streets? For that matter, how free do you feel to come out of your front door?

The U.S. Constitution guarantees us freedom, but it's no free ride. The preservation of our inalienable rights depends upon our willingness to behave in such a way that the freedom of others is preserved as well. You can't have freedom and take license at the same time. When people take license, they behave any which way they please, acting without forethought and taking no responsibility for the consequences of their actions. Freedom is an entirely different matter. In order to have freedom, you have to know things, think ahead, make judgments, and take responsibility for consequences. Teaching children to develop the capacity for freedom means teaching them about limits and rules and helping them to live within and understand them.

Where there is an absence of rules and everyone is free to do her own thing, no one is really free at all. Limits and rules are not just confining; ultimately, they are liberating. For as much as rules tell you what you may not do, they also tell what you may do. In the absence of boundaries and limits, there is chaos and danger. In chaos, your instinct is to retreat to keep yourself safe. No one thrives in chaos; and if we, with all our adult experience, can't cope well in such a circumstance, how can we expect a child to function when rules and parameters are not clear? Your children are no better suited to explore and grow in an environment in which boundaries for their behavior are not made clear than you are suited to drive in a world without speed limits and stop signs. Setting limits for children does not turn them into limited people. Rather, limits define the world in which children can freely interact.

When you set limits and enforce them, you not only teach your child about what constitutes correct and safe action, but you also convey to her that she is a worthwhile individual whose health and safety are worth preserving, even at the cost of an occasional temper tantrum. Considered from this point of view, limits are building blocks for self-esteem. You only say no to your child if you have regard for her and have a future in mind for her.

That said, it is important to note that not all rules, and not all methods of enforcing rules, are created equal. As important as it is for you to impose limits and standards, it is also important for you to be thoughtful about what limits you set and the way in which you go about making sure rules are followed. You can and should say no to children, but not always. What I want to do in this chapter is help you understand when and why no is appropriate and when and why it is not. You can then say no to your children for all the right reasons. And you can do so without guilt or remorse.

The Right Kinds of No

It's your child's job to explore the world. It's your job to facilitate this process while making sure no one gets hurt. It is appropriate for children to investigate and get into things. It is not appropriate for children to investigate and get into *all* things. You need to find a balance that's right for your child. How can you limit your child's activities to preserve everyone's health and safety while not stifling her curiosity, independence, creative spirit, and personality? A lot of this will have to do with the way in which you think about and use the word "no." "No" is a short word—just one consonant and one vowel. Nevertheless those two little letters can pack quite a wallop. And like most powerful things, "no" can be used well, and it can be misused.

The No That Preserves Health and Safety

A young child's curiosity is like water. It will go in every direction, and it will take your child with it. It is your job to make sure your child's curiosity does not take her over Niagara Falls; it's your job to place an obstacle in her way—"no"—to ensure that she stops well before the point of danger.

"No" is the right word to use when you want to stop a child from doing something dangerous. You do not limit a young child's potential for exploration and healthy curiosity when you say no to preserve life and safety. If your child is injured either emotionally or physically, she is not free to explore the world, nor is she likely to want to do so. If you don't protect your child from certain things in a manner that respects her developmental capacities and limitations, the world becomes a fearful place. A fearful child will not learn and will not grow. Ironically, it is the child who has been appropriately limited who is the least limited in her range and view in the long run.

Rules that are essential to safety and the preservation of life need to be put in place before your children have developed the capacity for rational thought. Your young child reaches to touch a strange dog, and you say no. You say no to a toddler who is reaching for the candle flame. When a child thinks to get in the car with a stranger, to eat berries off bushes at the park, to lean over the balcony, to play with the knobs on the stove, to run out into the street, or to eat all the bubble gum–flavored toothpaste, you have to say no or your child's health and safety may be at risk. You can explain the reasons for such rules as your children get older and have the capacity for abstract understanding. For a toddler whose physical capabilities far outpace her judgment, simple directives that make the essential point— "Don't touch! Dangerous!"—suffice.

A young child's understanding of danger is often inversely related to the expansiveness of her curiosity. Verbal limits you set will need to be backed up with actual physical barriers to destructive action. "No swimming without a grown-up!" needs to be backed up by a sturdy fence around the pool. "No eating! Dangerous!" is not a license to leave an open container of chewable vitamins within a young child's reach. You need to back your words up by shutting the childproof cap and storing the bottle on a high shelf.

Children do not have the ability to see how harmful the effects of their forbidden actions might be. The dinosaur vitamins taste good. What does a four-year-old know about iron poisoning? The pool is so much fun. What does a three-year-old know about drowning? Because children cannot appreciate the magnitude of the danger in which they put themselves, they often do not greet the limits you set to keep them safe with obvious expressions of gratitude. Setting limits on your children may occasion tears and whining. But like it or not, if your children are to make it beyond childhood, they need to learn about the dangers in the world and they need to be stopped before they are in jeopardy.

With young children, rules need to be repeated and reinforced over and over again. Your young child does not want to hear no, cannot understand the rationale for it in any abstract way, and will not necessarily remember that you said it fifteen minutes ago. The little pink pill she finds on the floor of your kitchen is tempting, and it can get from the floor to her mouth in an instant. Even if she could recite the "No eating things off the ground" rule if you asked her about it directly, there's no guarantee she will prompt herself to recall the rule at the crucial moment. To do so would require some self-awareness and self-monitoring, and young children don't have those capacities yet. Be prepared to repeat rules and actively enforce them until your children have developed the capacity for memory, and the ability to stop their first impulse to action and think about what they are doing.

Even when children get older—five, six, thirteen, fifteen—you will have to repeat and enforce certain critical rules until your children develop an ability to understand the reasons the rules were made and to appreciate the implications of breaking them that go beyond "I'll get in trouble if Mom or Dad finds out." The struggles will look different as children age and pass through different stages of development, but the underlying principle remains the same: You are always working with your child to establish a foundation for thinking, understanding, and making decisions that she will need to guide her throughout life. In thoughtfully setting limits for a child and enforcing these limits, you help your child develop enough of a sense of responsibility to be able to take over this function on her own behalf, and ultimately to pass it on to another generation. Your children may sigh and roll their eyes when you remind them once again that they need to wait for you to come to the backyard before they jump into the pool. It's better to risk being perceived as a broken record by a child who is alive and well, than to silence yourself in response to the eye-rolling of a child whom you later find at the bottom of the deep end.

The No That Preserves Civilization As We Know It

The right kind of no preserves health and safety. The right kind of no also prepares your child to participate in the social world outside your home. These are the noes that foster civilization. We are not a society of anarchists, so socializing children involves imposing order on the chaos of their feelings and behaviors and defining ways they can express themselves that are thinking, rational, and nondestructive. A child who has had the right kind of social "no" is a child who is later able to inhibit destructive impulses and has the potential to engage in more harmonious social relationships. A child who has not had such limits enforced is a child who will have her access to others limited.

> *Jimmy, a four-year-old boy from Miguel Marquez's preschool class, is a terror. If he doesn't get his own way, he pitches a fit, and he has been known to hit and kick others. He was at Miguel's fourth birthday party last year, and Mrs. Marquez doesn't want to invite him back this year. She says, "I talked to some of the mothers in the class, and they feel the same way. I get the feeling that Jimmy is getting left off a lot of party lists this year."*

Children like Jimmy tend to be excluded from social events, and rightly so. Some parents may feel a certain amount of social pressure to include all the children from a particular group, such as a school class, in a social event like a birthday party, but this only extends so far. And chances are, even when such children are included on the list, they will be ostracized at the party itself. Do you socialize with bullies? Probably not. And there's no reason to expect your child to want to do so. Bullies and kids with bad manners are no fun to be with. A child who always has to get her own way is a child who will eventually play by herself. While children vary with respect to their temperaments and some are certainly more prone than others to be irritable and aggressive, it is the parents' responsibility to work with a child to help her limit negative behavior so she is not left out of the fun with others.

Productive and civilized members of society respect other people. They do not speak loudly in a movie theater. They do not turn a restaurant table into a percussion ensemble and drum on plates and glasses with forks and knives. They don't push ahead in line. They don't grab what they want from other people's hands. They don't kick others when they are angry. A child who does not understand social limits is a child who will live a life of misunderstandings, repercussions, and difficulty. By contrast, a child who understands and abides by social standards is likely to have more freedom to move in the world and to be enriched by experiences she has with others.

This is not to say that socializing your child properly guarantees her a life of harmony and peace. Part of socializing children involves preparing them to come in contact with those who have been less socialized. You may keep a bully off the birthday party list, but that doesn't mean your child won't come into contact with her on the playground, and there may be times when you actually have to include a child in a gathering—a relative at a family event, for example—whose behavior is less than ideal. Your child may know what "no" means, but many with whom she comes into contact will not. The more capable your child is of understanding her own impulses and of understanding where the line gets drawn, the better position she is in to assess the behavior of those around her and to figure out how to cope in response. If she sees trouble coming and can identify it as such, then she can move to the other side of the street to avoid it. When she can't avoid it—if she's seated next to a bully, has a mean teacher, or ends up working for a cruel boss in the future—then she needs to be prepared to figure out how much of her self-respect is at stake, and what the costs of compliance versus noncompliance with the bully are going to be. We are not talking about finding some one-size-fits-all plan for coping in such circumstances because all of the situations a child will encounter are going to be different. Rather, we are talking about fostering character strength in your child on which she can rely to think her way through all the situations in which she will find herself over the course of her life.

Another Way to Think About No

What qualities do you value in others? Dynamic people are those with creativity and energy. Creativity and energy do not need to be manufactured in an individual over the course of her life; these are qualities that are there at the beginning. The spark is there in children. It is our job to cultivate it.

Children come to learn about the world through play and active exploration. With each new discovery, children ask new questions and uncover new directions to explore. Their energy for investigation seems limitless. The most important thing your child can carry into adulthood from this time has nothing to do with any one piece of information she uncovers. Rather, the most important thing she can carry into adulthood is the intact impulse to discover and investigate. We are not only talking about preparing your child for a satisfying life here. On a much more fundamental level, we are talking about ensuring your child's basic survival by keeping her alert to the environment. Keep your child's energy for discovery intact to keep your child alive, and in so doing, give her an opportunity to make the life she lives a richer and more interesting one.

How can you parent a child to give her the best chance of emerging from childhood with an inquiring and energetic mind? The answer has a lot to do with how you think about and use no.

The Levins can't stand what is happening in their household. Jacob, a very active two-year-old, is into everything. Mrs. Levin says, "I listen to myself, and I'm like a broken record all day long, saying 'no, no, no, no, no, no, no.' Yesterday, Jacob was playing with the fireplace tools. I told him no. Then he's pulling on the fireplace screen. No. He's climbing on the dining room chairs; he's banging on the glass of the china cabinet; he's playing with the knobs on the stove. No, no, no. I'm chasing him around taking everything away from him. I know I have to set limits or Jacob is going to get hurt. But I can't stand to listen to myself, and Jacob gets more and more frustrated as the day goes on. Last night, after what seemed like a whole day of no, he ended up running into the family room and pulling a pillow over his head. What do I do?"

Some noes are meant to stop progress completely. This type of no is equivalent to erecting a dam on a river. The Levins are constructing a lot of dams for Jacob. But while dams will certainly stop a child's progress toward danger, they will stop her progress toward other things as well.

A river with enough dams placed over its course can stop moving and become stagnant. Depending on the temperament of your child and the frequency with which you dam the river of her curiosity and exploration, you can end up choking the life out of her life, making her world small and slow. We are all familiar with stories about adults whose lives feel dull and repetitive, whose minds feel numb, who get into one routine or another, who can't seem to see beyond obstacles and who may not even try to do so. These are adults who have lost the passion and interest and curiosity of childhood. These may be adults with too many dam-noes in their pasts, so to speak.

There will be times when you need to erect a dam—if only temporarily—to keep your child safe. In the main, though, you need to think about allowing the energy of childhood to find expression while you steer your child away from areas where she is likely to encounter danger. This is not so much the domain of no as it is the domain of "not this, but that."

> *Instead of just stopping Jacob, Mrs. Levin was encouraged to provide him with alternatives and direct him to activities that would be acceptable. In the place of "Don't touch the stove," Mrs. Levin was encouraged to tell Jacob what he could do: "You can't touch the stove, but you can play with your toy kitchen." "You can't climb on the dining room chairs, but you can climb on your slide outside." After several weeks, Mrs. Levin reported that she felt the relationship between herself and her son change. She said, "I don't feel like a cop anymore. I feel more like a teacher. Doing it this way spurs me to think more creatively too."*

When Jacob is given options, the river of his curiosity can keep flowing. Dealt with in this way, he is more likely to grow up to see barriers as challenges to inspire him to creative action. He's likely to be fueled by faith that there is a way around things that obstruct his progress toward a goal.

Some children, like Jacob, if faced with enough "no, no, no," will hide their heads under a pillow and eventually shut down. Other children may

135

react differently. Just as there are slower-moving rivers, others are wilder and not so easily dammed. These rivers move with such force that they will sweep into their currents any rocks, logs, or other objects that have been applied in an attempt to slow their progress.

Mrs. Bingham's labor with her son, Kennedy, was fast, and anyone who knows Kennedy, now two years old, isn't at all surprised by this. This child gives new meaning to the word "active." And he doesn't take well to being thwarted. Mr. Bingham states, "This weekend I was working in my shop in the garage, and he came in, immediately got hold of a screwdriver that had fallen on the ground, and said "This?" I said, "No! Dangerous!" and I took it away from him. He found a nail on the ground: "This?" Again, I took it away and I said, "No. Dangerous!" Well, he lost it. Thank God there were no other tools in his reach, but he began to pound with his fists on the car, screaming 'Want it! Want it!' I had to physically remove him. He kicked and screamed all the way to his room. I have a black-and-blue mark on my arm where he connected with his foot."

While all toddlers are capable of temper tantrums, some children have shorter fuses than others. This is an issue of toddlerhood, but it is also an issue of temperament. While any child eventually might be provoked by being thwarted, it takes no time at all for Kennedy to reach a boiling point. But clearly a child cannot be allowed to play with screwdrivers and nails, so what was Mr. Bingham to do?

Mr. Bingham was encouraged to provide Kennedy with a child's tool set and workbench and some old, smooth wood scraps that he could pound away on while Mr. Bingham was working with real projects. He was encouraged to apply the same thinking to the innumerable issues that came up at home with his son, refocusing him—even physically turning his head at times, if necessary—to orient him to safer alternatives than the dangerous things that attracted him. A week later, Mr. Bingham reported, "I can't say it's been a week without temper tantrums, but I can say it has been a week with fewer of them. Overall, the temperature in the household has gone down a degree or two."

This raises an important point. Raising children is not a pass-fail enterprise, and the response to different approaches you take to parenting often will not produce all-or-nothing or immediate results. There is no intervention that is going to prevent your hot-tempered two-year-old from having an occasional tantrum. Expecting otherwise and judging the effectiveness of a strategy on that basis is being too rigid. It is a setup for failure. We are talking, after all, about human beings and human behaviors. Whenever you are taking a particular approach in parenting, it will help everyone involved if your expectations allow for gradual and nonmiraculous results.

Because the "not this, but that" approach presents your child with an alternative to something forbidden, when you take this approach you model flexibility in thinking. An adult with flexibility of thought rolls with the punches. He says, "I can't do it this way, but I bet there's another way to go about it." By contrast, if you tell your child "no, no, no" and don't provide any opportunity for the energy to be redirected, then your child may become an adult who is easily discouraged, who is more passive and less hopeful.

That said, while it is important to have a strategy that presents alternatives and invites creativity and problem solving, you are not mandated to take this approach *every single time.* There are going to be circumstances in your child's life in which there is simply no choice available. We adults pay our taxes. We listen to our bosses. We stop on red and go on green. We pull to the right when we hear a siren. A child whose parents bend over backward to make everything a game and to present an alternative in every conceivable situation is not being well prepared for certain aspects of living.

Dr. Bronski, a pediatrician, relates the following story: Erik Garcia, five years old, objected to having his throat cultured. Previously, Mother had offered Erik the choice that the procedure be done presently or in five minutes and he had chosen the latter. Now, Dr. Bronski had returned to find Erik still struggling. Mother said, "You can be on my lap or on the table." He chose her lap, but continued to struggle. Mother said, "I can hold you on the floor or on the chair." He continued to struggle and Mother offered him the

choice of Dr. Bronski or her partner. At this point Dr. Bronksi in-
tervened. Her partner was not available and she herself was out of
time. Here was the choice: The culture be taken now, or not at all.
"Mrs. Garcia accused me of being rigid. I'm not. I'm all for pre-
senting children with choices, but I think parents need to be aware
of when something like that becomes a tool in a child's hand."

In this circumstance, Dr. Bronski is not being rigid. In fact, Mrs. Garcia is the rigid one. Erik Garcia appears to have corrupted the concept of
alternatives in the service of resistance. Erik is not learning to be a flexible
thinker; he is learning to be a manipulator to avoid something that scares
him. And why shouldn't he be afraid? His mother is clearly communicating to him that there must indeed be something terrifying going on if she
is so willing to capitulate.

Mrs. Garcia appears to have taken the idea of modeling flexibility for
her son by presenting choices to him, and to have become very concrete in
its application. That is, in the process of bending over backwards to make
sure her son perceives alternatives, she has not left herself any alternatives.
Sometimes choices are an option. Sometimes they are not. It is up to you to
determine what the nature of the situation is. It is also up to you to determine when there have been enough options given. Children are clever.
Yours will not be the first to take a concept like this and use it in a way that
gives you that painted-myself-into-a-corner feeling. If you detect that your
child has figured out this system—or any system you are using—and is using it to manipulate you, you need to put your foot down. If you fail to do
so, you compromise your authority. Your children may have choices on a
number of matters. Respecting your authority is not one of them.

The Wrong Kind of No

Last night Mrs. Khalsa arrived home from work exhausted
and hungry only to realize that she needed to run to the store for
milk. She told Nerti, four years old, to put on her jacket and some
shoes. Nerti emerged from her room wearing her fancy shoes and
her pink kitty-cat raincoat. Mrs. Khalsa says, "I told her, 'No,
Nerti. Not those shoes. Put on the sneakers and your other coat.'

Nerti asked me why. I said, 'It's not raining, and those are party shoes.' She said, 'But I want to wear these.' I said, 'Just do it.' She started to whine. I started to snap at her. Then I thought, 'What's the big deal? So she wears her fancy shoes and a different coat from the one I had in mind. Will the world come to an end? Not likely.' So I told her it was fine and we got in the car. And you know, she looked absolutely adorable. Everyone at the market commented on how cute she was in her kitty-cat raincoat."

Just as there are noes that are necessary and good, there are noes that are for no good reason at all. At best, these noes serve no productive purpose. At worst, they do damage. These are noes that dampen spirits, squash creativity, and leave children mistrusting themselves and ultimately mistrusting you. These are noes that can easily come to dominate the interaction between parents and children. Whereas positive noes serve life, these noes insidiously take the fun out of childhood and the joy out of parent-child relationships.

Where do these noes come from? They often arise from parental exhaustion. Childhood takes energy, not only on the part of children, but on the part of their parents as well. Parenting is a full-time job that will take as much time and creativity as satisfying any employer, if not more. For parents who work outside the home, parenting is often transacted at the times of the day when there is the least energy available for performance. Rather than greeting children with vigor and inspiration at the end of a workday, parents often find that they are tired. One working mom stated it well: "By the time I get home, I feel all used up." A stay-at-home-mom of three children under the age of five said, "My oldest has outgrown his nap, but I still insist on an hour of in-room quiet time. *I* need it."

To cope with the many demands that are placed upon us in the modern world, we adults often go on automatic pilot. We depend upon a certain amount of predictability, routine, and control in our lives just to get through the day and to get everything that needs doing, done. To a certain degree, we impose this on our children, but we are not automatons and do not expect them to be so. Rather, we do this to give ourselves mental space. Sometimes we are just exhausted and don't have the energy to think about one more thing. It is not unreasonable, for example, for parents to have an evening routine for children by which the major items of eating, bathing, and being put to bed are generally accomplished. Structuring your child's life in this way helps her internalize a structure and a sense of order. If the bedtime routine starts around seven-thirty each night, your child will start naturally to wind herself down around this time. The thoughtful control you initially impose on your child becomes the self-control she can impose on herself over time. But it is important always to recognize that change is part of the "routine." Children change so quickly. Any routine needs to evolve along with your child to keep up with her needs.

It is not with the routines themselves that children are likely to struggle. Children like routine and dependability. Try to put a child to bed without her nighttime bedtime story and you are going to hear about it. This is not only because she wants the story and her closeness to you in the process of reading it, but most important, in failing to provide the story, you will have violated her sense of how things are supposed to run, her sense of where she fits in the process, and her sense of basic security. Your young child's sense of herself and her security are very bound up in her routines; they are the relative constants in a sea of developmental change. In an ordinary day, your child contends with many new pieces of information. Events that can be relied upon to be stable—the routines—give her a context and security for novel experiences. Children crave routine and structure for this reason, no matter how much they may appear at times to fight it.

While you need to provide children structure, you also need to provide them the opportunity to exercise some freedom and creativity within that structure. You may have established a routine for bath-dinner-story-sleep. You make a number of assumptions about how this will transpire. Surprise! Your child wants to dry herself with a washcloth, wants to eat her ice cream with a fork, wants to look at the pictures in a book and make up her own story to go along with them, and wants to sleep in a sleeping bag placed atop her covers. What?! Who would have considered such a thing? Children and nature, that's who. Many adults have predetermined ideas about how some tasks should go. These ideas tend to be so deeply ingrained that it is difficult to recognize that there may be another way. This is a perfect condition for the wrong kind of no—the no of convenience and rigidity.

While children's judgment about many things is not trustworthy, it is a major challenge of parenting to stay alert to those aspects of life in which children's judgment *is* trustworthy, and to honor it as such. You need to steer your children away from things that will hurt them, but you don't need to steer them away from silliness and fun. Your child cannot elect to leave the straps of her carseat unbuckled, but she may ask to have the seat moved to the other side of the car for no good reason you can determine. It is so easy to say no. After all, it's such a hassle to move the seat, and she's got no logical reason for requesting this change. There's so much left to do in the day, and while you're not running late, you just want to get home. You refuse, stick her in the seat where it is, and move on. She whines, is a little irritable. No harm done. Right? That night you are making her bed, and she says she wants her head where her feet usually go, and vice versa. Ridiculous, right? You say no. Why? Because this is the way you have her room organized. It makes sense to you. Imagine if your spouse asked you to switch sides of the bed. Spouses don't do things like that. But children do.

Some parents say no because they believe that someone else might look at them funny should they honor a child's idiosyncratic request. If that is your motive, then this is the wrong kind of no. Your children will come up with ideas you never considered. Just because you never thought of it is, in and of itself, not a reason to justify no. Children may develop interests that are different from yours and that are different from the interests you wanted for them. *Vive la différence!* If it's not harming anyone, leave it alone. Actually, don't leave it alone. Expand on it. This is a good time to initiate a communication of thinking with your child to help her to develop the whys and wherefores of ideas and wishes. Children are limited in many ways. They are not allowed to do many things. They are allowed, however, to have their own ideas and to determine their own personalities. To expect otherwise and to try to curb their very normal and creative expression with excessive noes is the emotional equivalent of foot binding.

How does a parent decide what is non-negotiable and what is the wrong kind of no?

- In matters of health and safety, there are no choices. Your child must take the prescribed medicine at the prescribed time. She must hold your hand when crossing the street. She must wear hand coverings outside in the dead of winter. She may not go her own way in the mall. She may, however, choose to take the medicine in a different spoon, walk freely after the street has been crossed, wear her gloves instead of her mittens, and draw your attention—and your feet—to a store at the mall you have not intended to visit.

- In matters of dress, there may be choice, but not in all circumstances. Nerti Khalsa may have been within the domain of self-determination to choose to wear her kitty-cat raincoat to the market. She would be outside the domain of self-determination, however, in electing to wear her bathing suit to religious services at her temple. Your child's choice of unmatched socks might be fine for a day at preschool, but might not be okay on the day you plan to visit the photographer to have the family portrait snapped.
- In matters of food, your child may refuse a meal once in a while. She may elect to eat her peas one at a time. She may not elect, however, to forego dinner and then to eat candy. She may not throw her peas at her brother or mash them into her hair.

You will have to figure out appropriate boundaries in your house and give everyone a little room for flexibility. You do not have to go along with every idea your children come up with even if it's not hurting anyone. Bone-weary is bone-weary, and after a particularly hard day, you simply may not have the energy to make up a game with your daughter involving a ball and running. Providing a less exhausting alternative for sharing time together is within your purview: "I'll lie down and bend my knees to make a bridge, and you pretend the ball is the boat going under the bridge on the river." Your children can be encouraged to stretch to accommodate your needs on occasion. This helps them to see you as a real person. This helps them to develop compassion. Sometimes parents need time and rest too. Your two-year-old can care for you in limited ways, and allowing her to do so gives her an experience of the power of her love. This will come as a comfort to her, and it will go a long way toward helping her develop into a caring, good citizen. Remember the tapes that are getting made all the time in the interaction between you. As long as she's recording, give her an opportunity to record compassion, consideration, and your ability to recognize what her capacities for caring are.

Stretch. Give up a little control. Find the energy from your childhood to meet the energy of your children. Allow your children to surprise you.

Allow them to recognize the relationship between you. Why? Because to squelch children, to put no everywhere is to limit everyone, including you. The opportunity to look at the world through your child's eyes is a gift she makes available to you. You give her a gift by helping her see, in a limited way, through yours as well. The opportunity to care for each other is a gift. Take it.

I Want to Say No, but I Don't Know Why

There is always a reason for children's behavior and feelings, just as there is always a reason for that of adults. Sometimes reasons can be understood. Sometimes they remain something of a mystery. There may be occasions when something apparently trivial becomes a huge and persistent battle in your house. The issue does not involve health or safety, but everyone behaves as if it were a matter of life or death. In such a circumstance, try to explore further to understand what fuels the situation.

> *Daria Baker, four years old, recently became intensely attached to the family dog, Degan. She drags him into the dining room during meals, and she brings him up on the sofa with her in the family room. This is making Mrs. Baker furious. Conversation reveals that there are other things afoot. Daria is suddenly clinging to her mother when she drops her at preschool. She calls Mother three times a day at the office to say hello. I suggest Daria may be struggling with feelings about separation, which are very normal for her age. Mrs. Baker comes to realize that some of her irked feeling also has to do with separation—that she experiences her daughter's attachment to the dog as a loss of her attachment to her. Once she comes to this understanding of her own feelings as well as those of her daughter, she is able to deal with the situation in a calmer, more understanding way.*

Pay attention. If you sense a molehill has become a mountain, this should be the impetus for you to do a little exploration into what the issue is for your child and what the issue is for you.

Not Enough No

Chances are you know of contemporary parents who, as a matter of principle, have decided never to say no to their children. Maybe you have made this decision yourself. In the service of not creating a "negative environment" or fostering circumstances in which children feel "stifled" or "criticized" or "frustrated," a number of parents have come to the idea that no is the root of considerable evil. This may well be a reaction to the authoritarian parenting days of yore, when "No" and "Because I said so" ruled the day. Maybe it is a consequence of parents never having been told no themselves. Maybe some parents see doing away with no as an easier way to go because it requires no commitment to a child. In a variety of ways, vanquishing "no" appears to be contemporary parents' reaction to how "no" was practiced on them in the past.

The decision to abandon authority is rife with problems. The cure for an overly authoritarian approach is not a democracy in which those with immature judgment are given an equal vote. Countries don't function without some type of government, and neither do families.

Parents who have decided to abolish no in their houses often can provide a variety of justifications for their decisions.

"I Don't Want My Child to Feel She Is Wrong"

Mrs. Nesbitt, the mother of three-year-old Todd, is referred by the preschool director because of Todd's penchant for hitting other children. Mrs. Nesbitt looks at the psychologist and says with peculiar pride, "I try not to say no to him when I don't have to." In the consulting room, Todd begins kicking the wall with his shoe. Mrs. Nesbitt says, "Todd, honey, that's not nice." Todd persists in kicking. Mrs. Nesbitt tries again: "Honey?" She says, "I would prefer you didn't kick, please." Todd's tempo increases.

This certainly prompts the question of what constitutes a circumstance in which Mrs. Nesbitt would feel that no was an appropriate response. But what is noteworthy is the pride Mrs. Nesbitt exhibits in taking such a position. Mrs. Nesbitt reported that she believed that saying no to Todd would limit him in his freedom of self-expression. She didn't want her son to grow up hesitating before taking action in his life, always hearing no in the background. Mrs. Nesbitt is certainly trying to do her best by her son, and her intentions appear honorable. But this is an example of a good idea, imperfectly understood and poorly executed.

"I Don't Want to Interfere with My Child's Creativity"

"I walked in and saw Jeremy crayoning on the wall," says Marla Macy of her two-year-old son. "I told him no and took the crayon from him, but he started screaming. And I was thinking, was I right? I mean, it is his room. And I don't want him to feel his creativity is wrong. So I gave the crayon back to him, and he was happy. I talked to my husband about it, and we figure he can crayon on his walls and we'll just paint his room when he gets a little older."

Not saying no in this circumstance is a mistake. Not only are Jeremy's parents failing to deliver a message about appropriate social behaviors, but they are conveying to their son their fear of his expression of negative feelings and their anxiety about being in charge. If your child is responding in a resistant or negative way to your imposition of a limit, this is not a reason to doubt your judgment.

Failing to enforce limits appropriately in this situation does not do Jeremy any favors. On the contrary, it adds to his problems. If his parents won't take decisive action to limit his crayoning on the wall in his room, Jeremy has nothing to stop him when he finds himself with a crayon in hand in the living room, kitchen, or any other room in his house . . . or in someone else's house. Not only are the Macys likely to be a good deal less charitable with him when they find him crayoning on the walls in the living room, but imagine their embarrassment when he takes to the walls at someone else's home. If this happens, the Macys or their neighbors are likely to react with less indulgence than they have at this first infraction, and any future reaction

145

they have is likely to take part of its strength from their anger at themselves for failing to intervene and set an appropriate limit to begin with.

"I Don't Want the Other Parents to Think I Am Being Mean"

"I was at a birthday party with Chelsea," says Mrs. Monroe of her four-year-old daughter. "She had already had a piece of cake and more chips and nuts and jellybeans than I could keep track of. She wanted more cake, and I said no. But a couple of other mothers thought I was being stingy. They said, 'Come on, it's a birthday.' One of them said she had read a book that said that if you let children choose their foods, then they will naturally gravitate to what is good for them. I didn't want to look like a prude. Besides, they were all skinny and, as you can see, I have a bit of a weight problem. I guess I felt foolish, so I told Chelsea to go ahead. Then she threw up in the car on the way home."

What has happened here? Mrs. Monroe has let a number of factors stand between her and her better judgment in this situation. She had an instinct at the party, which she ignored. Why? She didn't want to be perceived by others in a negative way. What is communicated to her child? "My concern over your welfare is not as strong as my need to be viewed well by others." Sometimes parents make decisions that have less to do with children's best interests than with their own best interests. Sometimes these decisions are made at children's expense.

Mrs. Monroe states that at first she felt awful about what happened, but her neighbor helped her feel better by explaining that letting Chelsea eat the cake and get sick from it gave Chelsea a chance to learn the lesson about eating too much cake for herself.

There is an age at which children can reliably learn from their past mistakes. That age differs according to the pace at which a child is maturing. But it is safe to say that a child of four is not yet there. Four-year-olds do not have the judgment, the capacity for memory, or the abstract thought to infer a les-

146

son from this circumstance. What Chelsea would be most likely to take away from this experience is not the idea that if she eats more cake she will be sick, but the feeling that she cannot rely upon her mother to take care of her.

"I Don't Say No to My Child Because I Don't Like It When People Say No to Me"

Mrs. Lassen comes for a consultation one morning with four-year-old Jared. She complains that he cannot stand being told no, and throws violent temper tantrums whenever he is thwarted. Jared begins whining, and Mrs. Lassen takes some crackers out of her bag. I tell her I don't allow food in my office and ask if Jared has had his breakfast. She says he's eaten, but she often gives him snacks during the day when he seems upset. As she says this, she is giving Jared a cracker. I repeat that I don't allow food in my office. Her face darkens, and she becomes indignant. I point this out to her. I suggest that talking about some of her feelings about having limits imposed might shed some light on what has been troubling her about her son.

Mrs. Lassen has failed to make an appropriate distinction between herself and her son. She's taking the way she feels about being told no and is projecting her feelings onto Jared. Perhaps she assumes that as she does not want to acquiesce to rules, he does not wish to either. Perhaps her son provides her with a channel through which she can express her own obstinacy, yet not be identified or held accountable for it. After all, Jared is the one with the problem, right? Jared may comply with her need, acting badly in order to make his mother happy. In so doing, he is unable, at his tender age, to see how sidetracked he gets from his own life in the process. The problem here is that Mrs. Lassen's projections onto her son are well on the way to becoming a self-fulfilling prophesy. Jared is evolving into a child no better able to contend with having a limit set on his behavior than his mother is. In addition to fostering an eating disorder in her son by feeding him when he is upset, Mrs. Lassen is failing to help him prepare appropriately for living in the world, in which there are rules and limits.

"I Don't Say No Because I'm Afraid My Child Will Be Angry (and Won't Like Me)"

Recently, upon returning home after having concluded a visit to the United States, a foreign dignitary was heard to comment something to the effect that he had never seen a country in which parents were so afraid of their children. It's not difficult to see what could give rise to such a statement. Contemporary parents seem to go to great lengths to keep their children from expressing strong negative feelings. Parents do not want their children to be angry with them. Parents seem to be afraid that their children will not like them. As many parents work and spend less time with their children than their parents spent with them, they often try to preserve the family time as conflict-free.

When parents fear their children's expression of feelings and go to great lengths to avoid them, it does not make children feel good. While outwardly they may wish to control things, children simultaneously know that they are not up to the task of ruling adults. As wonderful a concept as omnipotence seems to be, it is actually quite a terrifying quality to possess. Even Alladin's genie had his lamp. Children may *appear* to want that kind of power, but it does not comfort them to have it.

How do we know this? If ruling the house was comforting, children would appear placated and happy after emerging victorious from a struggle with a parent. They do not. Usually, after winning a struggle, a child will make another demand and then another demand within a short time. Often these demands will be increasingly unreasonable, as if the child is begging for someone finally to draw a line in the sand. Eventually, such a line needs to be drawn, and the episode ends up with the child in tears.

Your child depends on you to be stronger, calmer, and more in control than she is. When her emotions run wild, she depends on you to stay steady and calm so she can find her way back to balance. Your fear of your child's anger suggests to her that something within her is wildly beyond containment and control. It becomes important to provide your child with opportunities to discover that there are limits to her influence. Acquiescing to your child's demands when these demands are inconsistent with family rules is not the way to accomplish this task. Going to great lengths to suppress your child's anger only reinforces her underlying belief that her anger is tremendously powerful.

> *Troy, five years old, is brought in by his parents, who are concerned about his temper. Father says, "The littlest things upset him, and then he's so hard to calm down." He wonders if this is because Troy has raven-black hair. Mother reports that her father had black hair and had a similar temper. She says his temper used to frighten her, and she is concerned that her son will grow up to be much the same way. Troy, given an opportunity to speak, is a garrulous boy. When the session is over and I announce time is up, Troy says he wants to tell a story and begins to do so. I stop him, and he looks surprised. After a moment, he tries again, and again I stop him. His mother has turned ashen. She looks at me with a wide-eyed, horrified expression. She quickly tells Troy, "You can tell the story to us, honey, in the car!"*

Troy's mother is terrified of her son's anger, and this fear is contributing significantly to the problem at hand. Troy needs his mother to be stronger than he is. He needs her to provide a model of stability and control that he can internalize. When he gets carried away by his feelings, he needs to have confidence that he, in the process, cannot carry her away too. His mother, in responding to him as she does, is demonstrating quite the opposite. This five-year-old is well on his way to reaching the well-founded conclusion that his anger is powerful and scary enough to control adults.

Would driving around with what you believed was fifty pounds of dynamite in the trunk of your car make you feel powerful? In some ways, perhaps it would, but more probably, it would make you feel terrified. Suppose you went to an explosives expert to help you deal with the dynamite, and once you told her it was there, she tried to ignore it and did everything within her power to prevent you from opening your trunk to look at it. How much more frightened would you be? Conversely, if she listened to you, opened the trunk, looked at the contents, and showed you that it wasn't dynamite at all, but something that couldn't hurt anyone, wouldn't you be comforted? When children have angry and negative feelings, they believe they are toting dynamite. You, their parents, are the explosives experts whose job it is to look at these feelings with them and show them that they are not, in fact, so destructive at all. They can be tolerated, understood, and properly channeled.

Helping Your Child Channel Anger

As they develop, children must learn to regulate themselves and their emotions. Helping children to do so is part of the relationship between a parent and a child. Who is better equipped for adulthood—the child who has been allowed to weather emotional storms and who has the experience that she and others within the relationship emerged from them intact; or the child who is consistently prevented from feeling and understanding anger, frustration, or sadness by parents who rush to placate her whenever her lip starts to tremble or she narrows her eyes, the child who has never had the opportunity to test the real power of her feelings and more important, the real security of the relationship?

Angry feelings are a fact of human existence. It's important to acknowledge that your child has them, acknowledge that you have them, make it clear that it is all right to have them, and teach your child ways to express them that will not hurt her and will not hurt other people. It is common for parents to encourage angry children to "use your words." The general idea here refers to teaching a child to verbalize an impulse rather than to act it out. We can all agree that saying "I'm mad!" is a good deal more constructive than dumping a barrel of Lincoln Logs over someone's head.

While we need to help children put feelings into words, we need to recognize that not all words are created equal. It's fine and good for a child to say "I'm mad!" But it is not fine and good for a child to use profanity. It is not fine and good for a child to engage in an extended diatribe against her parents. Just because no one's nose gets bloodied by words doesn't mean words do not have lasting or damaging effects. Ranting and raving is no more acceptable from a child than it is from an adult. If a child is screaming "I hate you!" you need to intervene in this as quickly as you would intervene were a physical assault taking place. But what do you do?

While you need to stop a child who is being physically or verbally abusive, this is not so easily accomplished. The word "emotion" has its Latin origins in words meaning "to excite" or "to move." There is energy in emotion and it is not so easily squelched. A very angry child can't simply put a cork in it. You have to respect the fact that when your child is angry, there is a lot of energy in her anger that needs to find a way out, and you need to provide some means for the energy of her feeling to be expressed.

Some parents tell their children to hit pillows or pound on the mattress when they're angry. One mother who was having severe problems with her seven-year-old gave him one of those inflatable clowns that are weighted at the bottom and pop up after a blow. When he was mad at her, she told him to punch it and to pretend it was her. But these approaches are problematic. Children may wish terrible things on you when they are angry, and as your young child does not reliably differentiate fantasy from reality, the emotional repercussions for these wishes may be significant. In encouraging such behaviors, you will not end up making a child feel any calmer. Encouraging such behaviors is likely to increase her agitation.

To understand how to help a child with angry feelings, it's useful to look to what you foresee for her in adulthood. Perhaps you know an adult who has punched or kicked a hole in a wall when frustrated. Do you want to raise a child who does this? Do you think this is mature? This is not mature. A mature individual is someone who turns the energy of anger into something productive: an artist who makes a painting from the depth of her feeling, the victim of racism who channels her rage at injustice into a campaign for public office from which she legislates civil protections. Childhood is the time to teach your children to channel the energy of negative feelings into something productive. This is not something that comes naturally. When we use the energy of anger productively, we turn it in a positive direction. We don't try to squelch it or stanch its flow. We respect that there is a need to be active that goes along with the feeling, and we consciously make it work for us. How can we help our children to do this?

Consider the following example: Your five-year-old is enraged when she discovers her two-year-old sister has bent all her Pokémon trading cards. She starts screaming at her, and she throws one of her Barney videotapes on the wood floor, hard. You intervene. You say, "You are mad! You are so mad!" Her eyes are still blazing, and her fists are clenched. This is not a "use your words" situation. This demands action. What do you do?

- You could take your child out to the garden, give her a trowel, and have her dig up the dirt. By the time she has spent her energy digging, she may be in a calmer state of mind and can help you plant flowers in the newly turned earth.

- You could take her outside to run or ride her bike fast around the cul de sac, or put on music and let her dance, or give her a jump rope and some clear space to use it. Engaging in any physical exercise is a good and productive way for children—and adults—to let off steam.
- You could take her to the garage and turn her loose on the cardboard boxes that need to be broken down for the recycling truck. When she is calmer, the two of you can work together to stack the flattened boxes and tie them with twine.
- You could give her some art supplies—big pieces of paper and big crayons—and let her express her feelings this way.

In all of these instances, once some of the energy of anger has been discharged, there can be room for a little conversation. The words your child could not use when she was initially so overcome by the intensity of her anger may be more available to her now. Listening to her, being available to empathize with her or provide the words she cannot allows the feeling to be more completely reconciled and resolved.

The short-term value of such interventions is that they allow your child to express the energy of her feeling in a way that does not hurt anyone and ultimately has a positive impact. In the long run, you are showing her that she can take the energy of anger and direct it consciously in a productive direction. You are increasing her confidence in her ability to direct herself, to think, and to problem-solve.

Chapter 6

Boundaries, Limits, and Other Unpopular Essentials

At different times in history, children have been viewed as inherently bad and parents have felt the mandate to keep them on the straight and narrow to curb their wicked ways. Conversely, at other times children have been idealized and seen as inherently good. The truth lies somewhere in the middle.

What Your Children May Not Do

As your children are capable of affection and creativity, so are they capable of destructiveness and cruelty. When you find the latter, this is not evidence of bad parenting on your part any more than it is evidence of inherent evil on the part of your children. Rather, it is a reflection of the way people are, children no less than adults.

> *Mrs. Sander comes to consult because she feel helpless to control Gina, aged three. As she seats herself in my office, Gina begins to giggle and kick at her ankles. Mrs. Sander says, "Gina, stop being silly. You're hurting Mommy." Gina then pulls Mother's hair. Mother says, "Gina, stop playing like that." When Gina eyeballs a tall palm in my office and moves to rip one of the leaves, I say, "Stop, Gina," and when she does not, I pick her up and deposit her in a chair, which precipitates a full-fledged tantrum. I say to Mrs. Sander, "There's nothing playful or silly*

about kicking, hair pulling, or other kinds of destructiveness. Let's understand why you don't stop her."

If you are to solve a problem, you first have to identify clearly and accurately what that problem is. Deciding Gina is "silly" in this instance and treating her accordingly will do as much good as diagnosing a broken bone as an allergy and treating it with antihistamines. In this instance, Gina is acting aggressively and is being defiant. This does not mean she is a "bad" child, but her behavior is unacceptable. Seeing the behavior in this light is necessary so the appropriate response can be determined to make Gina stop.

What are the consequences for antisocial and aggressive behavior? Some consequences are external. In early childhood, there is Time Out. In later childhood, there is the principal's office. In adulthood, there is prison. All along, there is social ostracism. People who act aggressively not only end up in trouble with parents, police, school personnel, and the like, but often are rejected by others. Who wants a violent adult around? Who wants a child at a birthday party who cannot refrain from kicking others?

In addition to observable repercussions, there are subtler, more subjectively experienced consequences to bad behavior as well. Say you're late to an appointment and you cut someone off on the freeway. You glance at your rearview mirror with a bit of apprehension. Is the driver you cut off glaring at you? You switch lanes, and he switches lanes. Does he look mad? You exit the freeway, and he exits behind you. Your heart rate goes up. Is he following you? Chances are he is not. However, the fact that you have done something wrong is influencing your perception and your feeling. Some external consequences of aggressive driving are that others might not want to drive with you, you might get more tickets or get into more accidents, and your insurance rates might go up. But even if these things never occur, as an aggressive driver, you are likely to perceive the driving environment to be an unfriendly place.

Have you ever blocked an intersection and felt afraid to meet the eyes of the person you were blocking? Have you ever received too much change from a purchase, kept it, and looked behind you as you left the store thinking someone was following you? Have you ever gossiped about someone behind his back and the next time he made contact with you anticipated accusations and recriminations? Aggression sows the seeds for paranoia. The more aggression you perpetrate, the more aggression you will anticipate being visited on you. Because this principle is a reality of human life, children who are disruptive to others in a variety of ways are prone not only to be rejected by others, but also to perceive the world as a more threatening and more difficult place.

If we keep this principle in mind, it becomes apparent that there are a number of behaviors that your child may never be permitted to do, *under any circumstances,* as the observable as well as the more internal consequences for these actions are too great. These behaviors are not negotiable. You need to have conviction about their inappropriateness and be definitive in communicating your resolve to your child from the beginning, in your speech and in your actions. If children do not respond when told to stop these behaviors, they need to be physically stopped from engaging in them. They may need to be removed from the situation, despite whatever protestations they may make. What are these behaviors?

- Your children may not hit you or others, including pets.
- Your children may not kick you or others, including pets.
- Your children may not destroy property, including their belongings.
- Your children may not throw objects at you or anyone else.
- Your children may not bite.
- Your children may not spit.
- Your children may not push.
- Your children may not touch other people's private parts, other children's as well as adults'.
- Your children may not insult others.
- Your children may not use profanity or engage in extended diatribes.
- Your children may not ignore you.
- Your children may not litter.
- Your children may not go into your closets, drawers, or purse uninvited.
- Your children may not persist in their activities when you say "Stop!"

Many of these are behaviors that children will do naturally in the normal course of development. Babies "bite" when teething and touch their mother's breast when nursing. Young children ignore "stop" until they have learned what this word means. The process of teaching these limits will be gradual. This is not a license, however, for an "anything goes" policy to prevail at your house for your children until they reach a certain age. You will have a much easier time establishing these parameters for children if you are thinking about these issues early on and laying the foundation for them.

A five-year-old boy was having serious behavior problems that included some highly sexualized behaviors at school. No sooner had his parents seated themselves in my office than he nestled into his mother's lap, buried his face in her breasts, and put one hand under her shirt to hold what was presumably her bra. I drew the family's attention to this. "Oh," said Mother, "he didn't want to come here this morning. This just makes him feel more secure."

A baby or young toddler may have access to mother's breast and body when nursing, but this doesn't mean that it's all right for him to pinch mother's buttocks or fondle her. For this family, allowing their child to behave in this manner was the most significant force underlying the behavior problems. This boy is overstimulated by having this kind of access to his mother. All he can think to do to quell his anxiety is more of the same, but this makes the problem worse. A child's desire to do something doesn't make his judgment trustworthy. That an activity makes a child feel better in the moment does not justify parents' capitulating to something that is improper. Children have many impulses; you need to be the one who takes the larger view and sets the limits in this situation. If you lay the foundation early on for appropriate boundaries and limits, children have a chance to incorporate them as a natural part of how they grow.

In making decisions about what are off-limits behaviors for your child, you have to think about your value system. And you have to give some thought to how your values will go over in the larger world.

> *A woman was in the women's locker room at a health club. She was dressing after her shower when another woman walked in with what appeared to be a seven-year-old boy in tow. The naked woman quickly scrambled to cover herself. She said to the mother, "This is a ladies' locker room." The mother looked at her blankly. The other woman continued, "I need to get dressed." A light appeared to go on for the mother. "Oh," she said, "you don't have to worry. We walk around naked in the house. He's used to it."*

This mother has failed to appreciate that the rest of the world may not share her family's level of comfort with public nudity. Clearly, the woman who was walked in on was not comfortable with this approach. The behaviors your child is learning in your family have to prepare him to adapt to the larger world. A policy of not knocking on a bathroom door before entering is likely to create problems for your child at a friend's house when he walks in on a friend's mother on the toilet. It *should* create problems. Would you feel safe sending your child to a household in which the adults walked around in the nude or let children accompany them to the bathroom? Hopefully not. Looking at things from this point of view may be another way to get a clearer perspective on the standards you need to establish for your children. That is, protect your children in your household no less than you would protect a visitor.

Many inappropriate behaviors—kicking, biting, and other acts—are aggressive behaviors. While children need to have their destructive impulses toward others checked, this is especially true with respect to their parents. This is a critically important point. Parents can *never* allow children to harm them in any way, even in play.

> *Mr. Gumlumbi is worried about his two-year-old daughter, Sarai. "Always she is kicking and hitting. I tell her this is only something we can do in play, but she gets carried away." I suggest to Mr. Gumlumbi that while he may have a clear understanding of what distinguishes a period of play from a different sort of inter-action, Sarai does not understand this. Mrs. Gumlumbi pipes up: "It is even in the play that there is a problem. My husband will*

start out playing with her. He'll be saying, 'No! No!' as a joke, but then he means it. Sarai doesn't catch on, and she is then in trouble and he is angry."

Mr. Gumlumbi is setting up his daughter for failure. He is allowing her to hit him—mistake number one—and then he is expecting her to pick up on sophisticated nuances in tone to discern when she should stop. When she fails to do so—as she will—he holds her accountable. Everyone is irritated. The solution: No hitting games.

Children have many feelings about their parents, and some of these feelings are intensely negative at times. Add to the mix the fact that children don't discriminate fantasy from reality as reliably as adults do and that they are not reliable judges of the consequences of their actions. What is the result of this combination of factors? If you give your child permission to hit, kick, bite, or otherwise act aggressively toward you, then he can believe himself capable of doing great damage. The reality that he has not done so may be lost in his fantasy about the extent of his power. When your child is allowed to behave in these ways toward you, he is liable to feel anxious and guilty. If you allow your child to act in ways that leave him feeling anxious and guilty, your child is likely to mistrust your judgment.

On Being Formal in Informal Times

Once upon a time, not too long ago, children addressed their elders as *Mr., Miss, Mrs.,* and *Dr.* (Actually, adults used to address each other in these ways too, until invited to do otherwise.) Somewhere along the line, this convention has fallen by the wayside, and in many parts of the country, three-year-olds now call the forty-year-old friends of their parents by their first names. This may be the climate of our times, but I believe there are few adults around today who have not entertained at least a fleeting moment of discomfort when addressed by first name by a child. It simply doesn't feel right. Nor should it.

Formal address, in addition to being respectful, provides a feeling of safety and security. In any situation where there is unequal authority or knowledge, formal address can be a comfort. It is a way of acknowledging that one individual in a situation is being relied upon for greater wisdom and better judgment. Children and adults are not on a level playing field. Adults have lived on this earth longer than children, and they are in a position of responsibility any time they are in the company of children. We don't rob or show disrespect to children in any way when we recognize these differences. In fact, it is in recognizing the real differences between adults and children that we are most respectful to children and to what they need. Children and adults are not peers, and children need it to be this way. As grandiose as your three-year-old may be when he announces "I do it myself!" he maintains simultaneous awareness of his relative helplessness and dependency. He needs the security of knowing he is with a responsible person.

Perhaps it is because of the responsibility it conveys that we have tended to reject formal address. With the thousand and one things we are responsible for in the course of a grown-up day, the last thing we may want is another reminder of responsibility. For that matter, the last thing we may want is another reminder of the fact that we are aging. As one young mother said to me: "Do you have to call me Mrs. Shapiro? I keep thinking you're talking to my mother-in-law." Being on a first-name basis with children may be a way in which we preserve the fantasy that we are still children. We may stay one step ahead of our mortality every time a little mouth refers to us as John or Jane.

> *"I don't think the Ms. thing would make me very comfortable," says Ms. Boulet. "I want the kids in Dierdre's kindergarten class to think of me as their friend."*

The "Ms. thing" is not designed to make you feel good (though once you get used to it, it probably will). The Ms. thing is something you do to make your child feel good. It's done for his comfort and security, not for the purposes of fear or intimidation. Children do not think of adults as friends. They think of adults as people who can be relied upon to perform first aid, to transport them to a doctor, to find a lost parent, to soothe their hurt feelings, and to provide shelter, food, and safety. Adults are what stand between children and the terror of their real helplessness and vulnerability. Adults are there to facilitate the action, not to derive equal pleasure from it. Dierdre's classmates have friends. They need an adult around for security.

> *"I'm afraid the kids won't like me," says Claire Dumas. "I think they would laugh or look at me strange if I presented myself as Ms. Dumas."*

We should not need children to like us at all times. This places an unfair burden upon them. Your children can enjoy your company. You can enjoy their company. But you can never forget that you are the grown-up. It is more important for children to respect you than to like you, no matter how uncomfortable this may make you feel. Chances are if a child respects you, he likes you too, but you cannot make being his friend your main aim in your interactions. Formality is efficient. Formal address from child to adult means we don't have to reestablish our authority with every encounter. It is consistent with that authority. When you comport yourself in an authoritative, adult manner, this comes as a great relief to children. They know you can be counted upon.

> *"Kids in the neighborhood all know me as Ginny," says one mother of three. "Now I'm supposed to tell them to call me Mrs. Arlen? That seems so awkward."*

It is awkward to make a change in anything at first. But avoiding awkwardness is not a reason to persist in doing something that isn't right.

There has been a revolution that has gotten us from more formal times of yore to where we are today. Are you prepared to be a counterrevolutionary? If you are in a community in which children do not address adults formally and you decide to make this change, prepare for it to take a while before formality becomes automatic for your child and for you. You will not only need to help your children get accustomed to addressing adults formally, but to ensure consistency in your children's lives, when you speak to or about other adults to your children, you will need to use formal titles too. If you can't bring yourself to use last names—and in some communities this is so far outside the norm that it may feel like too great a stretch—at the very least attach formal titles to first names. Ms. Lynn,

Mrs. Shelby, and Mr. Bill still convey a differential in status in a way that Lynn, Shelby, and Bill alone do not. This will take a lot of getting used to for everyone. You can enlist your children to help remind you, as you will be reminding them, if you forget to use a title. You should also prepare for varying reactions on the part of other adults in your community who may not have given much thought to this matter.

What You Should Not Do

One would be hard-pressed to find a book for parents on child rearing that did not speak about the necessity of imposing limits upon children's behavior. There is little consideration given, however, to the need for parents to impose limits on their own behaviors as well. Just as there are things that children should not do, there are things that parents should not do in the process of parenting their children. We are not talking here about the gross and obvious behaviors. Of course, parents should not beat their children or invite children to take sips of their margaritas. These examples are at the extreme end of a continuum. There are a number of less extreme actions you may be doing with your children that may not be so obviously inappropriate and that bear some restraint.

You Should Not Do Anything You Don't Want Your Child to Do

Your young child is internalizing you. He doesn't sort through what he sees you do and decide what works for him and what doesn't. He is not the slightest bit discriminating. And the things your child will pick up on in you are often so subtle that you might never have imagined they could have been detected. For this reason, if you have an eye toward your child's future and the future of the society in which he will live and to which he will contribute, you will refrain from doing that which you don't want to see him do at some later date. In this light, you should not:

- *Lie.* In any way shape or form. A child who sees a parent lying is a child who learns that lying is acceptable behavior. A parent who lies and then reprimands or punishes a child for lying is a parent who is not being fair. Your child's sense of fairness is deeply ingrained and concrete. If your child knows you lie and you don't let him do the same, this is going to register with him. Chances are, you are going to hear about it from him at some point. How can you possibly explain yourself? Presuming you want to teach your child a respect for the truth, then you have to behave accordingly. Lying while not allowing your child to do so won't teach him about the sanctity of the truth. Rather it will teach him that there are double standards, that you cannot be trusted for your word, and that the truth is nothing special.

- *Cheat.* The government. Other people. Stores. If you are given too much change after a purchase, you need to give it back. In so doing, you take the opportunity to set the right kind of example for your child. If you fail to do so, you have no leg to stand on when you try to impart to your child a conscience.
- *Steal.* Anything from anyone or anywhere. Don't feed your child a container of cookies during a trip to the grocery store and then leave the empty box behind without paying: $1.39 is a small price to pay for your child's integrity. Or for that matter, your own.
- *Belittle others.* There are people who get taller by standing on others' shoulders, but this is not an attractive quality and the stature that such people gain is insecure. Remember "If you don't have something nice to say, don't say anything at all"? Practice this unless you want your child to become someone who bad-mouths others and who eventually may even bad-mouth you. This does not mean that if someone behaves badly or provides a negative example that you cannot talk about this with your child. It has to do with how you bring up and discuss such matters. If someone shows up at a function in a risqué outfit, there is a difference between saying to your child "Could you believe that Miss Sue was showing her bellybutton?!" versus saying something like "You know, that party got me thinking about style and fashion. Let's look at some pictures in magazines and talk about it together." You may still end up discussing Miss Sue's outfit, but you do so for the purpose of helping to foster thoughtful consideration in your child, and you do it in a way that is not gossipy or ugly.

- *Use profanity.* A civilized society is not populated by individuals whose potty training did not extend to their mouths. If you curse, you will hear all your colorful turns of phrase coming out of your child's mouth. And profanity is not only unattractive, but it is likely to get your child in trouble in school, in church or temple, and with other children's parents. This will not only be shaming for your child, but it is likely to embarrass you as well. Your child will pick up some curse words in the larger world. It's your job to teach him that cursing isn't smart, that people who curse can't think of anything else to say. You are going to have a hard time reinforcing this concept if you use profanity yourself.

You Should Not Put Adult Burdens on Children's Shoulders

While it is all well and good for us to be in touch with our feelings and attuned to those of our children, this does not give us license to burden children with feelings of our own that do not belong to them. You can acknowledge to your children at times that you are sad. They can see that you are angry or apprehensive, but the details that give rise to your feelings are usually best kept to yourself. In difficult family circumstances, as well as in response to the day-to-day events of life, you need to be the one who helps your child understand his feelings and hopefully feel better. You can't expect reciprocity. Your child does not have the life experience to be expected to comfort you, and you can easily overburden him by being too forthcoming about the details of your mental state. Rely on the memory of a nice experience with significant others in the past when you are struggling with bad feelings; call a supportive friend; go into therapy. But don't ask *from* your child the type of support that you should be providing *to* him. To do so, burdens him unfairly, and ultimately it can do damage to his basic sense of security in the world.

Carson Rennert, five years old, had begun bed-wetting, and his mother was worried that her recent divorce was responsible. "The other night, he asked if he could keep going to his school now that Daddy was gone. I told him I was doing everything I

163

could to earn enough money for us to keep our house, and even if we couldn't keep it, we'd try to stay in the neighborhood so he wouldn't have to change schools. I said maybe I would get a raise at my job, or maybe I would work extra hours, and if I did, he could start spending more time with his friends. I wanted to reassure him so he wouldn't worry. But he still looked so upset." I suggest that rather than reassuring her son, she is likely to be creating a great deal of worry in him. "Well, then what do I say to him?" she asks, growing teary. I tell her that Carson needs to hear something like "I know it's very different that Daddy isn't living here, but we are still your parents and we will always take care of you and make sure you have what you need." I suggest that to get her own needs met in this difficult time of transition, Mrs. Rennert find a therapist who can respond to her concerns.

There is such a thing as giving a child too much information, and Mrs. Rennert is certainly doing so here. Carson may eventually need to change schools, but there is no need to start preparing him for changes until they become more of a reality. At this point, Mrs. Rennert has no idea what is going to be happening in her life and she cannot say how it will affect Carson. She is understandably anxious about this state of affairs, but she needs to keep her worries to herself in the relationship between herself and her son. Mrs. Rennert's anxiety is overflowing its banks, and it is flooding Carson with a quantity and type of feeling he is even less equipped to deal with than she is. This is where the bed-wetting is coming from, and if Mrs. Rennert continues to relate to her son in this manner, chances are we will see a host of other symptoms develop in him as time goes on. Carson is already at his capacity for coping, given the impact that his parents' divorce is having on his life, and this is before his mother makes any comments about school or the house. Mrs. Rennert needs a grown-up to talk to. Carson needs his mother to be strong. He needs her to conduct herself in a manner that conveys dependability.

Certainly, it is our responsibility to prepare children for changes that we know are upcoming, but we have to remember that because our children are concrete thinkers, they have less of an ability than we do to understand possibilities that are not certainties. As concrete thinkers, children take everything that is said to them at face value, as fact. We should not start preparing our young child for a crisis unless we know for sure it will come to pass. If a relative has emphysema and is smoking, we may have a number of well-founded concerns about this person, but this is not the type of information to share with a young child. There is nothing concrete to prepare him for in this instance. The danger is not imminent and there are too many possible outcomes. If we speak to him about what *might* happen, all we will succeed in doing is burdening him with our worry. On the other hand, if a relative is terminally ill with cancer and the end is near, we are remiss if we do not help our child prepare for the transition to come.

When there is a real circumstance that your child needs to be prepared for, you will have to make a judgment about how far in advance to bring the topic up. As an adult, you can benefit from a greater amount of time to prepare for a loss. In making the decision about what time frame will be best for your child, however, you need to bear in mind that young children can't see as far ahead as adults, and they can't keep things in mind meaningfully for the same amount of time as adults can. For this reason, you don't give a young child nearly the advance warning that you would give an adult.

> *The Bettel family volunteered to be puppy raisers for the Guide Dogs of America. They took on Lucky, a Labrador retriever, when he was eight weeks old, knowing they would be able to keep him for only eighteen months prior to having to surrender him back to the foundation for his training and job assignment. They told Tess, their three-year-old daughter, about this early on, and periodically reminded her that Lucky was not theirs to keep. When the actual day came to turn Lucky in, Tess was confused and took it hard. The Bettels were surprised by her reaction. They figured they had prepared her for this loss so long in advance that the transition would not be so difficult for her.*

The Bettels may have had noble aims, but their approach was seriously flawed. At the age of three, Tess had no way of understanding the concept of giving back her dog eighteen months later. The more this idea was repeated over time, the less meaning the words had. From her point of view, her parents kept telling her she would lose her dog, and nothing ever happened. By the time the event actually occurred, the words were meaningless to her and the actual loss of the dog was shocking. The Bettels would have done better by their daughter if they broached this subject three or four weeks prior to the actual event, had taken her to the Guide Dogs of America office where she could see the program, and had worked with her to plan some meaningful last activities to do with Lucky to prepare to say a proper good-bye.

You Should Not Overwhelm Children with Feelings They Are Ill Equipped to Handle

It could certainly be argued that some of the cultural institutions of the late 1950s and the 1960s and 1970s were stifling compared to the way the culture is today. In the previous generations, there were certain ways that things were done, and that was that. People had less freedom to choose roles and less freedom of expression. Did your dad change diapers? Did your mom coach Little League? Did your family talk about feelings? Possibly, but if so, you are in the minority.

While some changes have been to children's advantage, there are changes that don't serve children well. We can certainly talk about the relative repression of the previous generation, but it is a mistake to then assume that all of the modesty of the past needs to be done away with.

Did your mother use the toilet in front of you? For that matter, did your parents use the toilet in front of each other? Chances are, they did not. This type of immodesty has arisen in our modern culture. This is not to say that all parents subscribe to it, but a fair number do. We are caught in the wake of a revolution. We are determined not to be the repressive parents of bygone generations, but in reacting against the principles of the past, we seemed to have skipped right by our own instincts or even common sense. The danger in coming away from a society in which there has been repression is to overcorrect for it. But one does not effectively correct for the presence of too many boundaries by creating a society in which there are no boundaries at all. People in the past may have been relatively conservative about revealing their bodies and the feelings their bodies contained, but the remedy for this is not the banishment of privacy.

Sex is not a shameful act, but we certainly don't let children in on it. Intuitively, we know this to be inappropriate. Children have a great deal of innate curiosity. That curiosity takes forms that are more and less acceptable to adults. Children are curious about many things in the world, from why the grass is green to where babies come from. Even before they can form sophisticated questions about sex and childbirth, curiosity about sexual and bodily functions is present nonetheless. Children are curious about their body parts, and they are curious about yours. This curiosity is evident in countless ways.

A mother in a parenting group talks about her four-year-old daughter: "You know, she's getting all these new skills. She can draw people with arms and legs with her crayons. She puts together Lego blocks to make houses and other buildings. And she's learned to button and unbutton. The other day, she was unbuttoning my blouse, but it seemed like it went a little beyond just practicing her skills. I really had the feeling she wanted to get at parts of me that haven't been her domain since I weaned her three years ago!"

A father comes for consultation after finding his six-year-old son playing doctor in a garden shed at the edge of his property. "I saw him through the window before he saw me. He had his pants down and, well, that little girl was really looking!"

A mother in a parenting group talks about her five-year-old son: "I love putting him to sleep at night, and we still read a story. He likes to nestle into my lap, but recently, I get the feeling he's doing more than the usual amount of scootching in to get comfortable. I get the feeling he's kind of rubbing up against my breasts. And sometimes he'll bury his face in them in a way that just doesn't feel quite right. Am I imagining this? Am I just being prude?"

167

During a family therapy session, an eight-year-old girl is complaining about her two-year-old sister. "She's totally annoying. She takes my stuff. She makes a mess of everything she gets her hands on, and she's got this fascination with Archie, our dog. I swear if he's laying on the ground, she'll go up to him and pull his leg up and just stare at . . . you know . . . his thing."

After her parents separate, a five-year-old girl spends her first night at her father's new apartment. He says, "It was time for her to go to bed, so I told her to get into her pajamas. Imagine my surprise when she took one of her mother's sexy nightgowns out of her overnight bag. She swore to me her mother had allowed her to take it; she put it on; then she wanted me to sleep in the bed with her. When I told her I would be sleeping in the other room, she begged me to stay with her. She was crestfallen when I wouldn't give in. It was a little surreal."

A mother describes walking in on her three-year-old son spread-eagled in front of the bathroom mirror. "I think he was trying to get a good view of his butt," she says.

Are these parents describing anything out of the ordinary? Not at all. This is not to say that all sexualized behavior in which children engage is benign. If a child masturbates compulsively or is intensely and persistently preoccupied with touching other people's private parts, this needs to be investigated further. This may be his only way to communicate a problem that he doesn't have the abstract thinking to conceptualize or the vocabulary to discuss in words.

But there is such a thing as garden-variety childhood sexual curiosity. The above examples fall into this category. All these behaviors are natural, bespeaking an underlying interest and curiosity that all children have. Parents should not be horrified or surprised or embarrassed by evidence of such interest. But beyond remaining unhorrified, unsurprised, and unembarrassed, how do you cope with this very natural curiosity? Parents in previous generations are more likely to have tried to squash such impulses, to pretend they didn't exist, or to shame or frighten children in order to get them to stop. "I remember clearly," says one father in a group, "I must have been five. I had just finished using the bathroom. My mother stuck her head in and said if I touched myself down there, my hand would fall off." Often, children were not taught the proper names for body parts associated with sexuality or elimination. Many contemporary parents consequently grew up with the feeling that their bodies were in some ways shameful or embarrassing, if not downright dangerous.

Think of how much energy in the culture has been expended over the last thirty years to liberate human sexuality. Contemporary parents of young children who have been witness to and participants in this revolution are determined not to foster sexual repression in their children. Parents want to ensure that their children grow up feeling good about their bodies, as opposed to feeling their bodies are dirty or shameful, attitudes fostered by previous generations. This is the new generation, and we do things differently, right? But how do we do them differently? It's one thing to know what not to do. But it's quite another to know what we should do instead.

> *The Gowitzes have an open-door policy in their house. Recently, Mr. Gowitz was preparing for a bath when four-year-old Louise walked in. She pointed to her father's penis and said, "I know what that's called. It's a penis." Mr. Gowitz felt a bit exposed, but proud of his daughter's unabashed manner. His discomfort increased, however, as his daughter continued to stare at his penis as he made his way past her to get into the bath. He found himself wanting to cover himself up, though he resisted the impulse for fear of sending her a message that there was anything shameful about his body. His daughter, however, continued to stare at her father's groin as he lay in the water. "Why is it floating?" she asked. "I don't know," he said. She asked, "Can I touch it?" At this point, Mr. Gowitz's discomfort won out over his desire to provide a shame-free lesson about body parts. He says, "I told her she couldn't and that she should leave the bathroom. I'm afraid I've damaged her. I was just so uncomfortable at that point. I didn't know what else to do."*

Mr. Gowitz has not damaged his child. His initial approach may not have been the best way to handle the situation, but what is important here is that he listened to his intuition and responded by sending Louise out of the room. Now he knows not to get into this situation again. If your child is staring at your genitals, there's a good reason to feel uncomfortable. Your discomfort is a sign that something is wrong with this picture. Similarly, there's a definite line between a child taking comfort on mother's lap, and a child nestling a little too intently into mother's breasts. An outside observer may not be able to discriminate when this line is crossed, but intuition is likely to be reliable. If something doesn't feel right, it probably is not.

There is danger in equating the idea of something not being shameful with the concept of letting it all hang out in front of our children. The danger of rebelling against preexisting cultural institutions is that we end up pressing on past the middle ground and too far into the domain of the opposite extreme. Rebellions are loud, and the voice of common sense can be much softer and is easily drowned out.

We are all just learning as we go along in life, in parenting as in every other domain. If a situation like this arises with your child and you get a clear signal that something needs changing, change it. That such a situation occurred doesn't mean you're bad or that the consequences for your actions will be dire. Rather, it's a wake-up call. In responding by changing your behavior, you show your children that you learn from experience and that they can learn from experience too. You can make a change without making a federal case about it. You can also make changes without shame. If your child questions you, you say, "Well, you know, I wasn't comfortable. I didn't feel right about that. Now that you are older, I realize I need some privacy." When you make a policy change like this, just as when instituting anything else that is new with your children, you can prepare to repeat the rule until it becomes clear to them that this is the new way that things are going to be. Be forewarned: If this is an area you are uncomfortable about, you are going to *really want* your child to catch on the first time, and you may feel less tolerant of the need for repetition. Hang in there.

Along with displaying a certain amount of sexual curiosity, children also tend to go through periods in their development when modesty is very important to them. In young children, modesty has a peak around the age of four or five. Often this modesty arises as a means for young children to regulate their curiosity about bodily matters and the feelings that their curiosity arouses in them. It can be seen as an adaptive defense that assists them in coping with this stage in life. It is important to recognize that children are not only likely to be more easily stimulated to strong feelings than are adults, but they are also less equipped than adults to handle whatever strong feelings may arise in them. It is important to respect modesty in children when it emerges and to see it as serving a regulating function for them. This doesn't mean you avoid using the proper names for body parts or that you need to act embarrassed about topics related to bodily functions. It does mean you don't push your child to face these topics.

Joy Smith and her husband, thinking themselves forward-minded, had bought a book about where babies come from, and they sat down with their four-year-old son, Billy, to read it. "My parents were strict and religious, and I grew up in a very repressed environment. I'm determined that won't happen with my son," says Mrs. Smith. "After we read a few pages, Billy pretended not to be interested and he tried to squirm off my lap, but I brought him back. It happened a couple of times. Billy got more and more antsy, squirming around my lap as the book went on. And then," she says with a horrified expression, "I realized he wasn't squirming. He was . . . well . . . playing with himself." At this point, Mrs. Smith states that she put down the book. It's been two days now, and Billy is still prone to stimulate himself as he walks around the house. "What should I do?" she asks, plainly distressed. "I'm afraid I've created a sex maniac."

Mrs. Smith was feeling awkward about the topic of sexuality, and she was so determined to push past her awkwardness that she was unable to see what was actually very awkward about this situation for her child. Had she been able to see more clearly, she might have waited until Billy indicated some interest before introducing the book. Or if she had introduced it in this manner and gotten this response, she would probably have been able to pick up on her son's discomfort and allowed him to leave much sooner. Has she created a sex maniac? No. She has created an uncomfortable situation. Billy appears to have been overstimulated by this encounter, and he is trying to discharge this energy in his masturbation. Mrs. Smith might talk to him about the strong feelings he has and reassure

171

him that he has been understood. She also needs to reconcile some of her own feelings about the encounter, as it is likely that some of her lingering agitation is fueling her son as well. Addressing the situation in this way may decrease Billy's need to stimulate himself. If it persists, Mrs. Smith can say, "I know that feels good, but that's something private that you do in your room." Mrs. Smith can trust that when Billy is ready to tackle this subject matter more directly, he'll say something. At that point, the book can be reintroduced.

You, an adult, have had many years to develop a system of coping with the various feelings that arise in you. Children don't have abstract thought to categorize what happens to them. They don't have vocabulary to express their feelings. They don't have a sense of self that would permit them to distance themselves from something by making a negative attribution about the thing itself. Adults can say, "Oh well, that thing is just stupid." Children can't. It would be a better arrangement if nature, along with limiting children's coping mechanisms, also limited the intensity with which they experienced things. But alas, this is not the case.

> *Three-year-old Dominick Sirola and his family were driving on a rural road. Another car flew into an intersection, sheared off their front bumper, went into a 360-degree spin, and hit the guard rail hard. Miraculously, no one was hurt. Mother states, "Dominick was very excited by the whole thing. He started to laugh, and then he fell into a deep sleep. Since then, he plays the same game over and over. He always has two things colliding with one another, and he makes a crashing sound. He does it with stuffed animals, silverware, books. Is this normal?" The Sirolas were asked how they had coped with the events on the road. Mr. Sirola said, "I called the police on the cell phone, and while we waited for them to arrive, I gave that other driver a piece of my mind. We drove our car to a nearby garage, and we got a rental. I still find myself checking and double checking before I pull into an intersection, but I think we're pretty much over it."*

All the Sirolas were exposed to the same event, but their experience of it was radically different. The Sirola adults expressed anger, they took action in the direction of repair, and they reminded themselves to be extra cautious to reduce the likelihood of such incidents in the future. They have regrouped. Not so for Dominick who, in repeating the experience over and over again in his play, is trying to master it with the resources available to him. He is dealing with what happened in the best way he knows how.

What does this mean? It reinforces what we intuitively know: Children do not have the same ability to cope with events as do adults. It is on this basis that the rating system for movies was developed. It is for this reason that children's books don't contain sex and brutality. This is why we do not turn on the nightly news in front of young children. Unfortunately, in our present-day culture with its fast pace and glut of media technology, it is not uncommon for children in well-meaning and conscientious families to be privy to things that are beyond their ability to understand and cope with.

> *Ms. Clark speaks of her five-year-old son: "This morning I had turned on a cartoon show for Jackson, but during the commercial, I watched him switching channels looking for different cartoons. He went past three news shows that were broadcasting images and stories from the latest school shooting, a commercial about erectile dysfunction, and a morning talk show that was doing a special about breast augmentation where they showed before and after with the nipples fuzzed up like they do on TV so you can't really see them. I was thinking, 'What has happened to the world?' My partner and I were talking about getting rid of the TV because I don't know how else to deal with this."*

It is easy to think that as the world, the media, and technology change, people have changed too. In fact, children and their experience of childhood have not changed substantively. Just because there are more images available to children in the present-day culture does not mean that children are any better equipped to cope with them than were children of previous generations. Parents need to keep in mind that children are inherently limited in their ability to understand that to which they are exposed and to process the feelings that arise in them as a result of their exposure. So what does this mean in concrete terms? It means you may need to alter your behavior. It means you should not:

173

- Be naked in front of your children (or anyone else's children, for that matter). This is too stimulating for them. It's fine for children to be curious, but this is not a signal to gratify their curiosity.
- Use the toilet in front of children. They will have ample opportunities in playgroups, in preschool, and when watching potty-training videos to see other children thus engaged. They don't need to see you on the toilet to learn.
- Engage in any sexualized play in front of young children. You have to keep the door closed when you are intimate with your mate, and you need to make sure your children are on the other side of it. If children are in your room, don't think it is all right to proceed with sex on the basis of your belief that they are asleep.
- Make negative comments about your spouse in front of your children. Your children have internalized both of you. Bad-mouthing a spouse is ultimately bad-mouthing a child and is liable to make a child feel rejected and vulnerable.
- Argue with your spouse in front of children. You and your mate are the world to your child. An argument is an earthquake that threatens to topple the world as he knows it. Your child does not have the same defenses that you do to overcome the threat of an argument. Having a disagreement or a somewhat passionate discussion in front of children is all right, but anything beyond this will frighten them because they have no way to understand the real meaning of such things.
- Have temper tantrums in front of children. Children rely on parents to be stable. You may be angry in the company of your child and you can let him know it, but you must retain control of your behavior. To do otherwise is to threaten your child. After all, if you lose your cool, what is to prevent you from going overboard in your behavior with him?
- Give children access to the TV or let them watch movies you are not familiar with. A G rating on a movie these days does not mean that your young child won't find something threatening or overwhelming in it. Watch out also for the contents of previews that are screened prior to the feature you are seeing.

You Should Not Act Out

"Acting out" is a term that refers to doing something destructive instead of putting feelings into thoughts and words. Acting out is something children do as part of childhood. Part of the process of socializing children and giving them a vocabulary for feelings is to help them grow beyond acting out. But acting out is not strictly within the purview of children. If you doubt that adults engage in acting out, watch the nightly news. Acting out won't always land you in jail or on Channel 7. There are infinite subtle and entirely legal behaviors that constitute acting out as well.

When parents engage in acting out, this is a type of regression to the past. It can shake a child's sense of security because an acting-out parent is behaving in an immature and destructive way and cannot be relied upon to provide the stability, rationality, and mature judgment that a child needs.

> *"I was at Playgym with Ellen," says Mrs. Antonio of her three-year-old daughter. "It was three o'clock, and we had to go to pick up Matt from a playdate with some other boys from his second-grade class. But Ellen was having such a good time, and she really didn't want to go. I remember my brother played baseball and my parents were always cutting my activities short to go to his games. I don't want Ellen growing up with that feeling, so I let her stay a half hour extra. When we went to get Matt, all the other boys had been picked up and the host's parents seemed a little upset at me. Did I do something wrong? I knew he would be safe with them, and it was only a half hour."*

Mrs. Antonio may appear to exist in the present, but she has been transported thirty-five years back into the past. The host's parents have become her parents, and she is rebelling against their demands. She might have wanted to resist her parents back then but was powerless to do so. Now she has power. She stalls a half hour before she gets in the car to pick up her son, who in this instance represents her brother, whose needs came first for all those years. Well, not anymore! She's not going to stop playing for his benefit! But of course, she has herself mixed up with her daughter.

175

The cost of transacting business from the past in the present is great. Mrs. Antonio has offended the host's parents with rude behavior. She has made herself untrustworthy in the eyes of her son. In reacting against favoritism and resentment, she is fostering resentment between her children as surely as she would have were she to wear a sandwich board stating "My daughter's needs come first."

Not only may parents with unresolved feelings from the past act out directly, but they may also engage in a phenomenon that could be called "acting out through one's children." When a parent is acting out through a child, the child takes on the parent's objectionable impulses and desires and enacts behavior that the parent might really like to do himself, were not prohibitions in place to prevent that.

One can suspect acting out through a child is occurring when a very passive parent spawns a bully. You can be surer of it when you observe this parent colluding with the child's behavior by failing to set and enforce appropriate limits. If you're perceptive, you may detect a subtle smile on the parent's face while the child clobbers a playmate. Don't think that this is a parent who would outwardly condone the child's behavior. On the contrary, it is often this parent who is the child's most vocal critic. In this instance, the child becomes the scapegoat, the carrier of that which is objectionable. Parents often don't enact these dramas intentionally. When these behaviors are made explicit, this is often the impetus to change. Though not always.

Mr. and Mrs. Vinnon complained that six-year-old Georgie was exhausting to interact with. There was nothing that was said to him that did not serve as the starting point for a negotiation. As we discussed the need to be definitive and to give clear commands to Georgie, his father, a politician, looked upset. "But don't you think he should get to have choices and discuss what he wants with us?" he asked. I pointed out that the fact that he was doing so was the family's main complaint. At the end of the session, I presented an agreement for the family to sign in which parameters for payment, scheduling, and the like are made explicit. Mr. Vinnon refused to sign it without making modifications in a number of the paragraphs. When I told him these items were not open for modification, the family elected not to pursue treatment.

Most parents would say that they do not act out through their children, but it happens nonetheless. None of us wake up in the morning and say, "Gee, I really want to saddle my kid with all the burdens from my past." It's nice to think every generation starts with a clean slate, but this is seldom the case. Often we are blind to the ways in which we act out, and we find it shameful when someone brings to our attention that we are doing the last thing we would want to perpetrate on our kids. As a parent, you have to be willing to explore avenues of yourself and make changes. You have to be willing to tolerate the feelings that arise in the process. The more you are aware of your own emotional dynamics, the less likely you will be to use your children as innocent conduits for the expression of your emotional residue. Your children must bear enough burdens of their own in this lifetime. The fewer of yours they need to shoulder, the better.

Boundaries and limits apply to everyone in our culture. In the parenting relationship, they apply to the children and the adults. Frustrating though it may be at times to have to impose and enforce limits—on ourselves and our children—it is essential for everyone's well-being. We may have certain inalienable rights guaranteed to us as part of our cultural heritage, but it is important to recognize that these rights rest on inalienable responsibilities. Taking these seriously and imparting this value to our children is for the good of all concerned in our society, for now and into the future.

Chapter 7

Beyond Crime and Punishment:
An Ounce of Prevention

What are young children? They are immature beings in a dynamic process of development. They are learning the ways of the world and of themselves and others, and they are looking to *you* for most of that information. And as much as parenting involves responding to the delightful aspects of children's process of development and discovery and encouraging that which is good, parenting involves contending with the more unpleasant and objectionable things children do too.

Do you discipline your children? Do you punish them? Do you think discipline and punishment are one and the same? If so, reading this chapter and the one that follows may very well change your mind.

Punishing children involves responding to a transgression with a penalty. A person who is punished is usually an unwilling participant in the experience, who may feel hateful and resentful. This is not a state of mind that allows for growth. Punishing children often ends up frightening, shaming, confusing, and angering them—outcomes that fall far afield of what we had hoped to accomplish. What do we hope to accomplish? To see to it that children learn what is and what is not acceptable behavior. This is the domain of discipline. Discipline is about teaching. The word "discipline" itself is from the same root as "disciple." It implies an agreement to be taught and a willingness to learn. A disciple is someone who is taught by a person with greater knowledge.

You and your children are not on equal footing. As the parent of a young child, you are the one with greater knowledge and experience. You are the authority. While sometimes it may feel as though your children have more power than any adult to drive you crazy, they do not have real power in the relationship. You do. You are the grown-up. When your children misbehave, you are the one who determines what has gone awry, and you are responsible for setting your children on the right road again.

Discipline is about establishing boundaries for children's behavior, teaching them about these boundaries, and helping them to remain within them. Discipline aims ultimately for regulation. A child who is disciplined well is eventually able to regulate herself—to keep herself within the domain of acceptable action and out of trouble to begin with. And when trouble nonetheless occurs, as it will, a child who is disciplined well knows how to contend with these circumstances too.

Thinking about discipline as teaching as opposed to as punishing gives you a lot more freedom and invites your creativity. Punishing children allows you only to respond to negative behavior. Discipline allows you—requires you, really—to intervene to prevent difficulty in the first place. In this chapter, we'll talk about that aspect of discipline which is oriented toward preventing negative behavior. In the next chapter, we'll talk about disciplinary issues that need to be considered once misbehavior has occurred.

Say What You Mean

Imagine the following: Your spouse asks you to pick up some meat so you can make hamburgers for dinner. You go to the store and buy a package of ground beef, but when you get home and hand it over, your spouse is annoyed and says, "Chuck? I didn't want chuck. I wanted sirloin." Your response to your mate? "But you didn't tell me which one you wanted." It hardly feels fair to be held accountable for failing to do something that wasn't made explicit in the first place.

Just as you are not a mind reader, your young children are not mind readers either. And not only that, but kids tend to be pretty poor at making educated guesses too. Why? Because they have not yet been educated. They lack experience in the world. They are literal-minded. In order to discipline your children, you must first know what your expectations are. You need to clarify them to yourself and then make sure to communicate them to your children clearly.

As in the ground beef example cited above, when young children do

179

not do what you want them to do, this is often not willful misbehavior. Often it's a product of their not having enough information. Their behavior is an indication to you that you need to be more explicit.

Mr. Tinker spontaneously adopted a twelve-week-old puppy from outside the market. When he got home, he presented his surprise to the family. To his horror, Joseph, aged three, greeted the dog by pounding on its head with his fist. "Stop it, Joseph," said his father. Joseph stuck his fingers in the dog's nose. "Stop it," said Father a bit louder. Joseph stuck his fingers in its eyes, and Father exploded. "That's it, Joseph!" he said angrily, sweeping the boy off his feet and heading toward another room. "Time Out!" Mr. Tinker thinks Joseph is just picking on a helpless animal. I suggest that this might be so, but by the same token, Joseph, in the absence of having had any previous experience with a dog, needs to be instructed in how one plays with a dog and not simply told what he cannot do. In only responding to the unwanted behavior, Father is relying altogether too much on Joseph's limited experience to inform him of proper action.

What has gone wrong here? First and foremost, Mr. Tinker failed to prepare Joseph for the experience ahead of time by defining the rules of the game. The introduction of a dog into the household begs for some prep work. Just as you don't jump from an airplane prior to learning how to pull the ripcord on your parachute, so too are you ill-advised to bring a new pet into a household without a little prior coaching. This is a safety issue.

Mr. Tinker is also off the mark when he interprets his son's behavior as arising out of cruelty instead of ignorance. Children are not born with an understanding of correct animal-person interaction. The difference between a stuffed and a real animal is not evident to a toddler. If Joseph can pull the nose of his Elmo doll, why can't he do the same with the puppy? Mr. Tinker sees his son's behavior as inappropriate in this instance, but the one behaving most inappropriately is Mr. Tinker himself.

Mr. Tinker's approach to his son in this situation reflects another common problem. Mr. Tinker sees Joseph doing something wrong and quickly moves to stop him by saying no. While "no" clearly defines what a child can't do, it does not tell her what she can do. In this example, Joseph will not learn how to interact with his puppy appropriately based upon his father telling him only what is out of bounds. But Mr. Tinker appears to expect this of Joseph, and he grows increasingly irritated as Joseph fails to meet his expectations. Figuring out what to do on the basis of being told what not to do would require Joseph to make an inference. Making inferences requires a mature brain and a certain amount of experience in the world. Joseph has neither. You know that age-old game in which you guide someone to a hidden object by telling her whether she's getting hotter or colder? This game may be fun, but it's not an effective way to teach young kids how to behave appropriately.

So how should Mr. Tinker have acted instead? When Joseph pounded on the puppy's head or stuck his fingers in his eyes or nose:

- Dad should have been right there to grasp his hand and guide it over the puppy's back, modeling how to pet a dog. "Don't hit the doggy, Joseph. Pet the doggy like this. Be gentle." Dad should expect to repeat this lesson and should remain close by to continue to guide Joseph in the process of teaching him.
- Dad could have shown Joseph the different toys for the dog and what to do with them. He could have shown him how to throw the dog a ball, or how to use the brush.
- Dad could have shown Joseph how to hold his hand out for the puppy to sniff and lick—letting the puppy come to him rather than encroaching on the puppy.
- Dad could have shown Joseph how to feed the puppy a treat.

Providing concrete, explicit information to children has everything to do with setting them up for success. Giving children all the rules of the game and letting them know what the parameters and expectations are gives them a fighting chance to fulfill them. Children are literal. If information given to them is incomplete and children must rely on guesswork, your children are going to guess wrong a good amount of the time. With so many unavoidable sources of conflict between parents and children, why not prevent problems that need not exist?

Defining the Rules

The Malones complain about four-year-old Cindy's penchant for interrupting them while they are on the phone. They attempt to hold her off. They try yelling at her. She persists in interrupting nonetheless, and they find they can't hold a coherent conversation with anyone. What should they do? Asked if they have ever told their daughter what is expected of her during adult phone conversations, they say, "Not exactly. But she knows. While we're on, we'll tell her to be quiet and wait for us to finish." I counsel them to sit down with her at a time when no one is on the phone and clarify their expectations. The Malones should lay out what appropriate behaviors are, and should describe how they will enforce these rules. It is suggested that if Cindy interrupts beyond one "Excuse me," they prepare her for the fact that they will not respond to her. If she persists in interrupting, she will be enclosed in her room until the call is finished. Once these rules are defined, the situation changes. There are two initial episodes in which limits are tested and Cindy ends up in her room. Over a short period of time, a look from Mom or Dad becomes a sufficient cue for quiet.

It is only fair to enforce rules that have been clearly defined for children to begin with. Parents commonly make the mistake of believing that their children understand what is expected of them in a situation because they have been in that situation with a child many times. This is not necessarily true. Before the age of six or seven, children do not make inferences and they don't generalize. As they age into the early elementary years, children are increasingly able to infer meaning beyond what they are directly told to do, but they may not draw the same conclusions that parents intend.

Defining rules and expectations with your children ensures that everyone is operating from the same set of assumptions. Such discussions allow children to ask questions to clarify what they don't understand, though often they will not do so. In these discussions, parents can inquire about what a child has understood to ensure that their meaning has been clear.

- "Can you tell me what I mean?"
- "Can you tell me what I just said?"
- "So if you do X, then what will happen?"

You can also test your child's understanding of a concept by providing a hypothetical situation for a child to respond to:

- "So if I'm on the phone and you want to talk to me, what can you do?"
- "So after you say 'Excuse me' once, if I don't answer you right away, can you say it to me again?"

It is essential that whatever is said be stated clearly, with all parameters and consequences clearly delineated so everyone understands where they stand.

> *Mr. Golina is a stay-at-home dad. Marty, aged six, is testing his patience. All summer, Marty has been going to a gymnastics class at a public park while Mr. Golina supervises Marty's younger sister and brother nearby in the sand. When it's time to go, Mr. Golina puts the younger kids in the double stroller, wheels over to the gymnastics building, and calls Marty from the door. As often as not, Marty ignores him. The double stroller won't fit through the door so Mr. Golina feels helpless, then angry, and he finds himself yelling at his son. Mr. Golina is counseled to have a discussion with Marty at a time when both can focus to clarify the expectations of Marty and to clarify the consequences for misbehavior. Mr. Golina returns for the following session and reports that this has not worked. Asked specifically what happened, he reports, "I had the discussion with Marty, as you told me. I said to him, 'Marty, today when I call you from the door of your gymnastics class, I would really appreciate it if you would listen.' But that afternoon, it went the same as before."*

Imagine you were studying traffic laws to prepare to take your driving test. You wanted to know the speed limit in a residential neighborhood and when you looked it up, the law said, "It would be appreciated if you didn't go too fast." Would you know what was expected? Of course not. Now imagine being pulled over and receiving a speeding ticket for driving thirty miles per hour. Do the words "Not fair" come to mind? A society cannot run well when the rules that govern it are so vague, and neither can your family.

When I told Mr. Golina the traffic story, he laughed, recognizing the parallels to the discussion with his son. The following week, he reported the situation was better. "After breakfast, I said, 'We're going to gymnastics today. When I pick you up, here's what I expect: I will call you once. When you hear my voice, you come to where I'm standing. If you need to say good-bye to your friends, you do it after you get to me. If I have to call you more than once, I will come in and pick you up myself and you will not go to gymnastics the next day.' I asked Marty if he understood, and he said he did. I asked if he had any questions. He asked what would happen if I had to tell him to come twice. I said, 'Think about what I just said.' He said, 'Lose gymnastics the next day?' I said, 'Bingo.' It worked great for two days, and I told him what a good job he was doing. Then, the third day, after I called, I saw him look at me and run to the back of the room where the balance beam is. I asked a lady I see at the park to watch the other kids, marched into the room, and picked him up. The next day, no gymnastics. He wasn't happy about it, but I stayed strong. We haven't had a problem since, but I know what to do if it happens again."

You may know what your expectations will be of your child in a certain situation. When you know them in advance, you need to clarify them.

- "When you open your gifts at your birthday party, good manners mean saying 'thank you' even if you don't like something you get or if you already have one like it. This doesn't mean you have to like the presents you're given, but it does mean you say 'thank you' and are polite."
- "When we go to the mall today, you have to hold my hand in the

parking lot, where there are cars, and I want you to be a good listener to my directions. That means listening the first time I say something to you. If you have trouble listening and I have to repeat myself many times, we will have to leave the mall."
- "When we go to the restaurant, we will bring crayons and paper. You can draw on the paper, but not on the table. You cannot bang your silverware on the plate. You can't rip your napkin into confetti and throw it on the floor. I expect you to use an inside voice in the restaurant."

In these ways, you can clarify rules for kids before problems happen. Sometimes, however, this will not be possible.

A mother picking up her son after his first day of nursery school was astonished to find him covered from head to toe with marker pen. She asked, "Don't they have a rule in nursery school about not drawing on yourself?" He replied, "They do now."

Your children are separate from you, and they have their own developing minds. It will occur to them to do things that are entirely outside the domain of your imagination. You may not know there is a need for a rule in a particular situation until your child does something that never would have occurred to you. We can't anticipate everything. You are going to find yourself in some "They do now" situations. If you haven't told a child that an action is unacceptable, you are not within your rights to hold her accountable for knowing this in the first place. It is important that you try to keep control of yourself in such circumstances and use these incidents as opportunities to clarify what your expectations are.

Whether you talk to your child about what is expected after a conflict or in advance of one, it is critical that you do so in an atmosphere that is calm and in which everyone has enough time and attention available to dedicate to the matter. It is all too tempting to try to establish rules in the heat of the anger or irritation immediately following an episode of misbehavior. Don't do it. Research has shown that when we're all riled up, physiological changes occur that make it impossible for us to store new information. If you are upset, you are not in the best state of mind to con-

185

struct a lesson. More important, if your child is upset, she won't remember what you are trying to teach her.

- If you are midway through backing your car out of the garage and your child reaches up and pushes the button on the remote, the sound of the garage door crashing down on the hood of your car should not immediately precede the conversation you have with her to clarify rules on such matters. You will need to cool down first.
- If your child has just stepped off a curb and narrowly missed being run over by a speeding bus, realize that you need to go over rules of the road with her, but also realize that your heart rate will need to stabilize before you do so.
- If you have just gone to put on your most expensive shoes and your toes have made contact with a wad of chewed gum in the toe, this would not be the time for the lesson on gum chewing manners. Clean your socks, take a few breaths, and then consider what to say.

If you are too upset when you talk to your child, rather than conveying any content, all you will convey is your anger. In such a situation, all your child is liable to feel is shame and fear, neither of which provides the soil in which learning something new can grow.

Talking about rules and correcting misunderstandings has implications beyond simply teaching your children. Having these discussions also models a process in which problems that arise are remedied. When we talk about modeling behavior for children, we are talking about providing them with examples that they internalize and that serve as reference points throughout their lives. In the future, after a misunderstanding with a spouse, a friend, or a coworker, a child who has been dealt with in this way is liable to have faith that the rift can be resolved, that the rupture in the relationship can be mended. This is an enormous asset in life; to such a person, misunderstandings and mistakes don't tend to feel so catastrophic. They don't tend to *be* catastrophic. A disagreement does not signal the end of a relationship. Rather, it's seen as an element in a relationship that needs attention and that can be resolved.

After a conversation in which you make clear your expectations and rules of conduct, your child's failure to follow a rule can be seen clearly and the need for consequences is made explicit. There is no respite to be taken in "But I didn't know" and "But you didn't tell me."

When your children comply with your expectations and rules, you are also in a position to catch them being good. Having such a conversation not only sharpens your child's awareness of what the rules are. It also sharpens yours. With such sharpened focus, you are liable to be more sensitive to perceive, and respond to, your child's compliance.

Accentuate the Positive

Chances are, when you think about disciplining your children, you think about responding to their misbehavior. If it's not broken, don't fix it, right? While this may be a useful strategy to adopt toward your toaster oven, it will not serve you well with your kids. The best defense is a good offense. This applies to sports, business, and parenting. It means preventing trouble before trouble happens. In parenting, it means telling your children about what they are doing right.

Why praise children for following rules? Some parents would argue that following rules is simply what is expected of children, so they needn't be praised for compliance. However, a better approach is that of positive reinforcement. Basically stated, the guideline is "Reward those behaviors you want to increase." Employees who are well compensated for their work are happier in their jobs. Those who have the opportunity to earn bonuses for better performance tend to perform better. Your praise is what your children can earn. The more of it there is to be had, the harder they will apply themselves.

- "Sally, good job cleaning up the sand that spilled from your sandbox. You finished playing and you saw it there and you cleaned it right up!"
- "Joseph, I like the way you said please when you asked me to give you your milk. When I hear 'please,' it makes me want to help you."
- "Sandra, I understand that you feel mad that I said no more TV. I'm glad you used your words to tell me how you were feeling."

- "Nathan, I liked the way you shared the Power Rangers figure with your brother in the car when he was crying. I know those figures mean a lot to you, and it's hard to share with him sometimes."

Responding to your children in this way makes them feel appreciated, gives them structure and direction, and increases the chances that they will repeat the behaviors you are rewarding with this kind of attention. Moreover, if as a disciplinarian you are only responding to negative behavior, you are teaching children that this is where parental energy and support are most plentiful for them. As a plant will develop in the direction of the sun, so will your children grow in the direction of more negative behaviors, if this is where they can most reliably find you.

"I don't understand my daughter," says Mrs. Morris, of four-year-old Karen. "Sometimes she has beautiful manners. Other times, I find myself constantly having to remind her. I'll tell her, 'When you don't use please and thank-you, I don't want to do things for you.' Nothing seems to be making an impression." I ask Mrs. Morris, "When she is behaving well, do you acknowledge her good manners?" Mrs. Morris responds: "I don't think that's necessary. I mean, things just go more smoothly at those times." I suggest to Mrs. Morris that the absence of her negative response does not have the same power that the presence of a more positive one could have on her daughter.

If Mrs. Morris is on the lookout for what is right as much as she is on the lookout for what is wrong, she and her daughter are likely to have a nicer relationship all around. As much as noticing your child's good behavior can have a positive effect on how your child behaves, it can have a positive effect on your behavior too. And it can have a positive effect on the way you feel about your kids.

Attending to what is positive seems to be a simple principle, but it is too little practiced. This is a mistake. The power of the positive approach is not to be underestimated.

Mr. Somes, an accountant with a home office, is being interrupted a lot by his children in the several weeks since school ended. In an initial session he was counseled to have a discussion with them to define the hours they would need to play with the sitter, and the time he would be available in the afternoon. Mr. Somes returns to report this worked "a little bit." One morning, he got forty-five minutes' peace while his kids read books in the adjacent living room. It was suggested that in the week to come, when Mr. Somes found his children behaving in this way, he get up from his work after ten minutes or so, tell them they were doing a good job of entertaining themselves, and then return to his office. He objected strenuously, certain that his children would construe this as an invitation to bother him. He felt when he lucked into a moment's peace, he should do nothing to jeopardize it. Eventually, he was able to see that not responding in a positive manner to what he had asked for was, in reality, the real jeopardy. He began to practice this approach, praising at more frequent intervals in the beginning. The children became more consistently able to leave him to his work, and Mr. Somes declared himself a convert.

The common wisdom is that the squeaky wheel gets the grease. The point here is that you should not take quiet wheels for granted. At best, you will miss opportunities to convey your appreciation to your children for a job well done. At worst, you will encourage the development of squeaky wheels where quiet wheels were before. If your attention is the prize and it only flows in the direction of problems, your children will be happy to create or perpetuate problems to ensure they get enough of you.

Paying attention to good behavior is not only a more effective way to help children develop good behavior, but it is a foundational building block for good self-esteem. A child whose parents see in her what is right is a child who is more likely to think of herself in these terms. We are not talking here about accentuating the positive while ignoring what is negative. Nor are we talking about acknowledging children for doing things that require little effort on their part. Imagine that you are an upper-level executive involved in an intensive development project at your job and your boss comes up to you and says, "Good pencil sharpening, Smith!" Reward your children with your attention for those things that have required some effort, restraint, or creativity, or that testify to their having listened to you or learned something you have taught them. Don't respond to trivia. Outside of a swimming lesson, the words "Good breathing, Jason!" are not likely to be appropriate.

When you respond only to what your child does that you do not like, you run the risk of doing psychological damage. Between spouses, this is called nagging. It is disrespectful and ultimately intolerable. It breeds no more good feeling between spouses than it will between you and your child. And when nagging exists in the relationship between a parent and a child, its effects are likely to be much worse. Your spouse is an adult with a sense of self that is fairly well established by the time the two of you get together. Your child, by contrast, is in the process of developing that sense of self, and she is developing it in the context of her relationship with you.

If you respond only to what is wrong in children, they will come to feel that they are the sum total of their deficiencies. This will color how they interpret their experiences in the world. What does this look like? Perhaps you or someone you know lives with an ongoing, self-critical internal monologue, sees only what she does wrong, doubts herself and her value, and anticipates criticism at every turn, certain of being rejected. This is neither a pretty nor a happy state of affairs.

Mrs. Foster comes to consult me about her daughter, Fontana, aged six. She says, "Fontana seems to be pulling away from everyone. And she's so sensitive. The other day I asked if she was planning to wear a particular leotard to her dance class. She said, 'You don't think it looks good on me?'" Mrs. Foster states that her husband can be very critical of Fontana, and she wonders if this is contributing to the problem. "She'll look adorable in an outfit, but maybe she'll leave a piece of hair sticking out when she makes her ponytail. He'll say, 'Cute dress, Fontana, but what happened to your hair?' Or she'll straighten up her room, and he'll say, 'You left two books out of your cabinet.' I have the feeling she only hears the negative part and I tell him he should lighten up, but he tells me I'm not helping Fontana prepare for the real world. He'll accuse me of coddling her and say that I'm being dishonest."

The opposite of criticism is not overindulgence. The opposite of criticism is support. Criticism doesn't build character. Rather, it can warp it.

Criticizing a child will not inspire her to achieve great things any more than tying a person's legs together will inspire her to swim the English Channel. People may succeed in spite of the handicaps that are imposed upon them, but they might succeed with a great deal less difficulty absent those handicaps.

You shouldn't lie to your children, but you can be selective about the truths you tell. Fontana Foster may have left a hair out of her ponytail, but this does not mean that she didn't put some effort into choosing her outfit, that she didn't match her socks to the color of her dress, that she didn't get her shoes on the right feet, and that she didn't stick with the difficult process of tying them. Emphasizing her successes is not the same as coddling.

The idea that criticizing children in the home prepares them for the real world is way off the mark. It's important to keep in mind that while there is a real world in which we all live, with its traffic lights, shopping malls, cola drinks, and a lot of other folks, how we perceive this real world is colored by the "real world" within each of us. Fontana's father is in the process of defining the "real world" for her according to how he interacts with her. If Fontana knows that when father looks at her, he likes what he sees, then Fontana's "real world" will be one in which she has confidence that she is fundamentally okay. In her "real world" she equals more than the sum total of her failures and imperfections. If she starts from this base of support, others' criticisms are not likely to penetrate Fontana so deeply, her failure to achieve certain goals is likely to be less disabling, and she will be more likely to trust her competencies, enjoy her successes, and then build on them.

Does accentuating the positive mean we never criticize children? Never correct them? Of course not. You are not obligated to come up with something positive to say in every circumstance. That's Pollyanna-land. We are talking about helping your children develop a base of personal operation that allows them to set out in the world with the security of knowing that they are fundamentally lovable. Your children believe they are okay if you believe they are okay.

Disobedience by Any Other Name

Disciplining children ensures that they respond to your authority, comply with your directives, and stay within the parameters of behavior you have set for them. When children don't comply, they can get into trouble. The farther this disobedience progresses, the more trouble and bad feeling it is likely to breed. As a parent engaged in preventive discipline, you need to recognize noncompliance in its many guises and stop it before it goes too far.

As children mature, their language develops. Around the age of two or three, the word "why" enters their vocabulary. In addition to driving you crazy with "Why? Why? Why?" children who have added this word to their vocabulary are now in the position to camouflage their insubordination in what appears to be a reasonable (and sophisticated) disguise.

Sara, five years old, comes to the office with her exasperated mother and father, who are determined to regain control of their household from their precocious kindergartner. Sara is told to sit in her chair by her mother. "Why?" she asks. "Because we are in the doctor's office and this is a place where people sit," answers her mother. "I don't want to sit. Why do I have to sit?" asks Sara. "Because this is the doctor's. You're being rude," says Mother. "But I want to play. Can't I play?" asks Sara, as she begins rummaging through her mother's purse. "No, you can't play. You need to sit down. Come on." "But why can't I play?" asks Sara. "Because," replies her mother, her voice showing strain, "we are at the doctor's and the rules here are sitting." Sara appeals to her dad: "Daddy, why do I have to sit?" Daddy responds, "We want to see what a good sitter-downer you are. Come on now, Sara. Show us what a good sitter-downer you are." "No," whines Sara, "I don't want to. Why do I have to?" Dad, looking stern, says, "Sara, do you want to go to the movies later?" Sara then sits, but just for a moment before the whole process starts again.

What has gone wrong here? It is not surprising that a five-year-old is negotiating. The problem is that the parents are negotiating back. What

192

does one do with the endless permutations on "Why?" that your children will introduce into the conversation in the face of being told what to do. Clearly, Sara is not asking why to gain more information. Sara is asking why to buy time. Wouldn't it be wonderful if there were a simple rule to follow that could put an end to many of these endless negotiations? There is: Any explanations your children request are provided after they have complied with your directive. For example, Sara is told to sit in her chair, and Sara asks why. Her mother repeats the directive to sit again and again, until Sara's bottom is firmly in contact with the cushion. Does her mother say "First sit, then I'll tell you why"? Perhaps, but she doesn't repeat this after saying it once. And if Sara says, "Why won't you tell me now?" does her mother then say "Because I won't"? No, she doesn't. She repeats "Sit down" and resists the temptation to fill in with any justification or explanation or threat until the behavior is performed.

This situation calls for definitive direction giving and unwavering parental intent to gain compliance. You cannot, as a parent, let yourself get easily distracted. And if you do not let yourself get led about in this way, you will probably find that your level of annoyance and exasperation diminishes markedly. After several family meetings, Sara's parents adopted this technique. They found, not surprisingly, that not only was Sara listening better, but she was demanding a whole lot fewer explanations as well.

Don't Give 'Em Enough Rope

How much trouble will you let your children get into before you intervene? Actually, this is a trick question because if you intervene in some situations early enough, your children need not get into trouble at all.

Mr. Perez, father of five-year-old Martin, has just received a gift of an old-fashioned radio. He has put it on the coffee table to enhance his décor, but Martin can't stop fiddling with it despite his father's repeatedly telling him to leave it alone. No amount of voices raised in the household can persuade Martin to keep his hands off it. And sure enough, when father turns his back, Martin picks up the radio and drops it. Now Martin is in big trouble.

What is wrong with this picture? Is Martin evil? Incorrigible? No. Martin is five. What is wrong is that dad is furious, Martin is in big trouble, and all of this was so easily prevented. Was father unreasonable in asking Martin to leave the radio alone? No, but he was unreasonable to expect Martin to comply when Martin gave him so much evidence that he could not do so. It is incumbent on you as a parent not to let your fantasies and wishes about your children's capabilities obscure what their capabilities, in fact, may be.

What might Martin's father have done instead? After telling Martin to leave the radio alone and seeing that Martin could not, he could have said, "Martin, I know you want to follow my directions, but I can see that this radio is too tempting right now. Let's play with it together for a while and I'll show you how it works, but then I'm going to put it away so nothing ends up happening to it that would upset us both." Father and Martin play with it together; then father stores the radio in a high closet for the time being. Nice shared experience between father and son. Little vote of confidence slipped in for good measure ("I know you want to follow my directions . . ."). No harm. No foul. No shame. Will father ever be able to display his new treasure on the coffee table? Of course, but probably not this month.

If you can see trouble brewing, you need to take action. If you give your children enough rope to hang themselves, they will take it.

Ethan Lane, almost four, loves to paint. Ethan is supposed to confine his painting to the downstairs playroom, but the carpet on his bedroom floor tells the colorful story of noncompliance. The Lanes have had it cleaned many times, but the residue belies the fact that the claim of "non-staining" on the outside of a bottle cannot be taken at face value. There has been a lot of yelling and punishment in an effort to make Ethan confine his painting to the playroom. His parents have tried to lock up the paints, but they are both working professionals and they tend to be inconsistent in remembering to do so. A week shy of Ethan's fourth birthday, the Lanes come to their appointment having discovered yet again that Ethan left a mess in his room. They have devised a plan. They have told Ethan that as a birthday present they will redo his room for him, complete with new furniture and carpeting. They are sure Ethan will appreciate the new things and that he will be inspired to take care of them.

The Lanes may wish to believe that at the age of four, Ethan is mature enough to curb his behavior, but he's not. They would like to believe that Ethan would make an extra effort to protect new things, but these are their values and Ethan is too young to possess the abstract understanding to permit him to share them. If the Lanes proceed according to their plan, they are setting Ethan up for failure. They will feel betrayed for Ethan's welching on a promise he never made in the first place. And as if he weren't already in enough trouble for messing up his old carpet, now Ethan will be in enormous trouble for fouling the brand-new stuff! Punishments and recriminations are likely to be more severe. This is all so preventable. How? (1) Let the Lanes wait to put down the new carpet until the problem reliably no longer occurs. (2) If the Lanes can't stand the stained carpet and must replace it, let them put in linoleum or a sealed wood floor, which are more easily cleaned. (3) Let the Lanes replace the carpet now only if they can guarantee themselves that they won't forget to lock up the art supplies.

We explore the topic of locking the supply cabinet. Mrs. Lane says, "You wouldn't think it would be so difficult to remember to lock up a stupid cabinet. After all, we're adults. It's not like it's rocket science." I point out that their anger at Ethan for falling short of their expectations of him appears largely to be fueled by their own feelings about having fallen short of what they expect of themselves. The Lanes ignore me. They say they believe that redecorating will work, and they have confidence that their son will value the new things so much that he will comply with what he's been told. I suggest that their logic would be akin to my suggesting to them that redoing their son's room should be sufficient motivation to ensure that they never again forget to lock up the paints. They immediately go on the defensive. They say they are doing their best. I say, "Of course you are. And so is your son. Instead of making decisions on the basis of what everyone should be capable of doing, let's work more with how things really are and not set everyone up for shame and failure."

In an ideal world, everybody does what she is supposed to do. Welcome to the real world. We may aspire to perfection, but we make mistakes. It's best to acknowledge our imperfections and work within what we are actually capable of doing. Your children do not get the most satisfaction from doing what they want to do if this displeases you. Children get the most satisfaction from feeling close to you. Misbehavior ruptures this closeness. If you want to raise an adult who can discipline herself and keep herself out of trouble, then you need to think about intervening in a child's behavior before a problem becomes a problem.

Time Out—Uses and Misuses

In the current parenting climate, one would be hard-pressed to find a mom or a dad who is not familiar with the term "Time Out." Unfortunately, with so many parents aware of the terminology, there seem to be few who really understand the usefulness of the concept and how to apply it.

In a football game, the coach calls a Time Out if he sees players lose their team unity or focus. He may call a Time Out if he assesses a need to change a strategy of approach. An experienced coach who knows his team can recognize a problem before it becomes a problem. A Time Out called at this point, before the game is lost, allows the team an opportunity to regroup. Can you imagine a coach screaming at his players that if they don't get their act together, he's going to call a Time Out? Hardly. In sports, Time Out is seen as an opportunity, not a punishment.

Well, Coach, guess what? Time Out in parenting is not that much different. Time Out is a preventive measure that respects the fact that in the course of living in the world, people occasionally need a cooling-off period. This goes for your child. And it goes for you. Many a parent has made joking reference to needing a Time Out for herself. It's no joke. Children do not have a corner on the market of coming unglued. So count to ten. Take a deep breath. There is nothing wrong with telling a child: "I cannot be with you when you are behaving this way. You are going to your room. I am going to my room. Why don't we meet when we both feel calmer?" Rather, there is everything right with it.

Unfortunately, rather than being appreciated for the opportunity that it is, Time Out is often seen and used as a punishment. Many parents give children a dose of shame along with Time Out. Rather than a respectful breather, Time Out is seen as shameful evidence that a child has misbehaved. Time Out has replaced the spanking. Whereas one might have heard in the past "Stop that or you'll get a spanking!" Now one hears in its place "Stop that or you'll get a Time Out!" Time Out, in this case, is a parent's revenge—a politically correct way to express anger at a child and assert authority and control.

Children may kick, scream, cry, and otherwise object to being sat in the Time Out chair. There are two main reasons this may happen. First, like the coach who waits until the team has fallen apart and the game and is nearly over before calling for Time Out, parents often wait far too long to implement it.

Mrs. Grinnler is a foster mother for Kileen, a seven-year-old girl who was drug-exposed before birth. Kileen flies into rages, and Mrs. Grinnler is at her wit's end. I ask Mrs. Grinnler to describe Kileen's rages. She states: "They're so predictable. It will start with Kileen just getting a little jumpy. I'll try to distract her. But she won't listen. Then she'll get really hyper. She'll start running around the house, or she'll run in circles in the backyard. I'll tell her to calm down. Nothing works. Eventually, she'll just do something dramatic. The other day she knocked over a table. By this time I usually lose it. I'll order her to her room for Time Out. She's screaming. She'll pound on the walls. It takes her a long time to settle down." I ask her why she doesn't put Kileen in Time Out when she is acting jumpy. She says, "Kileen hasn't broken any rules at that point." I suggest she use Time Out as a preventive measure. She agrees to try. A month later, I'm back at the foster care agency, and I run across Mrs. Grinnler. She tells me she cannot believe the difference in Kileen. Not only is Mrs. Grinnler happier, but Kileen seems happier too.

Children often unravel in a progressive manner. The time to start thinking about implementing Time Out is when you notice the first hanging thread. While not all children transgress dramatically, most children give a variety of indications that they are coming unglued long before they get into bigger, punishment-worthy trouble. You very likely have learned the danger signs in your child—eye rubbing, a certain tone of voice or facial expression, a shove to a sibling, a quick "No!" in response to anything you say even before you've finished saying it. If you see Time Out as an opportunity to regroup, you may be likely to implement it when these danger signs appear, before your child incurs considerable losses.

Children express negative emotions when in Time Out, but this is not an indication that a child doesn't like Time Out. This may very well be an indication that the child has finally come to a place—Time Out—where the feelings can be expressed safely and worked through. An employee who is criticized at the staff meeting and told to go back to her office to rework an assignment, and who waits until she's back at her office to burst into tears, isn't crying about being in her office. The office is a safe place, where the feelings can be expressed. The feelings expressed by a child in Time Out are the feelings that were percolating in the child and made the Time Out necessary to begin with. Time Out didn't create these feelings. Time Out was created *for* them. Time Out ensures that children needn't suppress what they're feeling, and it limits the damage they can do when they express themselves. It's a place to regroup.

Just as Time Out provides an opportunity for your children to work through a particular nonproductive state of mind, it also provides an opportunity for you to do the same. Actually, this is more than an opportunity for you. It is an obligation. Time Out is a chance for a new beginning. We want to teach children how to move on from their mistakes, yet all too often we stay stuck. Imagine the following scenario: The football coach sees his players making errors on a play. He calls a Time Out. The team meets and goes back to play the game with renewed focus. They feel positive and are reenergized. They are focused on the next play. As they get into the huddle, the coach yells, "And by the way, I hope you're not planning to make that same mistake and screw up again." Transitioning from Time Out does not involve ignoring what has occurred or pretending that it didn't happen. But it doesn't involve rubbing your child's nose in it either.

Time Out is a tremendous gift for all concerned. It stops behavior before the transgression is too great. Used properly, it is a tool for teaching self-control.

What Is an Effective Time Out?

Time Out situations range from very structured to much less so. Understanding your child's temperament and how much structure she responds to will shape the approach to Time Out that you take in your house.

Irrespective of how formal you are or are not with Time Out, you should always precede implementing it with a warning. Remember: You are not just trying to get through the day; you are trying to prepare your child best for independent functioning in the future. As you monitor your child's behavior, your aim is that your child will eventually take over this function for herself. Giving a warning is not the same as making a threat. It's an alert. It tells your child that you are paying attention to her and that you are seeing the signs that something is not right. It gives your child a chance to change on her own and lets her know you will help her bring things back into balance if she is unable to do so.

- "Gilligan, I hear you are using your grouchy voice with your sister. You will need some time in your room if your voice does not get friendlier."
- "Karl, you are playing too rough with the dog. If you yank him by his collar again, you will have a Time Out."
- "Loren, I have told you that you may not watch TV, and I have told you to stop asking for it. If you ask me again, you will have Time Out."

Formal Time Out

If you have a child who responds best to more structured situations, a formal Time Out is likely to work best. With this approach, Time Out occurs in the same spot each time. There may be a special chair in your home or a special area used for the purpose. It should be in an area free of distractions—preferably not your child's room.

A timing device dedicated for the purpose should be handy, and preferably one with an analog face as opposed to a digital timer. Ideally, it should have a bell. An old-fashioned kitchen timer is perfect. Time is abstract to children to begin with; digital time is more abstract than time that can be marked by the movement of a dial because to understand digital time, children have to understand number concepts. Analog time—the dial kind—is spatial in nature. Using an old-fashioned kitchen timer allows your child to "watch" the time while she is sitting and have some sense of when she will be liberated. Telling your child "When you hear the bell ring, you can come out of Time Out" makes the end of the experience clear.

When your child has not responded well to the warning you have given, you inform your child that she will now be in Time Out for a certain number of minutes. A rule of thumb is one minute for every year of age, but again, you will need to know your child and determine if this is right for her. Remember: The goal of Time Out is not to humiliate your child, but to enable her to regain possession of herself so she can resume her ordinary activities. Some children will be able to accomplish this more quickly. Some children may need a bit more time.

No matter how informal your Time Out is, there are certain rules that need to be adhered to. After you tell your child that she will be in Time Out, she must go to it. Some children go willingly. Some put up a struggle. Sometimes the struggle looks like a refusal. Sometimes the struggle looks like a temper tantrum. Sometimes the struggle looks like plaintive promises by your child that she will no longer do that which got her to this point to begin with. Do you capitulate in any of these circumstances? No. Going to Time Out is not negotiable. How a child gets to Time Out, however, may be.

If you have judged it to be the time for a Time Out and your child does not agree, here are the choices: (1) you will put her there or (2) she will go under her own power. She has until the count of three to decide. You will not be the first parent to carry a toddler who is kicking and screaming. At this age, children are portable; take advantage of it. Fail to act decisively now and you will find that when you try to exercise your judgment in your much larger teenager's best interests, carrying her to her room under duress is no longer likely to be an option.

Once Time Out has started and a timer has been set, the child needs to remain seated until the timer has gone off. If she gets up, Time Out starts again, from the beginning, and the timer is reset. This may occur several times.

There are occasions when a child who is put in Time Out will absolutely refuse to stay in the chair, even after you have issued and reissued the directive in no uncertain terms. What do you do? You let her know if she cannot remain in a chair under her own steam, you will put her in a room. Keep in mind that this is not to be a room filled with expensive electronics, glassware, or priceless family heirlooms. Often, it means the child's room, but you may have another that fits the bill. The room should have a door. If your child refuses to stay put, the door gets closed for a period of time. If she tries to open it, you block it. You may hear a tantrum. Things may be thrown. There may be kicking. Do you capitulate? No. You need to keep safety in mind of course, but so long as your child is not hurting herself or hurting anyone else, this is a storm that you need to ride out. Does this sound too harsh? Remember: Your child's expression of negative feeling is not an indicator that you are doing anything wrong. Give in to this and your child learns that if she raises enough of a fuss, she can get her way. This is certainly not a lesson that you would want to teach. It is tough to contend with a child in the manner I am suggesting. It may comfort you to know, however, that if you carry this out effectively and with the courage of your convictions, it will not be a frequent event. Your child will learn that you mean business and will not persist in testing the limits in this way.

Finally, at the end of such a Time Out, you need to provide a transition for your child. This is a time for you and your child to reconnect and move on. Bear in mind, however, that you need to be alert as to whether the necessary transformation in your child's state of mind has occurred. A child may give an indication that she needs more time to come into balance, and Time Out may need to be instituted again.

Less Formal Time Out

While some children need a very structured Time Out situation, it is inappropriate and will be ineffective with other kids. These children may respond to "Go to your room and join us when you feel ready." Often children who are more self-regulated can use this type of intervention quite well. You know your child best, and you will know whether she needs to be invited to rejoin you or whether she can do so on her own initiative. Remember: Time Out is not defined by how you enforce it. It is defined according to its purpose, which is to provide a break for cooling off. Any way you accomplish this goal is a success.

Chapter 8

Beyond Crime and Punishment:
The Right Kind of Cure

There will be times when you cannot prevent your child's misbehavior. You attempt to head him off at the pass only to arrive there to find a dust cloud and the sight of him galloping off into the distance.

Making Things Right Is a Process

Prevention and cure share the same goal: to bring children back to emotional balance with themselves and with the community. But where preventive measures are put in place before the imbalance is too great, curative measures, by definition, occur after there has been a more significant transgression. These are interventions that occur after a mess has been made, someone has been hurt, or a rule has been violated. They involve a different type of work because something has now gone wrong that needs to be made right.

We all make messes. We all make mistakes. The point is to be able to develop confidence in our ability to clean up and make things right again. If we can't prevent a child's misbehavior all the time—and we can't—we have to have some mechanism in place by which to help the child contend with its aftermath. Making things right when they have gone wrong has everything to do with personal accountability. It is an essential aspect of optimism and creativity. When our children have confidence in their ability to contend with the aftermath of their mistakes, they become effective citizens of the world, empowered to move more freely within it.

The Place of Guilt

Ms. Loveless gave her six-year-old son, Sandor, a severe dressing down for kicking another child at a playground. She then put him in the car, pleased to see the unhappy expression on his face. "He knew he did wrong," she said. "He felt real bad." Asked what her son had done to remedy the situation, Ms. Loveless looked puzzled. "I already told you. He felt real bad about it. And he felt that way the rest of the day."

When people think of guilt, they tend to think of a static place of bad feeling. One feels guilty, and this is considered a form of atonement or payment for wrongdoing. "I stole money from my company, but I feel really guilty about it." "I cut in line ahead of all those other people, but I feel guilty." End of story? Or is it?

Feeling guilty in and of itself doesn't fix a problem any more than noting that your roof needs replacing will make the rain stop dripping into your living room. Both are a step in the right direction, but feeling guilt is not a corrective action in and of itself, no matter how long you sustain the feeling. Guilt is not a final destination. Rather, it is a state of mind that you pass through in the journey to set something right that has gone wrong.

Julian, three years old, loves the riding car at preschool. He won't let anyone else get near it. One day, as he is pedaling with zeal around the track, Julian crashes into Johnny, knocking him to the ground. Johnny starts to cry. Julian takes off. When he is apprehended by the teacher and brought to the scene, he protests violently, kicking and screaming. He seems terrified of Johnny, and he objects more strenuously the closer to him he is brought. When he's plunked down next to Johnny, Julian starts yelling at him and striking out. In fact, now he's yelling at everybody.

Why is Julian crying when Johnny is the one who has been hurt? Why is Julian acting as if he's going to be attacked when he has been the attacker? Is he feeling guilty? No. He's behaving this way because he is convinced that because he has perpetrated aggression, aggression will now be perpetrated on him. Have you ever met a crook who was not convinced someone was ripping him off? A liar who did not accuse others of dishonesty? Children and adults are prone to interpret, and more often misinterpret, other people's actions and motives based upon how they, themselves, have behaved in the relationship.

A child in such a state of mind is not facing what he has done. If a child is in this state of mind, he is not ready to make things better. You cannot be thoughtful and take reparative action when you think you need to fight for your life. If you find your child in such a state of mind after a transgression, you first need to prevent him from lashing out and doing further damage, physically or verbally. You may need to remove him from the situation until he is calm enough to communicate and face the issues. You can use Time Out for this.

When a child comes back to a more reasonable state of mind, it is time to face what has happened. This will involve feeling appropriately guilty. When a child goes from a more persecuted state of mind to a state of feeling guilt, this should be seen as an achievement. A guilty child is living with what he has done for the moment. It's not a pleasant moment, but it is hopeful. A child who can feel guilty is a child who can face his actions and their aftermath, intended and otherwise. A child who can face what he's done is a child who has a chance of doing something meaningful to fix it.

The Difference Between Guilt and Shame

If guilt is meaningful and contains the seeds for reparation, does this mean you need to work to make sure your children feel guilty when they transgress? Absolutely not. You do not need to set out to foster guilt in a child. Guilty feelings will grow on their own when a child recognizes he has done something wrong. When we talk about trying to make another person feel guilty, we are no longer talking about guilt. We are talking about shame.

As productive as guilt can be, shame can be just as crippling. If guilt is an ice cube, shame is an iceberg: it's in the same basic category, but it's bigger, goes deeper, and can do a lot of damage. Guilt goes along with remorse, and it tends to be associated with a particular act of misbehavior. Shame, on the other hand, tends to pervade the entirety of the person in question. Shame goes along with disgrace and humiliation. Whereas a person feeling guilty can rouse himself to make amends, a person feeling shame has a much more difficult task.

Shame has to do with a feeling of being wrong, stupid, bad, inept. Shame is the hot potato of mental states: No one wants to be left holding it for long. No sooner do we find ourselves with it than we set about to find some way to hand it off to someone else. There is no wrong without right, stupid without smart, bad without good, or inept without competent. If you are to get rid of shame—if you are to feel right or smart or good or competent—then someone else has to be assigned these other, less desirable qualities. As such, shame tends to travel from person to person. It gets handed off. As you can well imagine, this does not make for pleasant or productive social interaction. Indeed, shame appears to be at the core of many of the troubling interactions that occur between people.

Where does shame come from? Babies do not feel shame. Shame seems to kick in during the toddler years as one of the legacies of toilet training. How does this work? Toilet training demands something of your child at a level at which nothing has been demanded before. Even though your toddler may physically be ready to learn to use the potty, he does not have the capacity for abstract thinking to allow him to understand all the concepts involved. Toilet training is also a complex physical skill involving body parts that he cannot necessarily see, and it involves substances about which he has built up many fantasies and has many feelings. Also, your many feelings about success, failure, excretions, dirt, smells, and so on get communicated to your child in subtle ways during the training process. Children will undertake this expedition as an act of love for you, though not without ambivalence. Before toilet training, what did your child have to commit himself to? Before toilet training, at what could your child fail? With toilet training, the world changes. With toilet training comes the capacity for failure, ineptness, disgrace, messes, and shame.

Many parents struggle terribly in the process of toilet training their children. Many are stunned to discover the intensity of feeling that embarking on toilet training their children arouses in them, not to mention their children. Many parents are ashamed that they struggle with this. For that matter, parents can feel ashamed that they struggle at any point in the process of parenting.

Shame seems to be hard-wired into humans. While someone can certainly set out intentionally to make you feel ashamed, shame will arise in the absence of another's conscious intent to inspire it within you. What can be done about this? Being aware of this state of mind can help you recognize it when it occurs in your children and can help you be sensitive to it. Thinking in this way can also sensitize you to your own propensity for shame. Being more aware may help you to not pass shame along to your kids.

The difference between allowing appropriate guilt to develop in children versus shaming them often can be found in how harsh parents are when kids go against a rule or when they violate a parental expectation. It's okay to be angry with children, but it's not okay to belittle them. If you are belittling your child, it's time to look within for your shame. Character assassination of a child by a parent is almost always undertaken when a parent is feeling especially frustrated or ineffective. It can be understood as an effort to transfer the shame that arises from the parent's feeling of incompetence.

Define your objectives: If you want to help a child move on from his mistakes, you will provide an environment in which he can experience appropriate and effective guilt. By contrast, if you want your child to stay mired in bad feelings and suffering, do all you can to make him feel bad about his behavior and offer no direction for hope or remedy. Within a relatively short period of time, you are likely to have a child who not only feels bad about his behavior, but who feels bad about himself as well.

Consider this scenario: Jason Herbert, aged five, was playing with the heater on his new tropical fish tank. He left the settings too high, and most of the fish died. Here's one approach.

Mother: For God's sake, Jason! You killed the fish! What were you thinking?
Jason: I didn't mean to do it.
Mother: How many times have I told you not to play with the heater? But do you listen? No. And now look what's happened.
Jason (crying now): I'm sorry, Mommy.

Mother: You should feel sorry. I hope you feel very sorry. Maybe next time you'll think before you do something like this again.

Jason is feeling guilty and trying to make amends here, but his mother will have none of it. She is understandably angry, but if she deals with Jason in this manner, he is likely to shy away from admitting wrongdoing because he will expect to be raked over the coals regardless of his efforts. People can only tolerate such painful feelings for a limited time before they start pushing them away by whatever means are necessary. Perhaps you know someone who is always quick to blame others? Who is defensive even when he's not being criticized? It's not difficult to imagine Jason turning out this way in an effort to push off the feelings of shame that grow from interactions like this.

So if Mrs. Herbert were to handle it better, what might the scenario look like?

Mother: I see the heater got left on, and the fish died.
Jason: I didn't know it would hurt them.
Mother: It is surprising how sensitive fish are.
Jason: I'm sorry, Mommy.
Mother: I accept your apology. It's not the end of the world. Why don't you help me clean up? You get the net, and I'll get a plastic bag.

Parenting demands you maintain faith in your children, and it demands that you practice forgiveness. It was not a demonic desire to murder fish that motivated Jason. His mistake reflected a lack of understanding. If Jason's mother can have faith in his ability to recognize his error and can resist the impulse to hammer home this concept with a shaming reprimand, Jason can proceed from this lesson with his self-respect intact and with the additional certainty that his mother's love and respect for him are secure.

When shame is present, people are not free to think or act. A shamed child can't be spontaneous, for fear that any impulse he feels will be a wrong one that will lead to more criticism and more shame. Jason Herbert, in the first scenario, has been shamed. It is entirely possible that while he knows that the fish died because of something to do with the heater, he has no clue what really has happened. A child who is shamed in a given circumstance may never fully understand what happened. He will be more likely to withdraw and form his own conclusions, no matter how incorrect, rather than risk further shame and humiliation by asking questions. In the second scenario, the environment is free of shame and therefore still open for exploration. A child treated this way is free to investigate what has occurred and learn from his mistake. One can well imagine that while Jason and his mother clean the tank, Jason might ask questions about aquarium heaters, what they do, what water temperature means, what temperatures are all right for fish, what temperatures are too low or too high.

Chances are, you have spent a fair amount of money on products to stimulate your child's developing mind. Did you buy the black-and-white newborn toys? The classical music CDs just for babies? The Baby Einstein products? Did you play your baby music in the womb? Providing opportunities for development such as these and then shaming children makes as much sense as training hard for a marathon and then putting sharp rocks into your shoes on race day. Shame, like rocks, interferes with forward progress. Why dedicate so much energy to opening a child's mind if you then introduce shame, which is unparalleled in its ability to stifle curiosity and paralyze creative thinking?

An Alternative to Shame:
Cutting Everyone a Little Slack

We will all make mistakes in our lifetime. People who are more prone to feel shame are often preoccupied with self-doubt. If they have a setback, it takes them a long time to recover. People who are less prone to shame are more forgiving of themselves. They can be more thoughtful about mistakes and move on from them without having to contend with the impulse to retreat to their room, draw the blinds, disconnect the phone, and hide under the bed.

Parents who are most prone to shame children are parents who start out with unreasonable expectations of their children, which ultimately means they start out with unreasonable expectations of themselves. If you expect your child will not make and repeat mistakes, you will see failure in your child, but even more profoundly, you will see it in yourself. After all, if your child should be able to learn concepts quickly and comply with rules and he does not, then it would follow that you are doing something wrong. You will see his errors as evidence of your parental failure. How long do you suppose a parent can live with such a feeling? Maybe just long enough for that parent to get angry with the child and start to see *him* as the incompetent one.

All young children at one point or another will spill milk, break dishes, chew with their mouths open, get mud on their clothes, leave telephones off hooks, wet their pants, forget their jackets in restaurants, dump pencil shavings onto carpets, feel jealous of their siblings, crayon on walls, leave toothpaste in the sink, feed cheese to the VCR, leave refrigerators open, dunk small electronic devices in the toilet, track dirt into the house, say mean things about other people, pour juice on computer keyboards, leave screen doors open, break windows, and rub peanut butter into the rug. Young children will do the things you tell them not to do. You will want to say at many points along the way "How many times do I have to tell you—?" Resist the impulse.

Remember: You are dealing with individuals in the process of learning about the world, and there is a lot of information for them to keep track of. They do not have the same capacity for memory as you do. You will do well to give your child the benefit of the doubt. The more faith you have in his essential good nature and the more you truly believe that he desires to do the right thing, the less likely you will be to hold grudges when he transgresses and the more of your faith in him you will communicate. As momentarily satisfying as it may be to unload some of your frustration by saying "Jeneane, how many times do I have to tell you to close the screen door when you come in the house?" chances are this will not ultimately increase the frequency of door-closing. A better strategy would be to say "Gee, Sandra, it sure is hard to remember to close the screen door after you've been playing. I bet when you come in you're already thinking about what we're having for dinner and which toys you want to bring with you into your bath." Jeanene is likely to feel shame, humiliation, anger, and defensiveness. Sandra is more likely to feel understanding. A child like Sandra, who is not at odds with a parent and struggling with feelings of shame, is a child with more available attention to focus productively on the issues at hand. Within a short period of time, Sandra is likely to come into the house thinking about her tub toys; this will remind her of the discussion about the door, and the door will get closed. More important, Sandra proceeds with a sense of herself as intact and competent, whereas Jeanene proceeds with self-doubt and a limited sense of her capabilities.

"Sometimes My Kids Make Me Mad"

We are talking here about facing children with the consequences of their actions. We are also talking about the need for a parent to remain dispassionate and objective in the process of doing so. Well, what about when these two worlds collide? What about when the very real consequence of your child's misbehavior is your anger? Are you allowed to express anger? Or will doing so somehow compromise your ability to be a good teacher to your child?

Confronting a child with his actions and their consequences will often require you to exercise some control over your feelings, particularly if the transgression has personally affected you. This doesn't mean you can't recognize your feelings, but it does mean that you are not at liberty to express them in their raw form. Easily enough said. Hard to put into practice. Remember Time Out? This may be the time for you to take one.

Fact: Sometimes children will do things that make you angry, and you owe it to them to let them know this. You do not damage kids by letting them know when you are angry. On the contrary, you run the risk of doing damage if you fail to do so. A child who is not taught that certain transgressions will result in angering others is a child with an incomplete education about people and the world. A child whose parents do not get angry with him on occasion is a child whose parents are not paying enough attention to him or investing enough energy in the relationship. Your anger or sadness may be one of the consequences of your child's actions. Disciplining children involves teaching them about this.

By the same token, as a parent, you need to prioritize. While getting appropriately angry at kids is part of their complete education, this does not give you license to make mountains out of molehills. It's no more fun for an adult to spend time around an irritable and hypersensitive child than it is for a child to spend time around an irritable and hypersensitive adult. You are served well by exercising some restraint and being able to separate the minutia from that which is more significant.

> *Mrs. Ling, exhausted in her first trimester of pregnancy with her second child, was shocked when she opened the kitchen door to discover the room festooned with an entire roll of paper towels. Sun, her four-year-old daughter, was severely reprimanded first by Mother, and then by Father when he came home later. Father said: "She said she just wanted to decorate the kitchen pretty, like the banquet hall at a wedding we went to over the weekend, but I told her she was a bad girl who tried to make more work for her mother. I made her stay in her room for one hour."*

There is a difference between behaviors that are truly destructive and behaviors that are more trivial. Sun Ling was, in her mind, being creative. It's true that children's creativity often produces results that are messy and annoying to parents and that certain materials—toilet paper, paper towels, mayonnaise, toothpaste—may be off limits for use in creative enterprises. But transgressions in this domain often provide an opportunity to teach children about such matters. Mr. and Mrs. Ling have clearly overreacted in this instance and, in so doing, run the risk of squelching further creative action on the part of their daughter.

There will be times when a child's actions are more directly destructive and the consequences of those actions are more significant and long-lasting. Just as there are molehills, there are also mountains, and they need to be responded to accordingly.

> *Mrs. Richards is set to take Marcus, aged five, and Nelson, aged two, to the pony rides. Just prior to leaving, she goes to the bathroom and finds that her new makeup brushes have been hacked up, presumably with her nail scissors, which she finds on the floor. She says, "I was so angry I couldn't see straight. I knew it was Marcus because Nelson doesn't know how to use scissors. Marcus knows the scissors are off limits. He knows my drawer is*

off limits. My first thought was, 'No way are we going to the pony rides now.' But then I thought that wouldn't be fair to Nelson. I confronted Marcus, and I told him I was very angry about my makeup brushes and my scissors. I said, 'Kid-scissors are for kids to use. Nail scissors are for grown-ups only. And paper is for cutting. Makeup brushes are not ever for cutting.' We went to the pony rides, but I didn't let Marcus have a ride. I told him I was too angry to want to do something nice for him. I tried to keep control of my voice, but I know I sounded stern."

For a mother to be appropriately angry in such a circumstance and then to turn around and offer pony rides to a child who perpetrates such a destructive action would be confusing at best. To cancel pony rides would be unfair to Nelson. This makes the point: "If you hurt my things, I get angry, and when I am angry, I don't want to do something nice for you." In reality, this is the way the world works.

If you are feeling angry in response to what a child has done, you are allowed to sound angry. Your tone needs to match the content of what you say. A stern voice will not damage your child; in such a circumstance it will make sense to him. Being angry is not license, however, to scream and yell and rant and rave. You need to remain in control of yourself, or you will frighten your child and you will end up with a host of other problems on your hands. But while you need to control yourself, you don't need to overcontrol yourself. Explaining how angry you are to a child in a cheerful voice defies logic and will most likely confuse your kids.

The most important point to keep in mind when you express anger at your child for some transgression is that the focus of your anger should be the act in question and not the child's basic personality or nature. What do we tell children to do when they are angry? We say, "Use your words." When we get angry, we should follow our own advice. Our anger provides a prime opportunity to model how angry words can and should be used.

- "I feel angry when I see marker pen on the wall."
- "I get mad when I see dirt tracked in from outside! I get so mad I want to throw all the muddy shoes out into the yard!"
- "I see that there has been eating in the TV room and that there is

peanut butter and jelly smeared on the easy chair. I feel so mad when I see that! I feel like a boiling volcano!"

Notice that while passionately expressed, these statements are directed at the consequences of actions and none are directed personally at a child. It is one thing to say to a child, "I get angry when I tell you to pick up your crayons and I find them on the hall floor!" It is quite another to say, "For crying out loud, how many times do I have to tell you not to leave your dishes in the sink?!" The former is explicit. The latter is insulting. You might as well be saying to a child "You idiot!"

It is important to bear in mind, however, that more than a shift in language use is involved here. You need to shift your perspective. It is possible to change your words while maintaining a tone and body language that are at variance with what you say, but children will continue to respond to your body language and tone.

> *Mr. Rubio has been consulting with me for several months in an effort to deal with the anger he finds flaring up in him toward three-year-old Jack and two-year-old Cammie. "I got home from work at seven-thirty, and Jack was waiting up. He said he wanted to sit with me and drink juice while I ate dinner. No sooner do I sit down than he spills the juice all over me. I was furious. My face was red. I was shaking. I wanted to say 'You jerk!' but I didn't. I remembered what we talked about. Instead, I screamed, 'I get angry when juice spills on my pants!' I gotta tell you, Doc, I can't say it made much of a difference. Jack burst into tears and ran into his room. I felt awful."*

Expressing anger about things that children do in language that takes the focus off them and puts the focus onto their behavior is more than a semantic parlor trick. It really invites a shift in perspective. It was clear from Mr. Rubio's voice and body language that he had not achieved this shift, and Jack had not been fooled by his words. Mr. Rubio is clearly furious with his son to a degree that is way out of proportion to the offense.

Just as it's not fair to take out your frustration by kicking your dog, so too is it unfair to take out anger on kids. Does this mean it will never happen? No. Chances are, you will lose your temper in the course of parenting your child and there will be occasions when something you do hurts your child's feelings. So what should you do? You need to remember that every time you act or don't act in a given situation, you are modeling behavior for your child. You cannot raise a child who can appropriately take responsibility for his misbehavior if you cannot take responsibility for yours. So just as you expect your child to apologize when he has gone too far in his behavior, so too should you apologize when you are out of line. Apologizing when you transgress models the same behavior you would expect of your child. Your apology communicates your respect for your child, and it shows that a misunderstanding need not be the end of him, you, or the relationship.

When you express anger to children, it is also useful to keep in mind the need to provide direction. More than any toy, more than any privilege, more than any dessert, what your children value most is your esteem and your love. What is most painful to them is to feel out of harmony with you. There is no more powerful negative consequence to a child for his misbehavior than the loss of this harmony. Any punishment or consequence you deliver is meaningful because it has this loss of connection to you at its core. Children want to make the situation right again. For this reason, when you express anger at your child about something he has done, giving him direction to effect a positive change can be immensely helpful. "I get mad when I see marker pen on the wall" educates your child about the emotional impact of his actions. Adding "Coloring books are for marker pens; walls are not for marker pens" educates him further and gives him clear direction for his behavior in the future.

Reparation: Putting the World Right Again

There are people who make messes in life and hurt others, and they move on from these experiences without addressing them. As unpleasant as this may be for the victims, the perpetrators do not fare any better. Uncorrected errors that people leave behind them interfere with their lives. They are not forgotten. If you have cheated on your income tax, correspondence with an IRS return address will make your blood run cold. If

215

you speak badly about someone behind his back, you anticipate harsh words from him next time you see him. If he doesn't mention it this time, won't you anticipate it the next time you see him? And the next? Living in this way is exhausting. You want to liberate your children's energies for creativity and constructive actions. You have to help them right wrongs for which they are responsible.

When a child strays from acceptable behavior, this damages connections. It may damage the relationship with another person if he has harmed someone in the process. The damage is in the relationship with you if he breaks one of your rules. Children need to reconcile the injured parties. They need to do this to make the people they have injured feel better, and they need to do it to heal themselves.

Guilt opens the way for reconciliation. If a child can face what he has done, he can make a correction. Often, this takes the form of an apology.

If your child apologizes, it is important to allow the apology to reach its mark. It is all too common for people to respond to "I'm sorry" with "That's all right." This fairly informal way of proceeding doesn't take into account the fact that an apology is a rather formal thing. If your child has acknowledged that he has done something wrong and apologized for it, you need to recognize this action for the responsible, reparative measure it is and accept the apology rather than passing it off. Rather than "That's okay," say "I accept your apology." You might say "Thank you."

This is more than a semantic exercise. Keep in mind that young children are concrete thinkers who are trying to learn their way through complicated matters of discourse. It is likely to be confusing to a young child who is trying to learn to be responsible for his behavior if, on the one hand, you make a big deal over his need to apologize, while on the other hand you trivialize the apology when he does so. Accepting a child's apology not only recognizes its import, but it lets your child know that the apology has reached its mark and healing has begun.

Sometimes an apology is not enough. Sometimes a child will need to make a larger gesture to make right something that he has put askew.

Johanna Fristoe, six years old, has dirt all over her outfit and under her fingernails. The neighbors come knocking on the door. Johanna admits she dug up their flowers, but she says she just wanted to give her mother some flowers for her birthday. Mrs. Fristoe says this was a nice idea, but the neighbors are not happy that it happened at the expense of their petunias. Johanna apologizes, and Mrs. Fristoe offers to replace the flowers that were dug up. The neighbors agree that this would be fair. Johanna contributes from her piggy bank to pay for the replacements. When she and her mother have finished planting them, they ring the bell and ask the neighbors if the garden looks all right to them now.

When a child apologizes in words, you need to tell him you accept the apology. When a child also apologizes with an action, you need a comparable moment of closure in which you communicate that his action has met its mark and the relationship is restored.

Making the Consequence Fit the "Crime"

When children have transgressed, they should be encouraged to find ways to make amends. But is it enough to let a child decide on an action to right a situation? Often, it is not, and particularly in the case of younger children. Often, you need to take action and make decisions too.

"Aha! Punishment!" you may be saying. Well, not exactly. Think in terms of consequences. The point you are trying to get across to children is that their behaviors have consequences. If they do something nice, chances are, something nice will happen. If they do something inappropriate, then they have to contend with some fallout. A good consequence is designed to ensure that something negative that has happened does not have an opportunity to happen again.

Kilroy Jamison, six, likes to watch the big television in his parents' room when he comes home from school. He also likes to go through his parents' bureau drawers. He has been reprimanded for this on several occasions, and he is clear about the rules. When he is found to have misbehaved again, he is told he will no longer be permitted in his parents' room. He complains that now he cannot watch the big TV. "Oh, well," says Mrs. Jami-

*son. "That's true. You can't be in our room alone, and that is
where the TV is. We know you will be able to learn to resist the
temptation to go into our things, and when you do, then we can try
again."*

This is good, logical consequence discipline. Perhaps you think of it
as punishment, but really it is not. A punishment is a penalty. It is mostly
about the past. If you are punishing children, you are saying: "You did
this, so here's what happens to you." In this situation, a punishment would
be "No watching the big TV because you went in our drawers." Discipline
is more about the future. "You have shown me you are not ready for this
responsibility, so we will remove it for now and we will try again later." In
this instance, Kilroy is not able to be unsupervised in his parents' room.
The loss of the TV is incidental, though it probably amplifies the message
to him.

*Karen Hill, three years old, has just been enrolled in a tap
dancing class. She has been carrying her tap shoes with her all
day since she and her mom bought them this morning. Here's the
rule: They can be carried, but they cannot be worn in the house.
Karen promises she'll comply. Unfortunately, she does not. Mrs.
Hill comes home from running some errands to find scuff marks
up and down the white linoleum hallway. She tells a tearful Karen
that the dancing lessons are canceled.*

The case could be made that Ms. Hill's reaction is a logical consequence, but it is not. It is excessively harsh and has a punitive flavor that
goes far afield of the objective, which is to ensure Karen doesn't scuff her
floor. What would a more effective and appropriate consequence be?
Given that Karen has illustrated that she cannot be trusted with the shoes
in the house for the time being, Ms. Hill needs to store them on a high
shelf in her own closet. This removes the potential for damage to the floor
and makes the point to Karen that if she cannot control herself, someone
will step in to assist her. This measure removes something valued from her
possession and, as such, could be construed as a punishment, but it is not
undertaken in the spirit of punishment. The discipline is consistent with

her offense, with teaching her about it, and with the need to protect the floor.

Part of child rearing involves responding to children's increasing capacities to be responsible for themselves and make their own decisions. From the baby state of utter dependence, children evolve until eventually they become independent adults. Fostering this is the job you signed on for. You will, in the course of parenting your children, make judgments about whether your children are up to handling a particular responsibility at a particular time. If your children demonstrate to you that they cannot be counted on to behave responsibly in a particular situation, then they need to be steered clear of it.

Chapter 9

How to Love Children
So They Will Love Themselves

Self-esteem is the feeling your child has about herself and her competencies. It develops and evolves throughout childhood and adulthood, but the foundations are being laid in the first years of life. You, your child's parent, are the most significant contributor to the process. Your behavior toward your child and your feelings about her will play the most decisive role in how she ultimately comes to feel about herself.

If you express love, concern, and respect for your child, she will see herself as worthy of these things. If you take real delight in her growth and development, empathize with her struggles, and have faith in her ability to move past obstacles, she will tend to treat herself accordingly. A child with good self-esteem likes herself. Behind every child who likes herself is a parent who liked her first.

In addition to genuinely enjoying your child, you are best prepared to help her through her earliest years in a positive way if you are knowledgeable about child development. If you are familiar with the competencies and the limitations that children at different developmental stages possess, you will understand the particular challenges that are most prominent at the different stages your child passes through. Outfitted with this knowledge, you can maintain expectations that are consistent with your child's real capacities. You will be less likely to burden your child with tasks that she is too developmentally immature to master. You are also going to be in a position to understand those that your child *can* handle, to ensure that she is appropriately challenged.

A Foundation of Trust

We don't think of babies as having self-esteem, and rightly so, because babies don't yet have a concept of "self" or the capacity for self-reflection that goes along with it. Babies are in the process of establishing the foundations on which all their later physical, emotional, social, and intellectual development will rest. For your baby to grow into a child who later develops self-esteem, she needs to develop *basic trust* in the world in which she is living and growing. This principle is discussed by Erik Erikson in *Childhood and Society*. Without trust, your child's self-concept develops in an atmosphere of threat and uncertainty. Trust makes the foundation under your child solid and frees her mind for further exploration.

Your baby can develop trust in a world that is, in the main, trustworthy. This is a world in which someone tries to meet her needs. You love her. Feed her. Hold her. Burp her. Change her diaper. You attend to her when she cries and try to figure out what is wrong. You respond to her smiles. You are sensitive to her participation in interactions and try to understand the nuances of her behavior, proceeding when invited and backing off when she needs space. You keep her away from dangers. Overall, you do your best to figure out what she needs and provide it. You do not have to be faultless. You just have to be genuinely interested and dedicated. You may not always be successful in figuring out what is necessary; it is enough for you to be interested in being successful and to do your best. It is also important that you be able to tolerate not getting it right immediately without being devastated by the experience and turning away from your baby in despair. When you are loving and interested and resilient, you communicate a trustworthy world.

The development of basic trust can go awry for a number of reasons. Certainly, a baby who is neglected or abused is not going to be able to trust her world. That's pretty obvious. But there are less obvious conditions that can negatively affect a baby in her effort to establish trust in the world around her.

An unresponsive parent may contribute to a baby's experiencing a lack of trust and safety. If you are depressed, for example, you may not be able to participate in the relationship in a way that gives your baby confidence. Other problems can arise with parents who, prior to bringing a baby into the household, have idealized infancy. If you idealize infancy and parenthood, you may be ill prepared for the nonglossy, unpredictable, sleep-deprived, loud, and messy realities of having an actual baby in the house.

> *Jane Ferguson brings newborn Lynwood home to a nursery with a drawer full of organic cotton clothes, cotton diapers, and a warmer for his wipes. The room is done in pastels and gets only filtered sunlight to protect him from any harsh glare. The crib rocks and vibrates for soothing comfort. In it is a bear that makes sounds like the ones Lynwood heard in his birth mother's womb. Ms. Ferguson imagines long stretches of time when she and baby will rock together in the glider, gazing into each other's eyes. But the first weeks go by in a blur of fussing, crying, and spitting up. Lynwood sleeps no more than forty-five minutes at a stretch, and fitfully at that. Ms. Ferguson thought she would understand what his different cries mean, but they all sound the same to her. She doesn't feel she is bonding, and she doesn't think Lynwood likes her. She finds herself feeling first helpless and then angry with Lynwood. She has never felt like so much of a failure.*

An already difficult adjustment is made that much more difficult if you cling to a fantasy that does not accord with reality and then resent having to accommodate the difference. A feeling of dissonance may come to dominate the relationship with your child, and this erodes trust. If you bring your baby home and find yourself feeling depressed or disconnected for any reason, the best action you can take for yourself and your baby is to get some help.

But it is not only abuse, neglect, unresponsiveness, or resentment that can make a baby's world difficult to negotiate. The trusting foundations for self-esteem can also be negatively affected by well-meaning parents who are too avid in their efforts to provide stimulating opportunities to enhance their babies' development.

> *The Ricardos bring baby Jessie home to what they believe is the quintessential baby nursery. The wallpaper, the crib, the bed-*

ding, the mobile hanging over the crib, and the ceiling are covered with high-contrast black-and-white patterns. Now that Jessie is born, Mrs. Ricardo can put away the apparatus she placed on her belly every night to pipe classical music into Jessie as she developed in utero. In its place are speakers that have been run into the baby's room to provide Mozart around the clock. The Ricardos have bought videotapes that promise to stimulate the different sides of Jessie's brain, and they have installed a television in the nursery to ensure that Jessie will get enough exposure to these for maximum brain development.

It's very contemporary in our culture to subscribe to the notion "If one is good, seven must be better." However, such a statement is not always correct. Stimulation is a good thing, but there is such a thing as too much of it.

We all need some downtime, and this is particularly true for babies. A safe environment is one where your anxieties over your child's achievements don't take precedence over a consideration for your child's whole self. The Ricardos communicate an implicit mistrust in Jessica's abilities to unfold naturally. Jessica's own competency and desire to develop are completely overlooked. If a parent mistrusts a baby so fundamentally at such an early age, what is the impact on the baby's eventual ability to trust herself? The assumption is that the baby, as is, is insufficient or wrong. This is the antithesis of self-esteem.

Helping Your Toddler Develop Self-Esteem

If you have spent any time around toddlers, chances are you have heard the words "I do it myself!" or some variation thereof. Toddlers are discovering themselves as independent agents in the world. They are as wildly intoxicated by their burgeoning separateness in one moment as they are threatened by it in the next.

Toddlers are intensely focused on performing many of the functions that you have previously performed for them. The ability to take over these functions—comb their own hair, brush their own teeth, and blow their own noses—is indeed one of the tasks of this stage of life. Toddlers particularly want to do those things that occur in proximity to their own bodies. That is, they don't care about doing the cooking, but they tend to insist upon feeding themselves. While their determination to perform functions on their own is gigantic, their capacity to accomplish these ends to your adult standards is considerably less so. That is, your toddler may insist upon feeding herself, but she does not do so with the same finesse you display when you sit down in the morning with your bowl of cereal. Similarly, your toddler may insist upon dressing herself, though the color combinations she comes up with and the ultimate orientation of different articles of clothing on her body are not likely to pass muster with Martha Stewart.

Your toddler's impressions of her own capacities are grossly out of proportion with what is likely to be fact, and her ability to conceptualize different tasks tends to far outpace her actual physical capabilities to carry them out. Your toddler has feelings about this. She gets frustrated. Your two-year-old may have every intention of putting on her pajama top and may fight strenuously against your efforts to assist, but shortly thereafter she screams because her head is jammed into a sleeve and she cannot extricate herself without your help. Then, when you come to the rescue at her insistence, she continues to struggle against you, displaying considerably less humility and gratitude than you might surmise should be your due.

How can your help your child traverse toddlerhood with the best chances for the development of self-esteem? You need to be savvy about the discrepancy between the enormity of your toddler's ambition and her level of real ability to perform the things she sets before herself. You need to give her room to try something on her own, and be ready to support her in bringing the enterprise to fruition when invited to do so. You are best situated when you are prepared to weather the bewildering storms of emotion that are likely to blow through regularly during this time in your child's life. And you need to use good judgment with respect to your toddler's capacities. Your toddler needs to have her developing autonomy supported while she is not overwhelmed by inappropriate demands.

The Shars are embarking on a trip across the country. All morning, two-and-a-half-year-old Alaya has been testy. When her parents take the stroller out of the trunk at the airport, she pitches a fit. "I a big girl!" she insists, stamping her feet. Mrs. Shar has had enough. "Fine," she says, and she puts the stroller back angrily. They haven't even made it to the gate, however, before Alaya is whining "Uppie! Uppie!" But neither of her parents has an arm to spare. Nine hours later, the situation is much deteriorated. Mr. and Mrs. Shar haven't spoke to each other since Alaya dissolved into a defiant heap in the middle of the gangway during their first plane change. Mr. Shar blames Mrs. Shar for not thinking ahead. And Mrs. Shar blames Alaya for telling her she didn't want the stroller in the first place.

If you are taking horseback riding lessons and you master the act of posting on an easy beginner horse, you might feel confident to take on a much more spirited mount, but your teacher would be remiss if she went along with your idea. If she puts you on an untrained stallion, this will have lasting repercussions on your confidence as a rider, not to mention lasting repercussions on your confidence in her judgment as your teacher. Similarly, your toddler needs some say in what she does, but the big, wide world that she is so eager to take possession of is broader than what she can really cope with. To preserve her feeling of competency, you need to punctuate the world for her in a way that allows her to be competent. You, her parent, are responsible for this. Mrs. Shar should have realized Alaya's fierce self-determination was likely to last only as long as it took her legs to get tired, and brought along the stroller anyway.

While you need to be careful not to overwhelm your toddler, you also need to be alert to the tendency to underwhelm her as well. While toddlers often bite off more than they can chew, sometimes they hesitate in the face of challenges that are within their purview. In these circumstances, they need encouragement.

Emily Johnson achieved the developmental milestones that indicate potty readiness at the age of two. She understood that certain things went in certain places, she had adequate fine and gross motor control, and she had a name for her bowel and bladder products and the ability to say when she was producing one or the other. Starting at the age of twenty-seven months, sometimes she would go in the potty, and sometimes she would resist. The Johnsons didn't want to push her, so they kept her in diapers waiting for her to let them know that she was ready to be a big girl. Now Emily is nearly four years old, and the Johnsons are still waiting.

Emily and her parents, in this instance, collude to avoid a task that is difficult. The Johnsons doubt Emily's ability to gain control over her bowel and bladder. Chances are, they doubt their own ability to see her through the process and cope with the feelings that arise within them as well. This lack of faith is communicated to Emily, who runs the risk of internalizing it. Self-esteem does not mean you have to be good at everything you do, and it doesn't mean you will not make mistakes along the way. Self-esteem allows you to value yourself for the effort you make as opposed to its product. Self-esteem gives you the wherewithal to stick with a job, even when the going gets tough. Self-esteem allows you to make mistakes along the way and not be crippled by shame. Without self-esteem, a mistake can land you flat on your face. With self-esteem, a mistake can be just a bump in the road, an occurrence that can be looked at and learned from because it doesn't threaten your sense of your basic identity. It isn't seen as proof of your essential ineptitude.

In the process of developing her skills and competencies, your toddler is not always going to look as good as she can if your standard has something to do with matched socks, shoes on the right feet, neatly combed hair, and pants put on right-side-out. It is important, during toddlerhood, not to place too much emphasis on appearances.

Mrs. Rillette is getting tired of fighting with two-year-old Laurent. "Every morning I drop him at the preschool, and he needs his shoes retied, his sweater will be all crooked and need rebuttoning, his hair will be messed up. To try to neaten him up brings on World War III." Asked why she does not let her son go into school the way he is, she states, "Well, he looks like a mess. I think the other children will make fun of him and hurt his self-esteem."

Laurent Rillette is very likely to arrive at preschool pleased as punch with what he has been able to accomplish in the domain of dressing himself. Mrs. Rillette devalues his accomplishment by redoing all he has been able to do on his own. The message is that his efforts have no real value and his accomplishments are worthless.

Your toddler does not particularly care what she looks like, and she doesn't judge herself by adult standards. If your two-and-a-half-year-old daughter goes to the mall wearing her firefighter's helmet, orange socks, purple shoes, and a blue-and-gray print dress, she is not likely to be embarrassed. Rather, she is likely to be proud of having dressed herself. But where a toddler focuses on the achievement of having dressed herself, parents are more likely to be concerned with the finished product. Parents are often worried about their own self-esteem in this case. You may impose your standards and taste to avoid being ashamed while in the company of a child who you think will be judged negatively by other adults.

If you are out to help a child develop good self-esteem, then you have to have it for her. That means you can't just bite your lip and tolerate her appearance. Your child will clearly pick up on this. You need to find it within yourself to be delighted at her initiative and to thrill at what she can accomplish on her own.

It's important to de-emphasize the importance of others' reactions as determining factors in your behavior. You presumably don't want to raise a child who is ruled by peer pressure, and this is the time to start setting a good example. Thus, you need not be ruled by the pressure of *your* peers. It is also important to recognize that what you imagine other people to be saying about you may not even be accurate.

A Montessori teacher spoke about eating at a local fast-food restaurant: "Behind me in line was the most pristine little girl— probably about three years old—and her family. She was wearing a fancy dress, and she had a hairband that matched it. She kept taking the hairband off and trying it on different parts of her body—her waist, her arms, her neck. I thought her mother would have a stroke. In front of me was a girl about the same age who looked as if her closet had exploded and she had been caught in the trajectory. She was showing her daddy her crooked ponytail, saying, 'Look, Daddy. I did it!' I know which family I would rather be a part of."

To paraphrase William Faulkner, "It ain't so much who's crazy. It's who's looking at you at the time." What does this mean in light of our discussion? It means that anyone who is savvy to child development is likely to give you a whole lot more credit as a parent if you are walking with a toddler who has been given appropriate self-expression, even if the socks she chose don't match and her hair looks as if it was done with an eggbeater.

The development of self-esteem can go awry when parents try to take too much control over toddlers. Your child needs to have the time to develop and master her self-help skills. You need to maintain the awareness that this process is essential and that mistakes are going to be inevitable.

Kirby Besseli, eighteen months old, is struggling to master the art of eating with a fork. Food is going everywhere, and Mr. Besseli, something of a neat freak, is not handling this well. When yet another piece of potato goes over the lip of the high-chair tray, Mr. Besseli can tolerate it no longer. He takes the fork from Kirby and insists upon feeding him. Kirby struggles briefly, but then capitulates. This is not the first time Dad has taken over for him in this enterprise.

Do you know how to drive a stick-shift car? Chances are, the person who taught you didn't take over the driver's seat the first time you stalled out. Your children will not master the skills they set out to learn the first time out of the gate either. To expect otherwise, and to see a false start as an indication that you need to take over the whole enterprise, robs your toddler of the opportunity to develop her skills and gives her a sense that her perfectly expectable errors are wrong and shameful. That's what is happening to Kirby Besseli. If Mr. Besseli has more difficulties with the mess than he can get a handle on, then his wife should take over feeding for a while until Kirby establishes more reliable control.

There are more and less effective ways of supporting a toddler's initiative.

Scenario: Your almost-three-year-old has been trying to master the act of buttoning his shirt. He has been exceptionally frustrated and tends to give up after a brief try. All the other kids in his preschool can do this task, and you are anxious about his slow progress. One day you happen upon him in his room, making his best buttoning effort, but growing visibly frustrated. What can you do?

- You could intervene, saying, "How many times do I have to show you how to do this? Why don't you just let me do it to begin with?"

This response uses shaming. It communicates to your son that there is something wrong with him, and it is likely to kill his initiative to keep trying.

- You could watch him try and eventually intervene, taking over to help him before he gets too upset. "See?" you could say while slipping the button through the hole in slow motion. "It's not that hard."

While you may be trying to reassure him by telling him it's not hard, in doing so you negate his experience and make him feel smaller and even more ineffective. When you take over for him, you communicate your lack of confidence in his ability to work through the task. Are you aiming to raise a child who can persist in the face of challenge? This is the place to begin. Let him.

- You could wait for him to give up on his own and then take over for him, reassuring him that one day he will be able to do the job if he just keeps practicing.

This approach is a bit better, but it still doesn't quite hit the mark because you have not acknowledged his struggle and communicated your recognition of his efforts.

- While watching him give it his best shot, you could say, "Boy, that's a hard thing to do, but look at how hard you are working!"

Eventually, if he invites your assistance, you could provide it. You might say, "Buttoning shirts is hard work. I remember when brushing teeth was so hard too. Remember how it was to try to get at your upper teeth in the back? But you worked hard at it, and you learned."

By responding like this, you let your child know that you understand how challenging the task is and that you do not expect him to find it to be otherwise. You respond to his effort and remind him of his prior success. This child is likely to persist and likely to feel a good deal more hopeful in the long run. When he gets older and is challenged by a particular demand, he can reference your understanding and champion himself in his own efforts toward the goal.

In addition to mastering skills to help themselves, toddlers are at a time in life when their personalities are emerging. More than supporting any self-help skill, more than facing a child with appropriate-level challenges for her capacities, the most important thing you can do for a child of this age—or any age for that matter—is to like who she is.

In essence, when we talk about a child with self-esteem, we are talking about a child who fundamentally likes herself. Absent your esteem, she likely will not be able to accomplish this. Liking your child is not a technical skill. You cannot practice liking your child, and there are no assignments you can do to make it happen. Most parents do like their children. Some parents have difficulties. Sometimes problems arise when a child's personality doesn't match what a parent hoped for. A father with three girls finally has a son, but the boy is sedentary and sensitive and doesn't have a particular interest in playing the sports his father always imagined they would share a passion for. In a household of readers is born a child with no interest in sitting down for anything. These types of experiences are not guaranteed to create schisms in relationships, but sometimes they do. If you encounter impediments to liking your child and they are persistent, you need to get some help. Not to do so cheats your child out of her birthright of having an adoring parent, and it will cheat you out of the joys of parenting.

Helping Your Preschool or Kindergarten Child Develop Self-Esteem

Between the ages of three and six, your child has mastered many of the discrete skills that go along with caring for herself. Her view of the world is expanding, and her memory and her concept of time are developing. She can imagine projects that are grander than simply the act of buttoning her shirt or feeding herself with a fork. These are the years when children start to imagine elaborate games to play and projects to undertake, and it's when they begin to have the capacity to sustain attention long enough to carry them out.

Your children are born with a spark—an inherent drive to master different challenges that the process of development will put before them. Your job is to make sure the spark stays lit. You do this by encouraging your children's interests and offering them appropriate help. At these ages, children need to be encouraged to act on their decisions. They need to be allowed to make things. They need to be permitted to conceptualize projects, carry them out, and bring them to completion. They need guidance—not too much and not too little. They need space, they need materials, and they need time to explore and investigate. They need the freedom to discover at their own pace and in their own way in the course of undertaking these enterprises. They need you to quell any impulse that may arise to have them proceed more efficiently.

These are the ages at which, as a parent, you need to reward initiative and not its product. If your four-year-old wants to help you bake a cake, you teach her how to crack eggs and provide a bowl for her to do it in. You also need to be prepared to fish some shell out of the bowl and to wipe up spills. If your six-year-old wants to have a lemonade stand, you do not wait to count the gross receipts at the end of the day before you deem it a good idea. "Great idea, Jenny," you might say, and then you support the process of bringing it to fruition. You still need to provide supervision, but at a slightly greater distance than you provided it when the child was a toddler. She can pick the lemons off the low branches of the tree by herself, but you supervise the cutting with a knife. She can carry the small chairs, but you might need to set up the table.

231

At this age of initiative, problems for later self-esteem can arise when children are placed in overly structured situations where they have few choices.

A local private school agreed to accept Dahlia Larmore into kindergarten when she just turned four. The Larmores had taught Dahlia phonics with flashcards and had used a computer math program for toddlers too. They were sure she would be bored by another year of preschool. In kindergarten, Dahlia could not stay seated in her chair and was regularly up at the art area, getting into the coveted crayons or trying to work on the Play-Doh projects from the day before. She would tolerate reading lessons, but she wanted to make up her own stories to go with the pictures in the books. At the age of four and a half, she was referred to be assessed for attention deficit hyperactivity disorder.

Dahlia Larmore provides a wonderful example of why we do not start four-year-old children in kindergarten. Dahlia is still developing her own ideas, making up her own projects. The part of her brain that might permit her to sit still reliably for more than five minutes is not quite yet wired in. She is having an experience of failure in school that is not her failure, but rather, is a reflection of her parents' failure to give her more time to develop before limiting her to the structure and demands of a school day. Of course, Dahlia will not see it this way. She is more likely to internalize the criticisms she gets in school and conclude that her very age-appropriate wondering and creativity are wrong.

School readiness is not only defined by a child's mastery of pre-academic skills. A child who is ready for school also needs to be able to meet the demands to sit and focus. A child of four may be able to grasp some academic skills if she is drilled as Dahlia was, but sitting still is a job of an entirely different part of the brain. Dahlia is being put in a situation that demands more sitting than she can accommodate, and she is encountering conflict. Dahlia has age-appropriate impulses to run, jump, and invent. She is continually being told these are wrong, but she is not yet developmentally able to quell them. We don't reprimand a child with allergies for sneezing. To do so—to tell her she is wrong for behaviors she cannot control—would certainly hurt her sense of herself. This is the situation in which Dahlia finds herself, and it does not bode well for her future.

Problems can also arise for preschool-age children when achievement is valued over process.

> *Soong Lee, four, has been practicing violin an hour a day since his mother started him with lessons on the instrument at the age of three. His mother listens to, and is critical of, his daily practices. She believes Soong must develop mastery of the instrument if he is to have good self-esteem.*

Mrs. Lee's demand that Soong practice the violin so rigidly robs him of the opportunity to discover his own projects and activities. A child who is at the point in childhood where she can conceptualize and innovate, and who is not permitted to do so, may end up with a lack of faith in her ability to create and solve problems. She may become an overly dependent adult, mistrustful of her instincts and reluctant to act on her own. She may be plagued by the type of self-doubt that is the antithesis of self-esteem.

Mrs. Lee is making another mistake, however, in assuming that Soong's self-esteem is dependent on a certain quality of external achievement. If Soong were never able to master his instrument and, rather, turned out to be only a mediocre violin player, would he then only be entitled to feel slightly good about himself? And perhaps more important to Soong at these ages, if he cannot perform well, will he be held in less esteem in his mother's eyes?

Self-esteem does have something to do with a child's sense of her competency, but it cannot depend upon objective mastery of a skill. A child who applies herself to a task, and disciplines herself in the process of working toward it, is demonstrating the kind of mastery that creates self-esteem. In Soong's case the task is being mandated by his mother. It would be more meaningful if it were a project that Soong had initiated.

Certainly self-esteem can exist in the company of achievement. However, as a parent, you should ensure that your child's value is not contingent on this achievement. A child with a positive self-image has the fuel to drive mastery. She has the self-confidence to persist through difficulty. When the going gets tough, she doesn't say to herself, "I'm lousy. I'm worthless." She says, "This is hard, but I'll keep trying." We have a right to feel proud of ourselves for sticking with what's tough. If self-esteem develops around your child's mastery of a task, it will be because she will have continued to apply herself to that job and not because you forced it down her throat.

Some parents err in the opposite direction. In an effort to avoid putting pressure on children to perform, they fail to respond to a child's appropriate desire for help in mastering skills.

> *Mr. Andover has Seth, aged six, in an alternative educational setting, and he strongly believes in letting children determine their own pace for learning. When Seth asks him to correct mistakes he makes when writing his letters, Mr. Andover will not accommodate him and, instead, simply praises his efforts. He believes that to correct his son would mean damaging his self-esteem.*

At the age of six, Seth is at the beginning of his elementary years. He needs to master the tools of the culture—reading, writing, and arithmetic—so he can be an effective member of that culture. Seth has identified the challenge and wants to apply himself to it. He has the faith in his own competency that will permit him to apply himself in this endeavor. Seth, however, cannot come to a mastery of his letters on his own. He needs correction and is asking for help. His father does not damage Seth's self-esteem by helping him meet this challenge and teaching him. He is more likely to do damage by failing to respond to his son's growth with a recognition of the developmental stage he has achieved and its appropriate demands.

School Readiness and Self-Esteem

"School readiness" is a relatively new issue. A generation ago, children were simply moved into kindergarten according to age cutoffs at their schools. We have learned more about child development in the last thirty or forty years, and curriculum and educational protocols have changed in the years since *Sputnik,* so contemporary parents now find themselves facing choices about the ages at which they will enroll their children in kindergarten. This is particularly the case for parents of children who turn five in the summer prior to the start of the academic year. In some school districts where cutoffs are in November and December, it is even an issue for those who will turn five after school has begun.

Until recently, parents have been very resistant to holding children with later birthdays back in order to permit them to develop for an additional year prior to embarking on kindergarten. Parents felt that to do so implied that their children were stupid, or they feared that others would look on them in this way. The pendulum seems to be swinging, however. Some parents, savvy to the idea that a child who starts school older may have an edge over younger classmates all the way through school, have embraced the idea of holding children back. Some are even entering their children in kindergarten at the age of six.

This is a complex subject, and it is beyond the scope of this book to tackle it in depth. For the purposes of this chapter, suffice it to say that a child who is developmentally ready to start school and who is prevented from doing so is at risk for future self-esteem-related problems as much as a child who is not ready to move forward and who is pushed. Both children are not respected when decisions such as these are made on the basis of something other than their specific developmental needs.

Don't Compare Your Child with Others

We are a culture that is particularly focused on outward appearances and visible accomplishments. It is therefore important to mention that when we talk about self-esteem, we are not talking about outer beauty. This is not to say that children with good self-esteem cannot be physically attractive. It is to say that being physically attractive in and of itself does not confer self-esteem upon a child.

At this very appearance-focused time in our culture, parents often engage in practices that may be psychologically and physically harmful to children in the service of creating a good outward appearance.

When Zubin Arafala brings his son Ahmed in for his two-year-old checkup, his weight gain is much less than expected. The pediatrician is alarmed. Mr. Arafala explains that in an effort to ensure Ahmed doesn't inherit his weight problem and the negative self-image that goes along with it, he and his wife have put their son on a low-fat diet.

In childhood, a child's sense of her own value initially rests upon the amount of value with which her significant others view her. She will also pick up on the attitudes that parents have about themselves. Unfortunately, Ahmed has already got a head start on a negative self-image. He is likely to base it upon his parents' views of themselves and their apparent view of him as someone with dangerous appetites whose own self-regulatory processes cannot be trusted.

"Georgia has great self-esteem," says Mrs. Petrie of her daughter. "She's the prettiest girl in her school, and she beat out forty other seven-year-olds who were competing statewide for the Little Miss Junior Beauty Pageant last weekend."

Georgia Petrie may be beautiful in others' eyes, but this does not mean that her opinion of herself is positive. Anyone who has ever picked up *People* magazine and read an article on this week's troubled movie star should not need to be convinced on this point. People with good self-esteem are often attractive, but this is often in large part because of the positive attitude they have about themselves. Self-esteem creates attractiveness, not the other way around.

The problems with Mrs. Petrie's approach go further. She doesn't say, "I think my little girl is beautiful." Rather, Mrs. Petrie seems to be measuring her child's beauty against the beauty of others, concluding that her daughter has a right to feel good about herself relative to the lesser appearances of her schoolmates and fellow pageant participants. Mrs. Petrie is making a mistake. Success that is measured according to someone else's failure is cheapened. It takes the focus away from your child and her achievement, and places the focus on others.

Your child's relationship to herself and her sense of what she is worth cannot be determined in the context of another child's value. If your child measures her value in this way or if you measure her value in this way, she can have no value when she is standing on her own. A child whose value exists relative to the failure of others is a child who is taller by standing on another's shoulders. By definition, this is a precarious position. A person who comports herself in this way does not proceed with self-esteem. She proceeds with triumph and paranoia. These are problematic. If your child has gained status by trouncing someone else, she must ever be on the alert for the one coming along who will unseat her.

Georgia Petrie's situation raises another important point. In a competition-focused culture, it may be common to believe that self-esteem is created in a child when she is the best at something, or when she wins over someone else. This is not so. External competitions come and go. Today's soccer match is tomorrow's checkers game. In the competitive external world, your child can have a good sense of self-esteem without winning a single blue ribbon, or she can take home all the prizes and feel terrible about herself.

The real struggle for a child is not with the visible competitors in the swim race. The real struggle starts much earlier in your child's life—at birth, if not before. The real struggle has to do with her pervasive and persistent jockeying for position with you, her parent. Any struggles against rivals on the football field pale in intensity when compared against the magnitude of your child's persistent striving for your deep and abiding approval. Self-esteem is not a sure thing, like eye color. In the emotional arena, we don't have such sure things. Rather, self-esteem grows in relation to the experiences your child has with you. To feel good, your child needs to know she is loved and accepted by you simply for who she is, for the fact that she exists. She needs to be cherished before she accomplishes a single thing and in spite of her lack of ability to excel above peers at anything.

A child's abilities may wax and wane. Her moods may change over the course of the day. Basic self-esteem does not wax and wane. Rather, it is a relative constant that is punctuated by moments of self-doubt. We are not talking here about pervasive self-doubt. We are talking here about transient episodes that seem to go along with being human. Self-esteem is the dominant relationship your child has to herself—how she feels about herself before she undertakes anything or demonstrates any of her accomplishments and abilities.

The fundamental attitude you have toward your child becomes

imprinted deeply inside her and becomes the reference point for how she feels about herself all the time. If she comes in dead last in a race, her feeling about herself will depend upon how you respond. We are talking about your real feeling here. If she can feel your honest respect for her effort and your abiding love, she may be frustrated or disappointed in not winning, but her sense of herself as a person of worth will remain intact. If you are ashamed or disappointed, or if she feels she has lost her position with you on the basis of her performance, her sense of herself will suffer accordingly. If you are ashamed or disappointed in her and try to pretend otherwise, you can bet that she won't be fooled. She may try to fool you into thinking that she is, so both of you can pretend to feel better in the moment, but this is a charade. In the long term, her sense of her value and her sense of herself will suffer.

Without the good foundation of your love and esteem, your child is on shaky ground. Some children show this more obviously in their behavior. They misbehave persistently, appear depressed, and appear never to try to achieve much of anything. Other children who lack a fundamental faith in their value look completely different. They may become stellar achievers and fierce competitors. So long as they win the races and get the A's, they may appear to be fine. But one blip on the screen—a B on a test, the loss of a contest, an insult by a classmate—and the whole charade is exposed. Such a child may be intensely focused on winning, not so much to support her self-esteem, but rather to keep from having to recognize that she doesn't have any. This child cannot take losses in stride. Rather, losses are experienced as a catastrophic confirmation of the negative self-image that all the winning is constructed to keep her from having to face.

Your self-esteem plays an important role in how you relate to your child and feel about her achievements. You are going to be best able to help your child develop a deep conviction about her value if you have deep convictions about your own. If you have a self-esteem problem of your own to contend with, you are more likely to need your child to excel. Her successes allow you to stay one step ahead of your shame and self-doubt, much as they may function for her if her worth is in question. On the other hand, if your sense of worth is more deeply rooted, then you are less likely to experience her mistakes as shameful confirmation of your own negative sense of value. When she botches her lines in the school play, you are likely to be more understanding and compassionate with her embarrassment because you will be contending with less of your own.

How Much It Helps to Feel Understood

Let's say you hate to travel by plane. You find it physically uncomfortable and confining, and you worry about the engines failing and the plane crashing in a fiery ball of molten metal. You avoid airplanes when you can, but one day you are summoned to a meeting that requires you to fly across the country on short notice. You feel your heart rate go up as you walk through the walkway, and when you step on board, the stewardess greets you and asks how you're doing. You tell her, "Not so well. I really don't like to fly." "Nonsense," says she. "You love to fly. Look, you've got a business class seat with a footrest. You have a blanket and a pillow. You'll get where you're going in no time. Flying is great!" "Still," you say, "I don't like airplanes." "Don't be ridiculous," she says. "Airplanes are wonderful. You've got uninterrupted time to do what you want. You'll eat a good meal. There's an in-flight movie. And we'll bake chocolate chip cookies for you and the other passengers before we land. What could be better?"

Now imagine a different scenario: You have all the same concerns. You board the airplane and tell the stewardess you are afraid to fly. She says, "Oh, I'm sorry. The plane is perfectly safe, but I know many people feel worried nonetheless. It's very normal. I wonder if there's anything I could do to make the flight more comfortable for you?" You tell her you don't like the confinement. She says, "Oh, I know what you mean. They do what they can to make the seats comfortable, but I'd take my easy chair at home over an airplane seat any day! Maybe when the plane's aloft and the captain has turned off the seat-belt sign, you could take a walk down the aisle. It won't get us there any faster, but it might make you feel less restless. Feel free to push your call button if I can be of any assistance to you, and I'll plan to check on you periodically in any case."

In this encounter, both of the stewardesses are transforming the experience for you, but in radically different directions. Next time you book a flight, which stewardess do you hope to have assigned to you?

239

In the first situation, you are trying to convey a feeling and the stewardess is trying to talk you out of it. Now you not only feel bad about being on the airplane; you feel bad about feeling bad. You have figuratively reached out for support and have found no hand to grasp yours. Instead, the stewardess has conveyed that you need to feel differently than you do. In the second situation, the stewardess has recognized that you have a feeling. She can provide evidence that suggests that your fears are groundless, but she does not convey that you are silly or unreasonable for feeling the way you do. Not feeling misunderstood or condescended to by her, you might even be able to take a little comfort in her mention of the fact that the plane is safe. You won't get to your destination any faster, but knowing she is on your side is likely to make your trip a whole lot more comfortable.

The same principles apply in parenting. Your child is going to have a number of feelings that you may think are silly, unfounded, unreasonable, objectionable, or inconvenient. The way in which you meet these feelings is critical. You can help your child diminish the difficulty of an experience by helping her feel supported and understood. Conversely, you can make the course your child travels with an experience immeasurably more difficult. You do this by conveying to her your refusal to recognize her upset, and by stating implicitly or explicitly that she is wrong in feeling the way she does.

When the Sayed family adopted Jamal, they did not anticipate how difficult the transition would be for their four-year-old daughter, Kiara. Prior to his arrival, she said she wanted a baby brother. Now, she says she hates the baby and wants her parents to send him back. Mrs. Sayed says, "I tell her, 'No, no, Kiara. You don't mean what you're saying.' I tell her I know she loves her brother, and it is very special to be a big sister." Asked how this approach is working, Mrs. Sayed admits that after the last of such interchanges, Kiara flushed Jamal's bunny down the toilet. I suggest that Kiara is struggling with very understandable feelings of jealousy and say it might be useful to communicate understanding to her about these feelings. Mrs. Sayed is very much against this. "I think that would make her bad feeling stronger, and I don't want to do that. I don't think it's true. I believe Kiara loves Jamal, and eventually she'll come around."

Even a parent who believes that giving a child a sibling is something of tremendous value may hesitate to follow through with the family expansion for fear of creating jealousy and rivalry. If we fear we will cause pain, we dread having to recognize evidence that it is there. So if an older sibling exhibits something short of unbridled joy when a newborn arrives, what are parents to do? Parents who remain open to recognizing jealousy may experience guilt, may question their judgment, and may revisit the doubt and trepidation that accompanied their decision in the first place. To avoid this, parents may do all they can to deny the child's expression of jealousy. They may call it something else.

Mrs. Sayed may wish Kiara to be uniformly happy about her brother, but wishing will not make it so. If Kiara suspected she lost her mother to this squalling new intruder, her mother is confirming this by so completely failing to hear and accept what Kiara has to say to her. By not validating the way her daughter feels, Mrs. Sayed is adding to her burdens. Now, Kiara not only feels jealous, she feels colossally misunderstood. And as if that weren't enough, there is the implicit threat of rejection if Kiara can't bring her feelings into line with what Mrs. Sayed finds acceptable.

Mrs. Sayed is not trying to make her daughter feel bad. She fears that validating her daughter's feelings would make them stronger. This is a fallacy. On the contrary, in attempting to blow out the fire, Mrs. Sayed is likely only to succeed in fanning the flames. Children are afraid of their strong feelings. They are not helped when adults are afraid of them too. It is a tremendous comfort to anyone—children and adults—to feel recognized. Recognition allows the person in distress to relax a bit, to not feel so alone. It's the balm that soothes. A voice of understanding may not alter a situation, but it alters a person's relationship to it.

Human beings are able to tolerate bad things happening to them. They are better able to do so if they can describe what they are experiencing to just one other person. In an environment that may feel threatening or oppressive, the existence of another who is aware of our plight is soothing and brings some comfort. So how should Mrs. Sayed proceed in this situation? Rather than being told she does not feel the ways she does, imagine if Kiara were held close by her mother and told instead: "You are feeling jealous of the baby. It's hard to have a new baby in the house and to have to share Mom and Dad. You can be as jealous or mad as you want. You can draw a mean picture or use your words to show how mad and jealous you feel. But

241

you cannot hurt the baby." This provides the closeness with mother that Kiara feels is threatened. It provides a name for the experience and parameters for Kiara's behavior. Kiara knows her mother is aware of her experience, and she knows that her mother is not rejecting her on the basis of it.

Kiara's mother's giving a name to Kiara's feelings is also helpful to her daughter. Imagine you have fever, chills, aches and pains, a runny nose, and a hacking cough, and you've never had this experience before. You go to the doctor, and she says, "Oh, yes. The flu." Suddenly, you are not at the mercy of an arbitrary and unknown process of subjective misery. You have something with a name, a predictable course, and you know what you can do for symptomatic relief. Your doctor did not run screaming from the room when you showed up. She did not tell you that your aches and pains were not real. She is not afraid of what you feel, and you need not be afraid either.

Babies are not born with the vocabulary to describe the external world any more than they have words to describe their emotions. It is as necessary for parents to teach children what the words "doggie," "house," and "milk" correspond to as it is to teach them what the words "mad," "sad," and "happy" mean. Being able to name things helps people feel a sense of order. If things have a name, they can be understood.

A child who has not had early experiences of understanding moves through life in a state of mental isolation. When the world feels threatening or difficult, there is little solace. She is not likely to see others as potential helpers. She doesn't expect to be empathized with, or worse, she expects others to compound her problems. This is a child whose parents denied her rivalrous feelings toward a sibling, who told her she was too old to be upset at being left for the day at preschool, and who told her that her fear of monsters in the closet was ridiculous and refused to check under the bed. Such a child cannot learn to name feelings accurately. When she says she is angry, someone tells her she is not. When she says that she hates, someone tells her that she loves. When she says she is afraid, someone tells her this is not so. Her self-awareness is being formed through a distorted lens. How does such a child come to have any faith in her own judgment? How does such a child come to learn to appraise her environment or her feelings accurately?

Children raised in this way are likely to misconstrue what they see.

They are being taught their perceptions are not trustworthy. They may be prone to respond to something benign as something threatening. Such a child is also likely to fail to see when help is available, because it is not part of her internal template. A child struggling with something reaches to a parent but finds misunderstanding instead of support. "Look at me!" she says. "I see you," says the parent, but the parent's eyes are looking in an entirely different direction. If this is repeated many times over a childhood, a child stops reaching and develops no faith whatsoever in an understanding or supportive world. This is a painful and isolating way to go through life. It is certainly not what you would wish for your children.

As damaging as it can be to fail to recognize a child's real feeling, it is as constructive to provide experiences in which children feel understood. The former sets the stage for a lifetime of alienation from the self and from others. By contrast, allowing children their feelings and communicating understanding of them prepares children for future self-awareness and for the development of empathy, sympathy, and compassion. Talking with children about their experiences sets the stage for them to be able to talk to themselves in the future. When you are not there in person, the internal model you established for your child can be drawn upon to provide comfort.

We don't always know what is wrong. All of us have had the experience of waking up on the wrong side of the bed, of being in a funk. Often, the cause of these feelings is not apparent to us. We feel better if we can understand the cause of something. This offers us a measure of control and makes the world seem less random. It reassures us that just as we can detect a beginning to our present concerns, so there will be an end to them.

Speaking It Will Not Make It So

Sometimes parents are afraid to speak to children about feelings they observe in them because they cannot be sure that they are right. They are afraid that if they are wrong, they will put ideas in their children's minds that were not there before and will create new problems.

"I was sitting at the kitchen table with Corinne," said Mrs. Maple of her four-year-old daughter. "She was playing with Play-

Doh, and we were talking about her friend Heather's birthday party. I said we needed to buy Heather a Barbie. Corinne didn't say anything. I asked if she thought Heather would like a Barbie. Still, no answer. I figured maybe this was a sharing problem. I said maybe she was feeling jealous that Heather would get a new Barbie. Still nothing. Now she started whimpering. I could not imagine what was wrong. Suddenly, she gave a huge burp. It surprised her as much as it surprised me. There was a pause; then she turned back to me. She said, 'My stomach hurt, but it's better now.' And that was that. It wasn't the Barbie at all. It was a stomach pain. We got Heather a Barbie, and Corinne was fine with it."

You will not always be correct about the roots of your child's feelings. What you think is sibling rivalry may be your child's response to your return from a business trip and her attempt to grapple with issues related to the separation. What you think is your child's anger at you when you stop her from repetitive toilet flushing may be guilt about having flushed your watch and anxiety about the anger you will feel when you discover this. But there is no harm in trying to understand what is going on and trying to talk it out, even if your initial impression is wrong. Mrs. Maple did not make Corinne jealous of Heather by asking if that was the cause of her distress.

Your children will not have ideas put into their heads that were not there before. If you say something that does not hit the mark, it won't register and you won't get a response to it because it's not how your child feels. But children, like adults, will respond when you have touched on something that has meaning for them.

Cassie Herman, almost four years old, screams bloody murder when her parents bring her to the potty. Her mother says, "I tell her she has nothing to be afraid of, but it doesn't help." I ask Cassie to tell me about the potty. She tells me her dog, Sparky, fell into the pool. Mr. Herman says, "Answer the doctor's question, Cass." I ask Cassie if she is afraid she will fall into the toilet and get flushed down, like Sparky who fell in the pool. Her mother interrupts, looking at me emphatically while speaking in a voice presumably directed to her daughter, "Well, that's just silly. No one ever got flushed down a toilet." I say that children do not get flushed down toilets, but many children fear this will happen. Mrs. Herman says to me sotto voce, "Is it such a good idea to mention this? She's already afraid. We don't want to give her new ideas, do we?" Cassie, meanwhile, has come alive in the session. She wants to talk more about it.

While Cassie may not have been able to put her fear into words, given her tender age and limited vocabulary, a fear of falling into the toilet and being flushed down—which is, by the way, a very common fear for young children—appears to have been exactly what she was grappling with. Sometimes, the best a child can do in such a circumstance is give you hints and hope you can use your experience to connect the dots and interpret the clues. Cassie's references to her dog and the pool were the only clues she could offer. When the pieces get put together and an adult provides the language, this gets her attention.

If your child is in distress and you are trying to understand the source of it, there may be instances in which something you suggest to her will become focal. You might think, in this situation, that you have created a new problem. This is not true. The feeling was there all along. You may provide a focus for it that it did not have previously, but you did not create the feeling itself.

Jilly Burnett, two years old, just came from the airport, where she and her grandmother saw her parents off for a weekend vacation—the first they have taken without their daughter. On the way home, Grandma pulls over at a park. As Jilly steps out of the car, a big black dog walks by and Jilly starts crying. Grandma asks Jilly, "Are you afraid of the doggie?" Jilly shakes her head. Later, outside the market, there is another dog and Jilly has the same reaction. When Jilly's parents come back, Grandma comments on Jilly's fear of dogs. They say Jilly loves dogs. Well, apparently the love affair is over because now she won't go near one. Mr. and Mrs. Burnett are annoyed and blame Grandma for creating this fear by putting ideas in Jilly's head.

245

Shortly after developing the fear of dogs, Jilly's fear started to generalize to other things and she was quickly getting to the point where she wouldn't let mother out of her sight. The Burnetts came to therapy with their daughter, traced the beginnings of the fears to the day they left on their trip, and started looking at the role their departure played in this chain of events.

Jilly Burnett did not go into the weekend with a fear of dogs. She did go into the weekend, however, distressed and angry about her parents' absence. Could she name these feelings? No. Were they real? Yes. In therapy, we put words to Jilly's feelings. From her perspective, her parents had vanished and could do so again, which was terrifying to her. All her current fears were serving the purpose of keeping her parents close by her to ensure they didn't get out of her sight again. And the anger she felt was terrifying her too. The dogs she was afraid of were not objectively ferocious, but some of her feelings were. Jilly was too threatened by her angry feelings and needed to distance herself from them. Jilly assigned the ferocious, dangerous feelings to dogs. It is no wonder that the dogs, imbued with all of her displaced strong feeling, became terrifying to her. In therapy, as we were able to speak about such things, put words to the feelings, and demonstrate to Jilly the real limits of her anger, Jilly's fears diminished.

Sometimes You Just Need to Cry

There are few honest parenting mistakes that are irrevocable, and those mistakes that are tend to fall not only outside the domain of good judgment, but outside the domain of lawfulness as well. Most parents aim to do their best by their children, and most parents do a fine job of it. Your job is to help your child grow. Your job is to help your child prepare for the time when you are no longer there to help. Your job is to do your best for your child, according to your best judgment. Your job is not to be faultless in the process of parenting. It is not your job to keep your child smiling all the time. Your child's tears are not an indication that you have failed as a parent. A successful parent is not the one whose child does not get upset and is never unhappy.

In the service of developing a capacity to regulate themselves, children and babies need to have an opportunity to shed a few tears. If you are a first-time parent, chances are you are going to have to learn that tears will not be the end of your child, and your child's tears will not be the end of you either.

Babies

There is a school of parenting whose proponents believe that a baby should not ever be left to cry. A recent parenting book suggested that a baby should never cry herself to sleep, as the negative consequences would be many. While babies should not be left for extended periods of time in tears, this is not to say they should not be permitted to cry. They need a chance to blow off steam, and this is the way they do it. Not allowing a baby to have such an expression inevitably makes for a tense atmosphere for everyone in the home.

> *Dylan was five when the Kleins brought baby Anastasia home. The first month, the Kleins walked the floor all night with her. She would bawl the moment she was set down. Dylan would then wake up, and he would cry. Mom and Dad were run ragged. Then, as if that wasn't enough, Anastasia, who had reliably quieted on being walked around, stopped being pacified by the walking. The Kleins tried everything they could think of to quiet her. The more desperate they became, the more Anastasia cried. I suggested that rather than trying to stop Anastasia from crying, they find a place in the house where she could cry to give her an opportunity for self-expression. They tried this. Anastasia cried briefly, and then slept through the night.*

Have you ever been in a bad mood in the company of people who can't do enough to make you comfortable? Far from a comfort, their relentless consideration becomes an irritant. Their need for your mood to lift is oppressive. Babies are a bit different than you are, in that they cannot do a number of things to make themselves more comfortable, such as change their own diapers and feed themselves. They clearly rely upon you for such matters. But when your baby is still crying and you have exhausted all your ideas—you've fed her, diapered her, made her warmer, made her cooler, burped her, rocked her, presented her with toys, and sung to her—it's time to try leaving her be. This does not mean you leave her alone in the house to catch a movie in the theater. It does not mean you reject her. It means making a conscious decision, as her caretaker, to give her a bit of time to express herself and bring herself more into balance. It means trusting her and respecting her competence to do so.

How long should your baby be allowed to cry by herself? Put away your stopwatch. The answer relies upon your judgment. How long you allow your child to cry will depend on her age, her temperament, and the context of the given situation. It will also depend on your state of mind. All parents, no matter how much they love their babies, have at some point of utter frustration fantasized throwing that baby out the window. They have not acted on that fantasy, mind you, but have certainly given it a moment's thought. Feeling this way does not mean you don't love your baby. It means you are human. Just as your baby may require some time on her own, so too may you. Leaving her crying for five minutes while you go in the next room to regroup may be best for all concerned.

It is important that you tolerate your own sense of helplessness and impotence in the face of your child's distress. This will allow you to avoid burdening your child with your need for her to feel better in a circumstance that simply does not lend itself to quick or neat resolution. A colicky baby feels dreadful already. A colicky baby with parents who cannot tolerate the feelings of helplessness that their child's cries arouse in them feels worse.

How long you let your baby cry will also depend on what happens over the course of the cry itself. In one situation, your baby cries, but the tone and volume of the cry diminish over the course of five minutes and it is clear that, in another five minutes, she will be calm or asleep. Leave her alone. At another point, in the five minutes since you put that same baby down, her cries have amplified and her distress level has increased markedly. What was crying is now squalling. In such a circumstance, do not leave her for another five minutes. Remember, the aim in this enterprise is to help her come back to equilibrium. If all indications suggest that she has gone more out of balance in the time since you have given her some space, then your purpose is not served by leaving her alone and you should try something else.

Toddlers and Preschoolers

As children get older, they can provide a bit more information than a baby can about what is bothering them. You cannot always make it better. You cannot bring back a beloved toy that fell out the window on the freeway. When the old family pet finally expires, you cannot make her come back to life and you cannot take away your child's grief. You cannot be with your child twenty-four hours a day, seven days a week, to prevent her feeling sadness at being separated from you. Well, perhaps you could do that, but it would not be good for her or you. It's important for children to have the experience of being sad and surviving. Sometimes all you can do is be there for a child who feels miserable, so she knows she is not alone. Being there doesn't always mean being in the same room with a crying baby or remaining chained to your preschooler throughout the day. Being there is a state of mind.

Respecting a toddler's or preschooler's need to blow off steam while respecting her ability to return to a state of emotional balance may look like providing a safe place for tears and issuing an invitation to rejoin the family when she feels better. Some children will respond well to this. They will have their cry and draw their ugly picture, and eventually they move past the feelings and everyone is ready to move forward again. Some children, in addition to crying, may express distress in a way that threatens to harm themselves or others. They may hit themselves or others in the context of a tantrum. This, you must stop. It is important that a child in a state of distress not be allowed to do damage.

Why We Miss What's There to Be Seen

There are many reasons that we may fail to recognize a child's bad feeling or try to talk her out of it. None of us intentionally try to create misunderstandings in relationships with our kids. Rather, these processes are often driven by forces in ourselves that operate outside the domain of our awareness.

Two weeks ago, the Slossons gave away Freckles, the family dog, after their two-year-old daughter became allergic. Subsequently, Clancy, their four-year-old son, has regressed in his toilet training, is defiant with his parents, and refuses to eat anything but mashed potatoes. The Slossons are racking their brains trying to figure out what's going on. Is he responding to something on TV? Is a new friend a bad influence? I suggest Clancy is responding to the loss of the dog. His mother states emphatically, "Well, I don't think so. When we got rid of Freckles, we got Clancy an aquarium, and we let Clancy pick out everything—the gravel, the filter, all the fish. It was really a great project." When I suggest this might not have softened the blow of the loss as they had hoped, Mrs. Slosson begins to cry. She says she knew her son was attached to Freckles, and she worries the loss will scar him.

The Slossons had no choice about giving Freckles away in light of their daughter's health, but they clearly feel bad about doing so. They had worried about inflicting pain on their son in this way and convinced themselves the aquarium would keep Clancy from being upset. Their intentions were honorable, but their measures have not worked. They try to assign their son's misbehavior to anything else they can think of, so as to avoid their guilty feelings—anything except what is most obvious.

As a parent, you suffer if your child suffers, but you suffer worse if you feel that your child is suffering because of something that you have done. We all have blind spots. In addition to trying to talk your child out of pain, if you think you've caused that pain, you may also fail to see or acknowledge a child's feelings because there are feelings of your own that you are trying to keep out of your awareness.

Karina and Pedro Gonzales are getting ready to move their family from Los Angeles to a small midwestern town so Karina can take advantage of a job opportunity. As the move approaches, five-year-old Juan starts hitting children in his kindergarten class, four-year-old Salina starts having night terrors, and the eight-month-old baby becomes colicky. Mrs. Gonzales says she has been reassuring the children and talking about how exciting it will be for them to have a new school, new friends, and a bigger house. I suggest that the coming change seems to be frightening the kids. "But there's nothing bad about it," she says. "It's going to be wonderful." I suggest that moves, while exciting, can also be stressful. "Not in this case," she insists. Mr. Gonzales, however, says he's been wondering how it will be for his wife to live so far from her family in Los Angeles. Mrs. Gonzales states she doesn't see the point in talking about that. When she is encouraged to do so anyway, she bursts into tears.

Mrs. Gonzales is trying to keep her distance from her own sadness. When her children are agitated, this brings her too close to her own feelings. She keeps trying to talk them out of feeling bad, without success.

To help your child get past something she is sad about, you need to be able to enter the world of her sadness and empathize. It is the same when a child is fearful. You look under the bed and pronounce "No monsters there." You look in the closet: "No monsters there either." Mrs. Gonzales cannot look at her children's monsters, because her children's monsters are her own. She cannot face her children's sadness and fear about leaving Los Angeles, because she is sad about and afraid of the same thing.

You will never be able to help your children get past any area in which you, yourself, are stuck. If you are trying to steer clear of a feeling, you will steer your children out of the vicinity as well. But your children do not have your sophisticated defenses for coping with what distresses them. If you maintain that their fears are groundless, they will not be able to repress them for you. They will find a way to express the feelings, though the feelings may become disguised in the process.

Never Can Say Good-bye

A baby and a mother start out physically attached to one another. From the moment the umbilical cord is cut, every developmental step that the baby takes, exciting though it may be, involves a separation and a loss. Growth is bittersweet. Each developmental milestone your child passes toward independence will take her another step away from her dependency on you.

Separation is a fact of human existence and is inextricably bound with growth. As much as we celebrate developmental achievements, we tend to want to ignore the losses that go with these steps because they are painful to face. Weaning a child from breast or bottle is a common "you're a big girl now" milestone, but the loss of intimacy in the feeding relationship for both baby and mother is significant. When a toddler takes her first steps, with all the emphasis on excitement and videotaping, parents may skip right by the simultaneous awareness that the child is now capable of going farther from them, and she will.

Children's mixed feelings about their growing independence is elegantly expressed in periods of progress punctuated by moments of regression. Toddlers are most obvious in demonstrating this struggle. One second they vehemently insist on putting on their own shoes, and the next second they are in tears, thrusting the shoes at you, saying, "Help me!" Your children's capabilities will ebb and flow not only as a function of their taking a while to master certain skills, but also as a function of their ambivalence about doing so. One day your toddler walks by herself in the mall. The next day she insists on riding in the stroller. Pacing herself in this way allows her to practice independence and cope with the various feelings that arise from the separation that goes along with greater competency.

So how do we parents cope? We allow ourselves the opportunity to celebrate the growth and to grieve the losses that are inherent in our children taking developmental steps. As one parent said tearfully as her daughter cut a first tooth, "It's not that I'm not excited she's getting her teeth; but I'm going to miss that toothless smile!" Often, we are not so willing to entertain those feelings. Instead, we employ a number of defensive strategies to protect ourselves. What do these defensive strategies look like? In the main, they fall into two categories: pushing children ahead too quickly or holding them back when they are ready to move on.

Some parents push their children right past any hesitation they express about taking steps forward:

- A mother dropping off her daughter at her first day of kindergarten sees her daughter's trembling lip. "Don't cry, Ginger," she says. "You're a big girl now."
- When a young boy who has recently learned to tie his own shoes asks his father to tie them for him, father says, "No, Jonathan. You know how to do it. I don't need to do it for you anymore."
- A toddler who is appropriately weaned from his bottle begins sucking his thumb. His mother panics and buys a bitter liquid from the pharmacy to paint on the thumb to ensure the behavior stops.

As thrilling as it is to see a child grow toward independence, there are feelings of loss and grief associated with separation as well. These parents, in trying to speed their children through these transitions, are very likely trying to avoid being aware of their sadness. In these circumstances, if children are allowed to be more in touch with their feelings, parents will be put more in touch with their ambivalent feelings too. If these parents could be more in touch with what they were feeling, they could help their children negotiate these stages with greater compassion. Ginger's mother might say, "I know that even though it is exciting to go to school, it is also hard to leave Mommy." Jonathan's father might say: "It's exciting to be a big boy who can do things for himself, but even though you are getting big, you don't feel big all the time and you still want to make sure you can count on Daddy to help you." The toddler's mother might simply acknowledge the reality: "It's hard to give up your bottle."

While some parents may push kids past a milestone, other parents may delay a child's achievement of certain milestones.

- In an interview, the mother of a six-year-old girl told the pediatrician that the girl was breast-fed. When the pediatrician asked when the girl had been weaned, there was an awkward silence. The pediatrician asked, "Not yet?" The mother nodded.
- A father persists in cutting up food for his seven-year-old. When asked why he doesn't give the boy a dinner knife and let him do it himself, he says, "Children shouldn't be allowed to use knives!"
- A mother breathes a sigh of relief when a diaper company comes out with an extra-jumbo size. She has had a hard time squeezing her son into the smaller sizes since he turned five.

What's the problem with these approaches? They are often enacted out of a parent's need to defend herself or himself against unwanted feelings. If a child's growth and development are slowed down, then this slows the pace of the separation between parent and child and limits the demand to cope with the attendant feelings of grief and loss. After all, if children aren't separating, then there's no loss to mourn. There is an age for weaning and toilet training, and it is long before five or six. A child of four or five is ready to start learning to cut food with a dull table knife. These parents are trying to keep their children small, trying to keep themselves young, trying to stop the flow of time. They will not succeed at any of these endeavors, but they will succeed in crippling their children if they continue these practices.

The problems with the approaches taken by all of the parents in these examples—those who try to speed their children past transitions and those who try to stave them off—is that none of these parents are responding to their children's feelings or their children's needs; they are responding to their own. Generally speaking, between parents and children, parents only come first when cabin pressure is lost and the oxygen masks drop from the ceiling of the airplane. Otherwise, it's children first.

So long as your child is alive and growing, there will be losses and separations to contend with for both of you. You must process your own feelings so your children won't have to bear the burden of them. You also must prepare your child for these losses and separations and help her cope with all the various feelings that arise in the course of them while you cope with them too. A child who is not taught how to cope with loss is a child who will be unable to move forward in life.

A Few Final Words

Like so much of what is valuable in life, parenting is all about relationships. Your children are on a journey through life, and you are their guide. That means you are on the journey too. Taking this journey will change you no less than it will change your children. I hope that this book will give you a bit of guidance—making the trip easier in spots than it might have been and helping you understand aspects of the landscape you will pass through together so you can negotiate them with some style and grace. I hope it will help you keep your bearings while, at the same time, orienting you to the horizon up ahead and giving you some influence over the kind of future your journey will lead you to. This is the future for you and your child, and it is the future of the world in which we all live together.

Suggested Readings

DeBecker, Gavin. *Protecting the Gift: Keeping Children and Teenagers Safe (and Parents Sane)*. New York: Dial Press, 1999.

Elkind, David. *The Hurried Child: Growing Up Too Fast Too Soon*. Third edition. Reading, Mass.: Perseus Books, 2001.

Erikson, Erik. *Childhood and Society*. New York: Norton, 1950.

Faber, Adele, and Elaine Mazlish. *How to Talk So Kids Will Listen and Listen So Kids Will Talk*. New York: Avon Books, 1980.

Ginott, Haim G. *Between Parent and Child*. New York: Avon Books, 1956.

McCullough, Donald. *Say Please, Say Thank You: The Respect We Owe Each Other*. New York: Putnam, 1998.

Index